Sales Control by Quantitative Methods

Sales Control by Quantitative Methods

R. PARKER EASTWOOD

New York: Morningside Heights
COLUMBIA UNIVERSITY PRESS
1940

COLUMBIA UNIVERSITY PRESS, NEW YORK

FOREIGN AGENTS: Oxford University Press, Humphrey Milford, Amen House, London, E.C. 4, England, AND B. I. Building, Nicol Road, Bombay, India; Maruzen Company, Ltd., 6 Nihonbashi, Tori-Nichome, Tokyo, Japan

MANUFACTURED IN THE UNITED STATES OF AMERICA

Dedicated
In Affection and Gratitude
To the Memory of My Mother

Preface

SPECIALIZATION has contributed immeasurably to the material welfare of society. Economists since the time of Adam Smith have emphasized the benefits to be gained from subdividing productive activities to accommodate differences in physical and human resources. Much less attention has been given the equally important process of coördination. Confusion and chaos would be the natural consequences of a division of productive activities were there no synchronizing forces operating to maintain the essential unity of the parts. How to keep the twin processes, specialization on the one hand and coördination on the other, moving at the same pace constitutes one of the major economic problems of our time.

The productice activities among specialized business units are coördinated through the synchronizing force of markets and price relationships. Within each business enterprise the system of exchange gives way to a system of conscious control. The specialized functions of selling, purchasing, production, personnel management, and financing are coördinated through various managerial techniques. The most important of these is the business budget and the keystone of the budgetary arch is sales. Hence, to establish a body of methods by which sales may be more effectively estimated and controlled becomes the most cogent business facing the managers of private enterprise. That is the general objective toward which this study is directed.

A variety of approaches are possible to a problem of such general character. For example, a series of detailed case studies might be made of a limited number of companies whose methods of controlling sales were distinctly superior to those in general use. A descriptive study of this sort would unquestionably provide many fruitful suggestions to companies whose methods were less advanced. If a much larger number of companies were made the subject of inquiry, a statistical tabulation might be undertaken in which the frequency of various attributes would be recorded. To be representative such study would have to include companies using a great variety of methods and presenting all degrees of efficiency. Just how significant a study of this sort would be is rather difficult to predict. It is more than likely that the only common attribute upon which a tabulation could be made would be so unimportant that the results, even if statistically sound, would be of little consequence.

A detailed running account of the actual routine work within the planning and sales control sections of some particular company constitutes a third possible approach to the solution of this problem. The tremendous amount of factual detail that would be required to present realistically the practitioner of sales control at work in his natural habitat seemed to provide the best possible argument against employing this particular approach. It is doubtful, moreover, whether any essential principles of sales control could be uncovered in this manner. Certainly the generalizations could be neither broader nor more instructive than the limited experiences of the particular company out of which they grew.

A fourth possible approach is that which undertakes a synthesis of all methodologies that are appropriate for the control of sales. Such an approach is not to be confined to the practices of any one firm or even to the techniques employed by the leaders in sales control activities. This fourth approach emphasizes the essential unity of techniques appropriate for the solution of the problem, regardless of whether or not the particular techniques are in current use. Hence, the outlook is definitely toward the future and the unexplored possibilities of employing more objective and refined analytical tools in controlling sales rather than toward the practices of either the present or the immediate past. Such has been the approach and the point of view that has dominated the making of this study.

It is a pleasure to acknowledge here my indebtedness to various faculty members of the School of Business of Columbia University. To Professor Roy B. Kester I am indebted for having been the first to suggest the general field of study as one offering rich possibilities for the application of accounting and statistical methods. No acknowledgment in this place can adequately measure the debt I owe to Professor F. C. Mills, who as teacher and colleague has given me so much in the way of friendly counsel and constructive criticism. Professor

Ralph S. Alexander read with particular care those sections of the study that deal with the measurement of markets. For his many helpful suggestions as well as for his sustained interest and encouragement I am deeply grateful.

Numerous obligations have been incurred to a great host of persons engaged in marketing and sales research—an activity so new that the trail blazers and pioneers still banquet as contemporaries with the newcomers in the field. To Dr. L. D. H. Weld, kindly counselor and trail blazer in marketing research, I acknowledge a particular debt for the personal and sympathetic interest he has shown in the study.

General acknowledgment is here made for the privilege of using certain illustrative statistical data gathered by market research organizations and published in various periodicals. Specific credit is given in the appropriate places in this study for all such data that have been employed. To Robert Jensen I extend my thanks for assistance in making the charts. Finally to my wife, Marcia Staton Eastwood, I desire to make a public expression of my sincere gratitude. To her goes the credit for having cheerfully assumed the onerous and monotonous task of typing the manuscript through the various stages of its preparation from the first crude draft to the final copy.

R. Parker Eastwood

Columbia University
October 15, 1940

Contents

Tables

Charts

CHAPTER I

Origin and Meaning of Budgetary Control

ONE OF THE most notable advances made in business management during the last quarter century consists in the systematic planning of the income and the expenses of the business enterprise together with the subsequent comparison of actual performance with these predetermined estimates. This is the principle of budgetary control.

ORIGIN OF THE BUDGET

The practice of preparing formal estimates of future operations began in the administration of fiscal policies of governments. Business managers borrowed the concept and adapted it to the problem of forecasting the income and the expenses of a business enterprise. Certain modifications in governmental budgetary procedure were necessary in order to accomplish this adaptation. The first of these relates to the sequence of making the estimates. The government budget makers usually begin with a list of estimated expenditures and then seek sources of revenue whose estimated aggregate yield equals the sum of the expected expenditures. In business this order is reversed. Business men usually start with a forecast of gross revenue, and their estimates of expenses are pared to permit the largest possible net profit or the least possible net loss. Even when no formal budgetary system is used, the business man thinks first of his expected sales income. If only a partial budgetary system is employed, the sales item may be the only one for which formal estimates are made.

The second distinction between a governmental and a business budget relates to the purpose of budgetary planning. Governments usually have no motive for profit. They are content if they can obtain revenue equal to the sum of their expenditures. A business man cannot be satisfied with this simple equality. He aims to achieve an excess of income over expenses, and one of the principal services of the budget is to direct the attention of management toward certain specific and desirable goals, which will, if achieved, provide this excess. Moreover, the business budget is less restrictive in purpose. Instead of establishing limits, it aims to provide flexible standards that will allow for variations under certain circumstances. Hence, coördination and comparison take priority as the two most important purposes of the business budget.

THE BUDGET AS RELATED TO ECONOMIC CHANGE

The importance of the budget as a tool of management is not to be measured by the number of firms which regularly prepare estimated balance sheets and profit and loss statements. The proportion which this number bears to the total is not impressive. The significance of the budgetary principle stems rather from the economic circumstances out of which it grew. These will prevail even when the objections to the use of the budget in certain specific enterprises seem to outweigh all the advantages that business men have urged in its favor. Only the outline of these broad economic tendencies can here be sketched to indicate their relation to the principle of budgetary control.

Within the last one hundred and fifty years industrial historians have recorded two series of changes, each of which has been of sufficient magnitude to warrant the designation "revolution." James Watt's invention of the steam engine has usually been taken as the starting point of the first, whereas time and motion studies made by Frederick W. Taylor in the Midvale Steel Company have been generally regarded as having inaugurated the second. In a larger sense, however, these series of changes had neither beginning nor ending. The technological changes typified by the Industrial Revolution of the latter part of the eighteenth century are continuously creating conditions in industry which make imperative certain changes in industrial organization and control. The era of scientific management symbolized by Taylor's studies may be regarded as a belated recognition that management is amenable to the same principles of science that had been used so effectively in the creation of new machines. The problems may be less tangible, but they are certainly no less cogent.

Although the important changes in the mechanics of production presaged changes in the realm of management, a great deal of interaction has obviously been operative. Improvements in the technique of management have frequently paved the way for further improvements in the machines themselves. The role played by the division of labor in furthering technological change, for example, is too well recognized to require comment. This process of interaction between the tangible instruments of production and the intangible methods of organization and management operates continuously to produce change in first one and then the other of these two related spheres. Budgetary control represents a relatively recent development in the realm of management, which has grown out of the circumstances created by previous technological changes. Only the two most important of these circumstances will here be discussed.

THE CIRCUMSTANCE OF EXPANDING MARKETS

The Industrial Revolution enabled producers to break the confines of their local markets. Perhaps the most important single factor in determining the effectiveness of the machine methods has been the size of the market. In the words of the late Professor Allyn A. Young "no other hypothesis so well unites economic history and economic theory than a persistence of a search for markets as the leading role in continuing economic evolution."

Mass production methods have extended the boundaries of markets until they are national and even international in scope. The serving of these extensive markets has called into being methods of mass distribution. In the process, the intimate personal lines of communication between those who make the goods and those who buy them have gradually disappeared. Advertising and consumer research have come in to reëstablish the lines of communication between buyers and sellers. The former serves to carry messages from the seller to the buyer. The latter relays opinions, desires, and reactions of buyers, both present and prospective, back again to the seller. The two lines of communication must be coördinated, and failure on the part of either constitutes a hazard to the capital which has been invested in the enterprise.

THE CIRCUMSTANCE OF DIVIDED MANAGERIAL RESPONSIBILITY

In a small business enterprise where a single individual manages production, looks after the selling, provides for the financing, and hires, trains, and supervises such help as may be needed, the problem of coördination of activities is very simple. Insofar as the manager's faculties are equal to his varied tasks, the activities which he supervises are coördinated. He may find accounting and statistical methods helpful, but usually such records as he keeps are quite informal and his methods of analysis most simple.

With the spread of mass-production technique and the increase in size of the business unit, managerial duties and responsibilities became too burdensome for one person to handle. There followed a division of responsibility and a delegation of authority along functional lines. This specialization of the managerial function unquestionably improved the quality of the supervision, but it created a tremendous new problem of coördination and control. The superior executive officers were confronted with the perplexing task of synchronizing the varied activities of the executives in charge of the various functional divisions. In the trading enterprise, purchases had to be coördinated with sales. If the business were that of manufacturing, production schedules had to be geared to sales expectation. In both types of enterprise there was need for financial planning to assure an economical flow of funds into the business to accommodate the maturing obligations.

The proper coördination and control of managerial functions within the business enterprise has constituted one of the limiting factors upon large-scale operation. Informal conferences and staff meetings have aided tremendously in letting the right hand of business know what the left hand is doing. Accounting records have increased in both number and detail. Formal statistical reports have become the order of the day in the larger and more technical business enterprises. Now the budget has been added as an instrument of managerial control and is destined to play an increasing part in establishing that twofold adjustment which is characteristic of the well-managed enterprise. Through it the activities of the various functional divisions are coördinated individually with one another and collectively with the general business and economic environment in which every business enterprise operates.

THE BUDGET AS A TOOL OF MANAGEMENT

In one sense the budget is not a new and distinct tool of management but rather a combination of techniques that have long been available as instruments of managerial control. Accounting, for instance, supplies the terms in which the completed budget is expressed. The forms by which comparisons are made and results of operations recorded and interpreted are likewise products of accounting. The preparation of the estimates that enter into the budget requires the use of methods most of which are a part of standard statistical practice. Finally, the budget committee with whom authority is frequently vested for the administration of the budget, represents a form of human agency that is as old, perhaps, as the human race itself. If, therefore, the budget is to be regarded as a new instrument for controlling the operations of a business, its novelty must rest upon the particular combination and application of elements rather than upon the elements themselves.

THE BUDGET, THE BUDGET SYSTEM, AND BUDGETARY CONTROL

The business budget presents in systematic form the estimates of revenue and expenses of a business together with a forecast of its future financial condition. This tabulation of estimates is to the business manager what the blueprint is to the engineer—a plan of future operations. But no plan is self-creative. It presupposes the collection, the analysis, and the interpretation of data essential for planning. Moreover, no plan is self-operative. It requires constant supervision, comparison, and correction while it is being administered. The processes of planning that precede the budget and the processes of administration that accompany and follow it are integrals of the budget system quite as much as the budget plan itself. Budgetary control is the objective toward which this triad of planning, formulation, and administration is directed.

The Policyholders Service Bureau of the Metropolitan Life Insurance Company has provided the following definitions:

A budget system has been defined as a systematic method of gathering information from the past and present, and of formulating plans for the future on this basis, and of reporting subsequently how these plans have been carried out. The application and use of this method of planning and recording give what is called budgetary control.[1]

Thus, the budget system is concerned not only with forms but also with types of organization and methods of analysis which are required in preparing and administering the budget. Budgetary control is assumed to exist when the budget system has been placed in operation.

MAJOR STEPS IN ESTABLISHING BUDGETARY CONTROL

The major steps in establishing budgetary control have their analogy in the behavior of a person setting out upon a journey. The traveler moves successively from the fixing of his destination to the planning of his itinerary and, finally, to the execution of his plans. If we assume the traveler to be an efficient person, we can imagine him setting a time for his arrival and checking his progress along the route by reference to a time table.

In a similar manner, management, operating under a budget system, first establishes the goal that it expects to reach within a specified time period. The immediate objective may be a certain volume of sales, but the ultimate destination is that amount of net profit that will provide a reasonable rate of return on the capital invested. The specified time is the budget period. The length of this period varies with the nature of the enterprise, the size of the business, the amount of experience upon which management can draw, and the temperament of the managers themselves. If one thinks of the budget program in terms of a complete schedule of income and expenses, the period is rarely less than three months or more than twelve. Specific items, such as sales, might be estimated for a longer period.

The planning of the itinerary consists in allocating responsibility

[1] Metropolitan Life Insurance Company, Policyholders Service Bureau, *Budgeting Manufacturing Operations,* New York.

for the attainment of the net profit goal. Definite tasks are assigned to specific persons and groups of persons. This process of assigning responsibility is three-dimensional. It extends both horizontally and vertically throughout the organization as well as laterally through time. The horizontal allocation consists in the breakdown of the total into parts that roughly correspond to a functional division of management (see Chart I). Then, since each major functional budget is itself a composite task, the process of allocating responsibility must be extended vertically to those of subordinate rank within each department. The establishment of quotas for each grade of selling agent, from the sales manager down to the man in the territory, illustrates this type of allocation (see Chart II). Finally, the lat-

CHART I. THE BUDGET AS A MEDIUM FOR THE HORIZONTAL ALLOCATION OF RESPONSIBILITY TO MAJOR FUNCTIONAL DIVISIONS

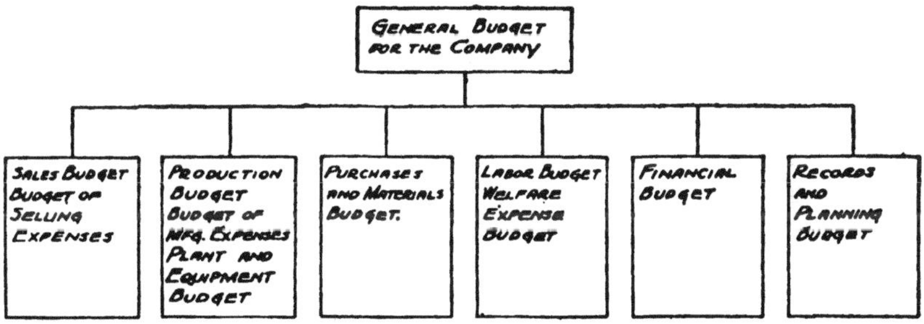

CHART II. THE BUDGET AS A MEDIUM FOR THE VERTICAL ALLOCATION OF RESPONSIBILITY WITHIN THE SALES DEPARTMENT

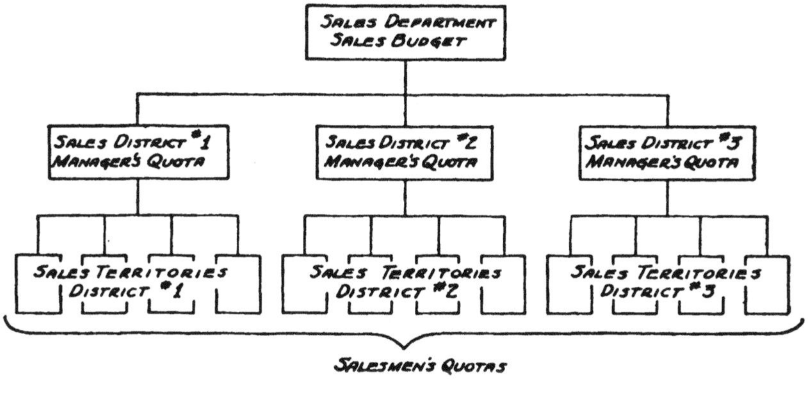

eral allocation of responsibility through time relates to the breakdown of each person's task into the parts corresponding to some convenient unit of time (see Chart III). This time unit varies with the nature of the business just as the budget period itself varies. The unit most frequently used is the month.

CHART III. THE BUDGET AS A MEDIUM FOR THE TEMPORAL ALLOCATION OF RESPONSIBILITY BY TIME PERIODS

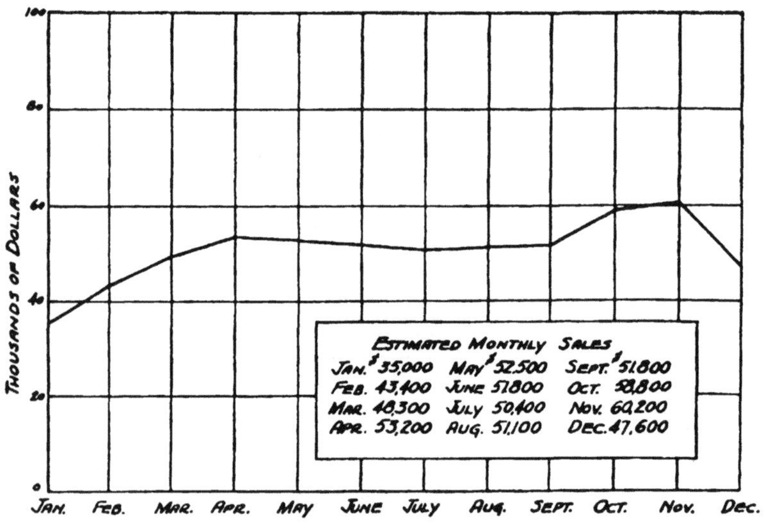

The breakdown of the budget by time periods provides the basis for the checking-up process. The schedule of expected performance laid out on some convenient time basis is the business executive's "time table," against which he checks actual performance. As each time period elapses he is provided with a dual check upon his performance. The first of these is the comparison of actual results with estimates for the current period, whereas the second is that of the accumulated performances with the accumulated schedules. Graphic methods have been found most helpful in presenting these data and in making the comparisons vivid.

RELATION OF BUDGETARY CONTROL TO BUSINESS FORECASTING

Anyone who buys or sells must make some estimate of the future. From peanut vendor to merchant prince, from shoe cobbler to auto maker, all are forecasters to some degree. The art and science of forecasting is as broad as business itself, whereas the methods of budgetary control are confined to a relatively small proportion of the total number of business enterprises. Forecasting has many purposes, and budgetary control is one of the most important. In point of time, forecasting takes precedence. It is inconceivable that a person could prepare a budget and apply the principles of budgetary control without having first made some sort of forecast.

Since forecasting provides management with the estimates which are the basis of budgetary control, there is danger of the two concepts becoming merged in one's thinking. Yet budgetary control may be appraised as something apart from forecasting *per se*. A budgetary-control system may have great merit as a means of coördinating and appraising the operations of the business, even though the forecasting is subject to a considerable margin of error.

If budgeting possesses an integrity distinct from that of forecasting, it is equally true that forecasting may possess an excellence that is not shared by the budgetary system. The business executive, for example, may possess that combination of ability, training, and experience that enables him to predict the course of business enterprise with considerable accuracy, and yet he may lack the managerial ability required to install and operate successfully a system of budgetary control. The plans and estimates which in themselves may be excellent must be fulfilled through organization. Budgetary control is the coördinating agency whereby the plans of each department are made to function in a harmonious system.

Finally, budgetary control provides the system for checking performance against the carefully laid and coördinated plans. Herein lies the ultimate test of efficient management. The discrepancies between results of operation and previous estimates may arise from either or both of two groups of causes. The first embraces all factors external to the business enterprise and are quite beyond the power of the individual business man to control. So long as these are operative the most carefully laid plans may never be precisely executed. The internal factors, however, offer a real proving ground to management. They may relate either to the techniques and methods employed in laying the plans or to the manner of their execution. Hence, planning, as well as performance, must be continuously scrutinized if the remedial sources of discrepancies between the two are to be removed.

RELATION OF BUDGETARY CONTROL TO ACCOUNTING

General accounting provides a record of the business transactions and summarizes them to show the financial status of the business as well as the net change that has taken place over a period of time. The balance sheet shows the status, and the profit and loss statement the process of change. Both are historical.

Budgetary control is coterminous with accounting to the extent that it treats of the financial condition of the business. Budgetary control, however, looks to the future, whereas general accounting records what has passed. By the lamp of this recorded experience management seeks through budgetary methods to give direction to its course. By projecting the items on the balance sheet and the profit and loss statement into the future it establishes a goal to which it later compares its accomplishment. Thus accounting had to come first, since no system of budgetary control could be operated without it.

RELATION OF BUDGETARY CONTROL TO COST ACCOUNTING

Cost accounting is a child of general accounting. Like its parent, it is retrospective. The data provided by the cost records become available only after the close of the fiscal period. The general books of account classify the income and the outgo of a business along functional lines. For example, expenses are listed as rent, insurance, superintendence, light, heat, power, direct labor, materials, supplies, and so forth. Cost accounting takes the expense side of the ledger accounts and seeks to apportion these general items to departments, processes, products, or services. The purpose of such apportionment is threefold: (1) to aid in estimating total expenses; (2) to aid in the determination of prices; and (3) to provide a basis for the establishment and modification of administrative policies. Thus, cost accounting touches budgetary control only on the expense side of the ledger and then only as an aid in making estimates. The previously mentioned study of the Metropolitan Life Insurance Company [2] shows the cost department to be the source of data, either entirely or in part, for estimates of forty-six out of fifty-five factory expense items.

RELATION OF BUDGETARY CONTROL TO STANDARD COST ACCOUNTING

John H. Williams, author and consulting management engineer, says that cost accounting has become confused with budgeting through the development of what is known as standard cost accounting, which is a hybrid of budgetary control and cost accounting.[3] Standard cost accounting involves the comparison of actual costs for each department, process, product, or service with certain standard theoretical costs. These standard costs may represent a series of average costs over a period of time or they may represent something like ideal costs which would prevail were the company operating at 100 percent (or some other hypothetical proportion) of its capacity.

The standards used for budgetary purposes differ from standard costs in several respects. First, they embrace the income as well as the expense side of the profit and loss statement. Secondly, they relate primarily to the responsibilities of individuals, whereas cost standards usually relate to departments, processes, products, or services. Even when the standards coincide, the emphasis in budgeting is upon the individual and his job, not upon inanimate objects or services as in cost accounting. Finally, the standards set for budgetary control are usually more flexible than standard costs. Like tailor-made suits, the budgetary standards are cut to fit the particular company, the particular items, and the particular conditions of operation. Standard costs, on the other hand, usually mean average costs. These may be derived from the company's own experience or from the experiences of a group of companies in the same industry. Thus, the basic data used in establishing standard costs will frequently exhibit considerable variation, so that allowance for indi-

[2] Metropolitan Life Insurance Company, Policyholders Service Bureau, *Budgeting Manufacturing Operations*, New York.

[3] Williams, *The Flexible Budget*, p. 3.

vidual differences in operating conditions must be made in applying the averages. Since adjustments for individual differences have presumably been made in the budgetary standards, a much closer agreement between actual results and estimates can usually be expected.

In recent years cost accountants have made great strides toward increasing the usefulness of the cost department in the budget-making program. By first classifying the expenses into fixed and variable cost items, they have been able to set up variable standard costs that depend upon the volume of production. These costs may be applied directly to the budgeted output in estimating expenditures. Later, as the actual volume of business becomes known, management can modify the budget of expenditures accordingly and can allocate the variance of net operating profit to its true cause. "Change in volume of business will be charged or credited with its proper share of the variance and variance in efficiency will be charged or credited with its just amount without the complicating factor of volume variance." [4]

RELATION OF BUDGETARY CONTROL TO STATISTICS

Statistics deals with the collection, classification, analysis, and interpretation of numerical facts. Some of the numerical facts needed for budgetary control are external in that they pertain to conditions common to the industry. Data collected by trade associations pertaining to production, sales, deliveries, and stocks on hand in the industry fall into this category. Most numerical facts used in budgetary control, however, are internal and come from the accounting records kept by the business.

The analytical methods that statistics provides for revealing the significance of numerical facts may be classified as either static or dynamic depending upon the part that time is assumed to play in producing variety and change. In the static analysis time is assumed to be an unimportant element. The averaging of ratios derived from a series of balance sheets and profit and loss statements illustrates

[4] Hovey, "Cost Accounting and Budget Making," Taylor Society, *Bulletin*, XVI (No. 3), 100–103.

this type of analysis. The averages are set up as standards with which individual ratios may be compared.

A more refined and flexible statistical procedure for the establishment of standards is that provided by correlation technique. Typical of the studies in this field are the correlations between costs, either in total or in unit form, and such variables as sales and volume of output. Both for controlling current costs and in estimating future costs correlation provides one of the most effective tools.

The dynamic or time-series analysis is concerned with the classification, measurement, and prediction of forces that operate over a period of time to produce variation in any series of values. Just as the items within any specific balance sheet or profit and loss statement are related to one another, so are corresponding items related over successive periods. The first group of relationships is revealed through ratio and correlation analysis; the second is the subject of time series analysis.

The two types of analysis, static and dynamic, supplement each other in appraising the present status of the business enterprise and in predicting its future position for purposes of budgetary control. Forecasts derived from a dynamic analysis can be checked by the aid of ratio analysis, which relates each forecast to the other projected items. Forecasting for budgetary purposes is very largely a matter of consistency. Each item on the projected balance sheet and profit and loss statement must be consistent with itself as revealed by its record over a period of time and consistent with the other projected items when considered at any given point in time. Statistics provide the tools for the establishment of these consistencies.

RELATION OF BUDGETARY CONTROL TO SCIENTIFIC MANAGEMENT

Scientific management has been mentioned heretofore as one of the two major and complementary series of changes that have transformed the medieval handicraft economy into our modern mechanized industrial order. Budgetary control has been represented as an extension of the scientific management principle, and both are developments from forces that were previously generated by the Industrial Revolution. The purpose of the present section is to indicate briefly the stages by which scientific management has extended its limits so as to include budgetary control.

Beginning as a series of time and motion studies made upon a particular production process or centering in a particular production unit, such as the machine or the work table, scientific management reached out to embrace a series of processes or machines and tied them together in a harmonious group by means of scientific methods of routing. This was shop management. From shop management to factory management was the next logical step as scientific management extended its boundaries to include all the production departments, such as the foundry, the machine shop, the carpenter shop, and the assembly department.

Once production had been subjected to the principles of scientific management, distribution began to be considered as a great new world to conquer. The intangible and subtle human motives began to replace human motions; psychological forces gradually took precedence over mechanical forces in the minds of those who were seeking to apply the methods of science to the problems of management. The years of the great depression following 1929 gave impetus to this trend. As Frank R. Coutant [5] has stated, the difficult and troublesome times have served to make clear the necessity of finding some means "to keep the stream of goods and services flowing from producer to consumer freely, more smoothly and more profitably; to raise the per capita consumption of present users of goods and services; to bring the output of production within reach of new and greatly enlarged fields of consumers and to eliminate every form of waste that now inflates the cost of distribution." These are, in general, the aims of scientific management as evidenced in marketing research. In comparison to the progress which has been attained in production research, little more than a beginning has been made in distribution.

The third and most advanced stage that has been reached in the gradually expanding area of scientific management is represented by the attempt to coördinate according to a systematic plan the three major functions performed within a business enterprise. Pro-

[5] Foreword to American Marketing Society, Committee on Marketing Research Technique, *The Technique of Marketing Research.*

duction, distribution, and finance must be coördinated with one another and with general economic conditions surrounding the business enterprise. This is the purpose and scope of budgetary control. It represents, by all odds, the most difficult assignment that has been essayed by those who seek to apply scientific method to the problems of management.

CHAPTER II

The Place of the Sales Budget In the Budgetary System

WITHIN THE MATRIX of general budgetary control a considerable number of individual budgetary problems are to be found. Each part of the general budget is of sufficient importance to warrant detailed and specific treatment. To distinguish the various parts from the whole which they comprise, the term "budget" has come to be used in a dual sense. The general budget may be defined as a composite of related estimates pertaining to the future operations of a business unit. Each of these individual estimates may, in turn, be designated by the word "budget." For example, we have budgets for sales, production, plant equipment, materials, labor, and each of the various items of expense. Even some of these specific budgets contain elements of sufficient importance to warrant a further breakdown. The budget of advertising expense as a major subdivision of the budget of selling expenses may be cited as an example.

IMPORTANCE OF THE SALES BUDGET

Of the various divisions and subdivisions into which the general budget may be divided, that which pertains to sales is the most important. No other item in the estimated profit and loss statement contains quite so much uncertainty as the forecast of sales. Such items as rent, interest, taxes, and insurance are relatively fixed. Those that are variable are usually tied to sales by the common practice of using a percentage of sales as the basis for their allocation. The projected net sales minus the projected cost of goods minus the projected expenses plus estimated income from nonoperating sources gives the projected net profit or net loss of the enterprise. The projected net profit or net loss finds its way into the projected balance sheet by way of the net worth section. Obviously, whatever change is projected between the present and some future net worth must be the result of changes between present asset and liability values and those of some future date. The allocation of these changes among the various items of the balance sheet cannot be accomplished without knowledge of the projected sales. Thus, the task of estimating sales easily becomes the most cogent business which the budget maker has before him. As one writer has expressed it, "the sales budget is the natural starting point of the budget system." [1]

If formal apology were needed for the selection of sales as a significant item for intensive study, it would emphasize such factors as: the importance of sales in establishing any system of budgetary control, the difficulty that usually attends the forecasting of sales, the scarcity of comprehensive analyses dealing with sales control, and, finally, the opportunity afforded by the problem for applying various statistical methods of analysis. Such elements have been dominant in dictating the choice of the sales budget for the specific and detailed treatment to which the remainder of this study is devoted.

THE SALES BUDGET DEFINED

The wording and emphasis of a definition is often affected by the point of view. This is certainly true of the sales budget. The factory manager might say that the sales budget represents a certain quantity of goods to be manufactured and ready for sale at certain stated intervals of time. His emphasis is on the physical units, since these are the terms in which most schedules of production are prepared. The purchasing agent is likely to use similar words and phrases. To him the budget of sales represents a requisition for a certain volume of materials and supplies to be purchased and ready for delivery at certain stated intervals of time. The emphasis is once again on physical units, since these are the terms in which purchase orders are placed. Finally, the sales manager, were he called upon to place his conception into words, would probably say that the sales budget

[1] Blocker, *Budgeting in Relation to Distribution Cost Accounting.*

represents an allotment of goods, measured either in physical units or in dollars of value, which he expects to sell within a specified period and in accordance with a specified schedule. If the sales pertain to a single uniform and homogeneous product, the sales manager is prone to think of his task in terms of physical units. The same is true if the units of the product are of considerable value, such, for example, as automobiles or electric refrigerators. The monetary unit tends to become his means of measurement when the products are numerous and of small unit price.

Although it is fitting that each person within the business organization should view the sales budget in its relationship to his own particular job, a conception much broader is needed for the framing of a definition. From this larger viewpoint the sales budget may be defined as that part of a company's financial plan of operation which consists of a schedule of expected sales income over a specified period of time. Since income from other sources is usually small and insignificant in comparison to the magnitude of sales, one is justified in regarding the latter as comprising practically the whole of the budgeted income.

The phrase "that part of a company's financial plan" is of special significance in the definition. It emphasizes the two important aspects of a sales budget. As a part of the general budget it must be related to and coördinated with every other part. Every item in the operating budget is financed either directly or indirectly out of sales income. If we grant that the central purpose of business is to make a net profit, the wisdom of any estimate of sales cannot be gauged without reference to the other items on the projected profit and loss statement. The definition properly recognizes this financial aspect of the sales budget. It implies the necessity of keeping the estimate of sales in proper proportion to other estimates and the entire system of estimates moving in the direction of the common financial goal which is net profit.

RELATIONSHIP OF THE SALES BUDGET TO THE PRODUCTION BUDGET

Procuring, distributing, and financing represent three basic and interdependent functions of a business enterprise. Their simultaneous consideration is imperative in the establishment of any well-coördinated budget system. The special budget committee with a membership representing these various functional divisions offers an effective means for achieving the proper degree of coördination between interdependent activities.

The problem of harmonizing estimated sales with estimated production is twofold. The first part is concerned with adjusting the total sales budget to the total plant capacity. If estimated sales exceed the current plant capacity, new plant and equipment may be added, or the existing equipment may be operated overtime. Neither solution is likely to be attractive to the production manager, who is ever on the alert to keep his unit costs low. The more probable condition is that estimated sales will be considerably less than the productive capacity. The production program must then be pruned to fit sales prospects or sales pressure must be increased to obtain a larger volume of business. Both procedures are expensive. The first results in higher manufacturing overhead costs, the second in higher unit selling costs. The problem of adjustment consists in reaching that compromise volume of business which results in the greatest over-all economy.

The second part of the problem of adjusting sales and production pertains to discrepancies in the rates of selling and production. The difficulties met in synchronizing the two schedules are due primarily to the seasonal factor. Either or both sales and production may be subject to a pronounced seasonal variation. Unless the seasonal factor in sales just happened to coincide with that in production, the problem of adjusting the two schedules would arise. Perfect adjustment between the rates of production and sales would require a schedule of sales and deliveries so nicely synchronized with production that no inventory of finished goods would exist. Sales would deplete the stock as rapidly as production added to it. In the absence of this ideal condition the problem of inventory control arises.

RELATIONSHIP OF THE SALES BUDGET TO INVENTORY CONTROL

The essence of inventory control consists in deriving from previous experience limits of variation known as "maximum" and "minimum" points for each of the various articles manufactured and stocked. In the determination of the minimum point an estimate of sales for the ensuing production period is required. The maximum point for each article manufactured is ascertained by simply adding the quantity under manufacturing order to the previously determined minimum.

The sequence of relationships involving sales, production, and inventory may be most conveniently visualized from the brief tabular arrangement shown below. From the schedule of estimated sales a schedule of estimated production is projected. The schedule of differences added algebraically to the initial inventory provides a schedule of finished stock.

TABLE 1

SCHEDULE OF SALES, PRODUCTION, AND FINISHED GOODS INVENTORY

(In terms of units of product)

Month	*Initial* [a] *Inventories*	*Estimated Sales*	*Estimated Production*	*Estimated Closing Inventories (Min. 3,000; Max. 5,000)*
January	3,000	8,000	8,500	3,500
February	3,500	7,500	8,500	4,500
March	4,500	9,000	8,500	4,000

[a] The initial inventory for January represents the actual quantity on hand. For the other months the quantities are estimates.

A slight modification of the table is sufficient to transform it into a schedule of inventories for a trading enterprise in which purchase orders replace production orders as the source of supply. A schedule of raw material stocks is easily developed from a similarly prepared table with purchases and factory requisitions serving as source and outlet, respectively. To the extent to which management is able to regulate the flow of goods into and out of the various reservoirs, it has achieved inventory control. The power to regulate, however, is not absolute. Through the determination of minimum and maximum levels for each of the various inventories, management makes allowance for certain unavoidable discrepancies in the rates of two or more activities related in sequence. Since sales provide the terminal outlet through which all other activities must eventually be released, an adequate system for controlling sales constitutes the first step toward the establishment of that synchronization of functions characteristic of the well-managed business enterprise.

RELATION OF SALES BUDGET TO PLANT AND EQUIPMENT BUDGET

Plant and equipment are quite as essential as raw materials and supplies in the production process. The sales budget provides the basis for judging the merit of proposed expenditures in both instances. Betterments and additions to plant and equipment are made for the benefit of future income. Consequently, a long-range forecast of the probable effect upon sales income is the first step toward evaluating any proposed capital expenditure. An estimate of the probable effect upon costs is much more easily made. A combination of the two provides a series of estimated future increments to net income. Such a series discounted at prevailing rates on borrowed capital should yield a present value at least equal to the present estimated capital outlay. Unless management can look forward to receiving annual increments to its net income sufficient, at least, to pay interest on the new capital expenditure, it had better place its financial resources in the custody of others until the prospects of future returns improve.

RELATION OF SALES BUDGET TO LABOR BUDGET

Estimates of the labor required to transform schedules of production and of sales into accomplishment differ from estimates of materials and capital, since labor is a human factor and much of the company's good will depends upon the character of its labor policy. Instead of regarding labor as something to be purchased when needed and dispensed with as soon as sales decline, the more enlightened personnel administrators strive to develop such a synchronization of sales and production that a uniform labor force becomes possible. Among the various methods employed for stabilizing production and sales schedules and making for a lower labor turnover are: the building up of inventories when sales are slow, the addition of auxiliary products whose sales exhibit seasonal patterns of an inverse and complementary character, and, finally, the offering of special inducements to customers or salesmen or both for increasing sales during dull seasons.

Three principal methods are available for estimating the direct labor needed to transform a proposed schedule of production into accomplishment. In some industries standard labor rates per unit of product are available, and the estimate is readily obtained by multiplying the standard by the schedule of production. The labor estimate arrived at in this manner may be either total man-hours or total monetary cost depending upon the form which the standard takes. In other industries, ratios may be available for estimating labor requirements. Relationships such as direct labor cost to the cost of goods manufactured, man-hours to machine-hours, and direct labor cost to material cost provide possible bases for making labor cost estimates. Finally, correlation analysis provides a basis for estimating labor requirements from relationships that have been developed from experience. This last method is perhaps superior to either of the other two, since it makes allowance for changes in the proportion between factors at different production volumes. The increasing realization of the need for flexible cost standards will make the application of the correlation method more and more desirable.

RELATION OF THE SALES BUDGET TO THE BUDGET OF MANUFACTURING EXPENSE

Among the budget items less directly related to sales is that of manufacturing expense, a title covering a rather heterogeneous group of production costs that cannot be easily and economically charged directly to the product. Some of these indirect production costs, such as taxes and insurance, are affected scarcely at all by the volume of output whereas others, such as repairs, depreciation, power, heat, light, and lubrication, tend to vary with the volume of production, but not proportionately. These differences in the behavior of the items and the lack of centralized responsibility for their control make a separate estimate of each item of expense desirable. Whatever part the schedule of sales may play in making these estimates is of a rather circuitous nature, since the production budget provides the immediate basis for estimating the less rigidly fixed items of cost.

RELATION OF THE SALES BUDGET TO THE BUDGET OF SELLING EXPENSES

The setting up of cost standards for future sales is the logical complement of cost analysis for previous sales. Both aspects of the control of distribution costs have evolved from earlier and more highly developed systems of cost control in the field of production.

Since sales are made for profit, the sales budget can scarcely be formulated without reference to some estimate of the selling expenses. The sales department must have an estimate of expenses if it is to appraise its own sales program. The personnel department needs an estimate of the labor requirements in order to engage and train the sales personnel. The treasurer must know what funds are to be expended in order to plan to meet the expenditures as they are incurred. Finally, the budget officer must have the estimate of selling expenses along with the estimates of all other expenses if he is to prepare an estimated balance sheet and profit and loss statement for the ensuing period.

For budgetary purposes selling expenses may be grouped into three categories. The first includes expenses that tend to vary in direct proportion to sales. These may be estimated by applying the appropriate ratio directly to the budget of sales. The second includes expenses that are either fixed or relatively constant. These give rise to ratios that vary inversely to the magnitude of sales. Management's efforts to increase sales and thereby reduce the ratios of these fixed items of expense has created a third category that may appropriately be referred to as "pressure costs." These tend to increase relatively faster than sales.

The problem of control as applied to the three categories of selling expenses might be summarized as follows. The selling expenses that are directly proportional to sales can be left to care for themselves since their constant relationship holds them consistent with whatever volume of sales is estimated. With the two remaining sets of expense ratios, one tending to decrease with increments in sales and the other to increase, the problem of control resolves itself into something approximating a mathematical relationship between variables. The most economic magnitude of sales would be that for which the net profit would be a maximum.

RELATION OF THE SALES BUDGET TO THE FINANCIAL BUDGET

The financial plans of management provide the coördinating mechanism by which the two basic functions, production and distribution, are made to contribute to the net profit of the enterprise. Both production and sales may be subject to efficient control, but if the business has been saddled with a poorly devised financial structure, or if the current financial needs of the enterprise have not been provided for through a carefully planned system of commercial loans, most of the meritorious work of the production and sales departments will have been dissipated before it can be reflected in the net profit figure.

Financial planning as applied to the business enterprise simply means making provision for future contingencies in the supply of its working and fixed capital. The general growth of the business plus the seasonal and cyclical variations in its sales create certain demands, both temporary and permanent, for additional funds to carry on the business. The temporary demands are usually provided for through the medium of commercial loans whereas the demands for a permanent increase of capital are usually met by the issuance of stocks and bonds and occasionally by long-term notes.

The amount of a company's fixed investment and the rate of increase in sales are the two most important factors determining the extent to which management should go in planning its long-term financing. The American Telephone and Telegraph Company, for example, has found that estimates must be made as far as 25 years in advance if the needs of the public are to be economically served. In general, the period of long-term financing varies directly with the magnitude of the investment in fixed assets and the rate of growth of the business.

The most important factor influencing short-term financial planning is the rate at which current assets can be converted into cash. If funds on hand plus expected receipts fail to equal total estimated cash disbursements, new loans must be obtained or old ones must be renewed. Neither a simple equality nor an excess of receipts over expenditures will be sufficient, however, unless there is a reasonable degree of synchronization between the two rates of flow. If each day's cash receipts were to equal each day's disbursements there would be no problem for the financial manager. In the absence of such an ideal relationship management must keep a cash balance to synchronize the inflow and the outflow of funds in the manner that inventory serves a similar purpose for merchandise and raw materials.

The principal source of cash for most businesses is the receivables arising from the sale of goods. From a knowledge of estimated sales and their probable terms an estimate of the inflow of cash from this source is made. If the sales are made only when cash accompanies the order, the estimated sales schedule is also the schedule of estimated cash receipts. When payment is made on delivery, cash receipts will coincide with billings, so that the schedule of production and estimated shipments provide the basis of the prediction.

The forecast of cash receipts from credit sales requires a double estimate involving, first, the ratio of cash to credit sales and, secondly, the time lag between sales and collections. Such disturbing factors as seasonal changes, fluctuations in interest rates, and variations in the state of general business render the prediction of both these variables difficult. If previous experience is to be safely used in forecasting the probable relationship of cash to credit sales, as well as the most probable time lag in collections, cognizance should be taken of each major source of variability. Possibly each month of the year may require treatment as a distinct problem for which a normal ratio and a normal time lag are computed. In any case, the schedule of expected sales provides the base from which the schedule of expected cash receipts is developed.

On the cash disbursements side of the financial budget the problem of forecasting is relatively simple, since expenditures are very largely a function of income. Moreover, management can more easily take the initiative and control the rate of expenditure, whereas the rate of cash income is largely dependent upon the good intentions as well as the good fortune of its debtors. Materials, labor, and manufacturing expenses constitute the major items of cash disbursements in productive processes, whereas the purchases of merchandise and selling expenses constitute the bulk of expenditures made by a mercantile enterprise. The relationship of each of these items to the sales budget has been previously discussed and requires no further comment.

ANALYSES EMPLOYED IN THE ESTABLISHMENT OF THE SALES BUDGET

The preceding discussion will have served to indicate the central and dominating position occupied by the selling function. The many points of contact between the sales budget and other budget estimates make the prediction and control of sales the most important part of the budget program. Analyses designed to aid in the control of sales are, therefore, indirectly applicable to the other functions.

The formulation of the sales budget calls for a series of compromises, one of the most important of which is bringing the estimate based on previous experience into line with that derived from an appraisal of the market. Various analyses of the sales data provide the best basis for estimating future sales, if one assumes that what has been done is the best index to what can be done. Rarely, however, does human accomplishment correspond to the optimum, and one of the special purposes of a market analysis has been to reveal sales possibilities in each of a company's territories. There is need of terminology that will distinguish these two estimates, one derived solely from an analysis of internal data, and the other a more or less independent estimate developed from a study of the market. "Probable sales" is offered as a provisional designation to indicate the general statistical nature of the first concept, whereas "potential sales" [2] has already become accepted as legal-tender terminology to represent the second. Any discrepancy that may appear between probable sales and potential sales calls for a high degree of judgment in effecting a compromise. The standard should be high enough to call forth the best efforts of everyone in the organization, yet low enough to be capable of attainment. This stimulation toward more effective application of sales effort and the check on efficiency provided by the comparison of performance against estimates represent the two most important services rendered by the sales budget.

TYPES OF SALES ANALYSIS

"Sales analysis" has become a sort of chameleon phrase in the literature of business management. It has been made to assume several hues of meaning depending upon the background and the experience of the writer. To the accountant a sales analysis usually refers to a classification of sales invoices upon one or more bases

[2] "Potential sales" has been defined by the Committee on Definitions of the American Marketing Society as "the possible sales of a commodity or a group of commodities or a service in a given area or market within a period."

selected in accordance with the purpose of the study and the facilities for making the analysis. A summation of the various classes provides management with a microscopic picture of the source of its sales income and helps it to identify and correct the low spots of its distribution.

Among the bases most frequently used for classifying sales are the following: geographical areas; customers; size of orders; products, groups of products, or subdivisions of products; selling units; sales outlets or channels; terms of sale; methods of delivery; and advertising media.

To the financial analyst, and to all those interested in appraising the credit standing of the business and the efficiency of its management, a sales analysis is likely to emphasize the distribution or allocation of sales income rather than its source. This type of analysis involves the computation of a series of ratios indicating what part of the sales dollar is represented by each item on the profit and loss statement and the subsequent comparison of these ratios with a series of standard ratios developed for the industry. Implicit in the computation of standard ratios is the assumption that a well-managed company will have ratios approximating averages of those in the industry. The limitations of this and of other assumptions made in the computation of standard ratios will be indicated in Chapter IV which deals specifically with ratio analysis.

To the statistician a breakdown of the sales income, either by source or by destination of the funds, is inadequate. Both forms of analysis reveal variability, but they do little to explain it. The accountant, for example, may classify sales by geographical areas, but the tools by which one accounts for the variation in sales among territories are those of the statistician. The application of correlation technique to the problem of analyzing the sales of a business enterprise represents a relatively new development and cuts across both types of analysis referred to above. Differences, both in sales and in ratios derived from sales, may frequently be explained through the statistical process of relating such differences to various internal and external factors.

All of the preceding types of analysis are static in that the comparisons are assumed to be made as of some specific period in time. The three analyses in combination provide a microscopic picture of the source, the destination, and the interrelationships of the parts of sales income during any specific accounting period. There is need, however, for an analysis that parallels the stream of time. The fourth and final type of analysis provides a means for discovering consistent behavior patterns within sales data ordered in time. An extrapolation of the patterns provides a forecast of future sales. The purpose of this dynamic type of analysis may be summarized as follows: (1) to discover and classify the forces that cause sales to fluctuate over a period of time; (2) to measure the influence of each of the various classes of forces; and (3) to forecast the probable future sales by projecting patterns of previous sales behavior.

In order to illustrate the mutual aid provided by static and dynamic analyses in the making of a sales forecast, we may assume a company that classifies its sales by territories and by products. If these two static analyses have been made continuously for a term of years, the analyst will have available three sets of data, two of which are breakdowns of total sales. By applying time series analysis to the total, as well as to the two series of classified sales, a triple check is provided on the forecast of future sales. The behavior patterns that are found typical in the sales of the several territories should, when projected into the future, check in total with the sum of the estimated sales for the several products, and the twain should agree with the sales forecast as derived from a dynamic analysis of total sales.

OUTLINE OF STEPS FOR THE CONTROL OF SALES

In approaching the problem of sales control through the broad gate of general budgetary principles, one finds the field roughly divisible into two parts. The first is represented by methods and techniques appropriate for making the budget estimates. The second is concerned with means and methods for making the estimates effective. The activities connected with the first call for the knowledge and abilities of a business forecaster, whereas those associated with the second require administrative abilities. Of the two spheres of activity, forecasting has been the more neglected. A number of books have been written on the methods and practices of general business forecasting, and magazine articles galore have appeared to explain how individual companies predict sales. Little, however, has been done to synchronize these two substantial bodies of information. The information relative to general business forecasting is fairly well organized, and the various procedures employed have been classified into categories which have become sufficiently well known to be considered almost standard nomenclature. No comparable degree of organization of materials and of standardization of procedures has yet been achieved in the field of individual business forecasting.

The chaotic state of the information relative to specific business forecasting can be regarded either as a boon or as a challenge. The absence of signs and guideposts to direct the activities of the forecaster is a boon to the extent that his mind is left free to explore each problem without any hampering tradition as to how it should be done. To minds intent upon placing knowledge in order, the piecemeal treatment of individual business forecasting is more of a challenge. The outline presented below represents an attempt to organize the materials and the methods used in the control of sales and to merge points of view of persons with different backgrounds and experiences. The topics cover fields of interest shared by the statistician, the accountant, and the market analyst. The methods of analysis involve procedures that have become well established in each of these three major spheres of activity. Whatever novelty may be contained in the program consists in the organization of analyses into a systematic approach to a common problem. The aim has been to indicate the complementary character of the various analyses in the control of sales rather than to emphasize the efficacy of any single method of approach.

I. Classification and analyses of internal sales and cost data
   A. Analyses of the static type
      1. Classification of sales and cost data as a first step toward the discovery of weak spots within the sales organization
      2. Establishment of significant relationships through various forms of ratio and correlation analyses
   B. Analyses of the dynamic type
      1. Discovery, classification, and measurement of forces affecting sales and costs over a period of time
      2. Synthesis of forces and establishment of sequences preliminary to the making of forecasts
II. Discovery and measurement of the market factors influencing and conditioning the sales of a business enterprise

A. Static analysis of basic factors upon which the existence of a market depends
B. Dynamic analysis of current business and economic conditions which exert a temporary influence upon the market

III. Combination of analyses and merging of divergent points of view into a sales program

CHAPTER III

The Classification of Sales and Costs

ANY COMPANY, whether it is a peanut stand or a public utility, has the raw material out of which a sales analysis can be made. The material has its inception with the writing of the first sales invoice and tends to increase in direct proportion to the volume and variety of sales transactions. A single sales invoice is a relatively simple thing, yet thousands of them taken together provide a problem as varied and as intricate as the transactions out of which they grew. The analyses with which Chapters III, IV, and V deal are static in contrast to the dynamic analysis of Chapters VI and VII. An appropriate classification of sales and costs constitutes the first step in any program for sales control. Not infrequently weak spots in the selling activities may be uncovered by the classification process. Subsequently management may use the results in establishing certain normal and significant relationships.

PRELIMINARY PREPARATIONS

The old adage "a task well begun is half done" might be modified to read "a task well begun is more than half done," and it would still represent a substantial truth as applied to the job of the accountant in planning for the recording of sales transactions. The most important part of the making of the analysis of sales begins even before the first sale is made. The preliminary preparations fall naturally into two categories. The first is concerned with setting up the forms into which each sales transaction is to be recorded. The second consists in making provisions to insure the correct recording of each sales transaction. An adequate system of internal check aims to provide a maximum degree of independence between the activities of selling and those of recording. The extent, however, to which the principle of division of labor can be invoked to separate the chain of activities is conditioned by the volume of transactions. A complete internal check would require that each person's activities would pass in review before at least one other person. Since this problem is primarily one of administration, it is of less interest to the sales analyst than is the setting up of forms by which sales data are collected and interpreted.

PLANNING THE SALES RECORDS

The planning of sales records requires that the accountant determine what information is needed and what classes he will find profitable to use in tabulating and analyzing that information. The volume and variety of data that are collected at the point of sale set the conditions for preparing the form of the original entry. The number of classes and the volume of sales transactions are the determining factors in setting up the permanent record. Neither the original entry forms nor those for the permanent record can be safely prepared without intimate knowledge of a particular company's operations.

Perhaps the most distinctive characteristic of any adequate system of sales control is the economy of effort that goes into it. Collection, analysis, and application represent the three major steps upon which effort must be expended if control is to be achieved. When the expenditures incurred for establishing control exceed the benefits derived, the source of the difficulty can usually be traced to an overemphasis upon the collection of data. The piling up of sales information has so frequently been mistaken for sales control that conscious effort is needed to keep the analysis and the application of analysis from degenerating into second-rate control functions. The cumulative effect of the following specific failures is a top-heavy planning and records department: (1) failure to ask for the purpose of each item of information; (2) failure to determine the probable value of the information to the company, either for increasing income or for cutting down expenses; (3) failure to determine the probable cost of gathering the data and of weighing this cost against the estimate of income that would be either added or saved; (4) failure to plan the original form of the record so as to obviate frequent future revisions; (5) failure to plan the forms so as to avoid needless duplication both as among departments and as between head office and branch offices.

On the positive side, the following significant factors may be said to determine the volume and variety of sales data required for adequate control:

1. *Size of the business.*—The intimate and personal supervision so characteristic of small enterprises gradually disappears as the business grows larger, so that formal accounting and statistical records must supply the need.

2. *Number of products sold.*—A company selling a large number of products requires more records than one which concentrates its attention on a few. The diffusion of interest arising from a large number of products must be counterbalanced by a greater amount of information.

3. *Nature of the demand for products sold.*—Other things being equal, the person who sells goods of relatively elastic demand requires more information than one who sells goods having a more uniform and stable demand. In general, the need for records and data increases in proportion to the hazards of loss, and these tend to be greater for products of elastic demand.

4. *Financial resources available for the collection and analysis of data.*—One of the distinctive advantages of operating a business in accordance with a budget is the proportionality and harmony of interests that careful planning tends to foster among the various functions. Fact gathering and record keeping can become a fetish, so that the scale of operations in this particular direction must be watched quite as closely as those of other departments of the business.

THE MECHANICS OF CLASSIFICATION

The technique of classifying sales is conditioned primarily by two factors—the volume of transactions and the number of classes into which the sales are to be grouped. If the business is small and the number of classes is very limited, the process of classification can be carried out on the books of account. By setting up the sales book in columnar form and summarizing the columns periodically a total of transactions by classes is readily obtained.

When the volume of transactions is large or the number of classes great, some mechanical method for classifying the sales becomes desirable. The punched card forms the basis for most of the mechanical methods of classification. When all the pertinent information from the sales invoices has been entered upon specially designed cards, an electrically operated sorting machine quickly provides any classification of the sales that may be desired. Large companies have been able to classify 25,000 invoices a day with a relatively small working force.[1]

The volume of sales transactions and the number of classifications required for the economical use of mechanical methods tends to vary with each type of business enterprise. Provision with some tabulating equipment company for the periodic classification of sales invoices on a service-charge basis is occasionally the most economical arrangement for a company whose sales transactions are too numerous for manual methods and yet are insufficient to justify the installation of a thoroughly mechanized system that will provide a continuous flow of information by sales categories.

THE SELECTION OF BASES OF CLASSIFICATION

In selecting the basis or bases upon which sales are to be classified management should be able to identify the factors that are most likely to effect the magnitude of its net profit. Not every variable, however, is worthy of being made the basis of a sales classification. Unless the influence is of sufficient magnitude to justify the additional expense of classification, the variable is not to be considered significant. The selection of the significant factors can usually be made from a general knowledge of the business and *a priori* reasoning. In doubtful cases decision must be reserved until the basis of classification is put to the test and the net profit by categories ascertained.

Justification for the adoption of the net-profit test as a criterion of significant classifications rests upon the legitimacy of the profit motive and the desire to make net profits a maximum. And, in any particular business enterprise net profit is something less than it might be unless each line of goods sold, each customer served, each order filled, and each territory covered, yields an income that exceeds the allocated outgo by the greatest possible margin. The rigorous application of this principle implies a detailed system of sales classification on the income side, matched by an intricate system of

[1] Childs, "Methods of Analysis of Sales Records."

cost accounting on the expense side. The manner in which these complementary systems function will become apparent in the following sections in which the major bases of classification are discussed.

CLASSIFICATION BY PRODUCTS

The number of products which a company sells may range from one to several thousand. The Regal Shoe Company, for instance, sells a single product of uniform quality at a standard uniform price. Sears, Roebuck and Company, on the other hand, sells thousands of products in a great variety of styles, sizes, materials, and so forth. Both companies find a classification of their sales by products useful as a means of control.

The decision to classify sales by products should be made only after careful consideration has been given to the various characteristics of products sold. Physical characteristics are the most obvious and should be among the first to be studied. Some of the company's products may be heavy, others light in weight. Some may be bulky, and others very compact. These are characteristics that affect the cost of handling, storing, and shipping. If the differences in these costs are not made up by proportionate differences in sales income, the net profit is affected. The probable extent of the variations in profit occasioned by these physical characteristics determines the wisdom of classifying sales on this basis.

Again, products sold may vary as to their demand characteristics. Some may be staple goods, whereas others are affected by the style factor; some may be durable, and others nondurable; some may be nationally advertised, whereas others are private brands of the distributor. These demand characteristics affect both the sales income and the costs. Durable goods, for example, do not lend themselves well to repeat orders. On the other hand, they represent a rather low cost of deterioration and obsolescence during the inventory period. Again, nationally advertised goods usually provide small gross margins for the retail distributor, yet the costs of selling are presumably less than for privately branded or little-known articles. All sources of dissimilarity in the demand characteristics of a company's products should be carefully explored to determine their probable effect on net profit.

Another product characteristic that might be mentioned as affording a basis for classifying sales and expenses is the service element that is frequently a part of the contract of sale. If the original sale price of an article is assumed to include a period of free service, or if the guarantee is such as to obligate the seller for various uncertain outlays in the future, the income and the costs incident thereto are quite different from those for a product which does not possess these service or guarantee features. Usually, the difference is great enough to warrant a separation of income and of costs pertaining to serviced or to guaranteed products from the income and the costs of products lacking these features.

No general rule can possibly be laid down respecting the characteristics of a product that warrant a classification. Much depends upon the volume of transactions, as well as the facilities of the particular company for handling a variety of products. Every characteristic, however, should be examined as a possible source of significant variation in net profit.

The benefits to be derived from an analysis of sales along product lines are most apparent in estimating future sales. The total of a series of sales estimates, distinguished as to products or groups of products, provides a very helpful check upon the probable accuracy of an estimate made independently of these distinctions. Other applications for such analyses are: the setting of quotas by products and classes of products to represent a well-balanced selling program, the checking of performance against estimates to determine the weak spots of each salesman's selling effort, the compensation of salesmen on the basis of the kind and quantity of each product or group of products sold, the gauging of relative popularity of products and changing trends in consumer buying, and finally, the formulation of selective selling policies for which it is necessary to determine the extent to which each product, group of products, or division of products has contributed to the final net profit or net loss of the company.

CLASSIFICATION BY SELLING UNIT

The term "selling unit" is used here to designate any coördinate member of a sales group within the company's organization. Thus, "selling unit" might refer to a salesman in the field, to one of a series of branch managers, or to one of a series of retail store outlets. Although the selling units are assumed to constitute a homogeneous selling group, there is obviously a variation in both the income and the expenses that are associated with the different units. The one question of significance, however, from the point of view of one who contemplates a classification of sales by selling units, is whether or not the dissimilarity among the members of the group is sufficiently great to warrant classification along these lines.

The analysis of sales by products and that by selling units may occasionally coincide, as, for example, in the classification of sales by departments in a department store. This is an analysis by products as seen from the angle of the objects sold, but from the viewpoint of one who does the selling it is an analysis by selling units. No possible confusion can arise provided one keeps in mind that the analysis by selling units always relates to the active selling agent.

The sales manager is quite definitely the chief beneficiary of information obtained from an analysis of sales by selling units, since without this information he could neither compensate the salesmen nor direct their efforts. Even for the payment of straight salaries he should know the sales of the various salesmen, and this knowledge becomes imperative as soon as he contemplates the payment of bonuses and commissions, the establishment of quotas, the awarding of prizes, and the promotion of salesmen.

For the general executive, interested in controlling profits, a combination of sales analysis and cost analysis by selling units provides a basis for determining the relative profitableness of various branches, stores, departments, and salesmen. In fact, any measure of efficiency that might be adopted with respect to the sales organization would require that sales be classified on the basis of selling units and supplemented by a cost classification along identical lines.

CLASSIFICATION BY SALES CHANNEL OR OUTLET

A sales channel or outlet differs from a selling unit in several respects. The former denotes a member in a homogeneous group; the latter may represent widely different categories, ranging from the specialty salesman to the large department store and the mail-order house. Moreover, the selling unit can be assumed to be a part of the company's organization, whereas the sales outlet or channel usually extends much beyond the limits of the company's organization in the direction of the ultimate consumer. Consequently, the analysis is appropriate only for enterprises that operate at some distance from the consumer, such as wholesaling, jobbing, and manufacturing enterprises.

The determination of the relative popularity of several sales channels in distributing specific products, the framing of advertising policies to reach the greatest possible number of customers, the budgeting of sales by sales channels, the checking of subsequent performance against sales estimates, and the appraisal of several channels or outlets as to relative profitableness are a few of the important purposes served by a classification of sales by outlets.

CLASSIFICATION BY CUSTOMERS

If customers were identical with respect to the quantity of goods they buy, the quality they desire, the frequency of their purchases, their nearness to the seller, their promptness in paying their bills, and so forth, there would be no need for an analysis of sales along these lines. Since they are obviously different, each of the various sources of their unlikeness must be examined to see whether or not the variety is great enough to produce any decided difference in the profitableness of one customer compared to another. Even significant differences may not offer an opportunity for saving in distribution costs. The corner groceryman, for example, must serve any person who comes to buy regardless of how difficult the customer and how small his patronage.

A classification of sales by customers may serve a variety of purposes. The sales manager, for example, may use the information in directing the sales force toward a larger volume of business. By comparing the company's sales to each customer with the customer's financial rating and capacity to buy the sales manager can point out those customers from whom a greater volume of business can reasonably be expected. Possibly some salesmen may be spending too much time on small customers; others may be covering their territories in a haphazard manner. For revealing such low spots in the daily routine of selling, a carefully prepared set of customers' records constitutes an almost indispensable aid.

The setting of sales quotas represents a second possible application for an analysis of sales by customers. Assuming a small number of customers in each territory, a forecast can be made of the amount of business that each can reasonably be expected to provide. A summation of the several estimates provides a territorial quota for the salesman.

Finally, the analysis of sales by customers may be used to introduce a selective selling policy. A modern trend in distribution emphasizes the necessity of segregating income and expenses according to their source, after which policies may be so modified that the non-profit elements can either be eliminated or substantially reduced in number. The application of this principle of selective selling to customers' accounts assumes that management not only knows the relative profitableness of its various accounts but also is able to place its finger on the reasons for an account being either profitable or unprofitable. Aside from the obvious factor of volume of purchases, such variables as the location of the customer, the size of his orders, and the kind of products purchased are the most significant in determining the profitableness of any particular account. Analyses made along these lines can profitably supplement the analysis by customers in establishing the reasons for profit or lack of profit in each account.

CLASSIFICATION BY SIZE OF ORDERS

Other things being equal the net profit per customer will vary in direct proportion to the volume of sales per customer. The size of order is one of the many "other things" that are seldom, if ever, equal. Brown may have purchased the same volume of goods during the year as Jones but because Brown purchased in a few large lots and Jones in many small ones Brown's account was profitable whereas Jones was served at a loss. The hypothetical data of Table 2

TABLE 2

Relative Profitableness of Two Customers' Accounts

	Customer Brown		*Customer Jones*	
Number of orders		10		100
Total income from each customer		$1,000		$1,000
Cost of goods sold to each customer	$600		$600	
Cost to dispose of goods:				
12 monthly calls of salesmen at $5 per call	60		60	
Cost of filling orders at $4 per order	40		400	
Total costs charged to each customer		700		1,060
	Profit:	300	Loss:	60

will serve to illustrate the importance of size of order as an element in the profitableness of customers' accounts.

Inspection of the data given above reveals that the difference in profitableness of the two accounts is to be found in the number of orders. Experience has shown that certain costs connected with putting through an order and billing the customer are much the same whether the sale is for $10 or for $1,000. One of the most suggestive analyses of such distribution costs is that given by Eldon Wittwer, market analyst. The five groups of costs and their content are as follows: [2] (1) order costs (expenses connected with the receipt of the order which tend to vary in direct proportion to the number of orders); (2) invoice costs (expenses connected with the billing, filing, and recording of accounts receivable and affected very little by the size of the orders); (3) item costs (expenses connected with the keeping of cost records, the operation of the shipping room and the stockroom, all of which tend to vary with the size of the order); (4) financial costs (selling, administrative, office, and shipping expenses that are not capable of allocation in the categories above); and (5) call costs (expenses that are definitely associated with the salesmen, such as salesmen's salaries, commissions, bonuses, and traveling expenses).

By dividing the sum of the expenses in each category by the appropriate number of units a series of unit costs are obtained that are helpful in setting the size of minimum orders. Assuming the following unit costs in each of the five categories and a gross profit margin of 30 percent, the break-even point for a simple order of five items may be readily determined.

TABLE 3

UNIT COSTS AND BREAK-EVEN POINT FOR A SIMPLE FIVE-ITEM ORDER

Order cost	$ .50
Invoice cost	2.50
Item cost at $.10 per item	.50
Call cost	4.50
Total costs (excluding financial)	8.00
Gross profit margin (less 10 percent for financial costs)	20%
Break-even order size	$40.00

[2] Hovey, "Cost Accounting and Budget Making," in Taylor Society, *Bulletin*, XVI (No. 3), 100–103.

Under the hypothetical conditions assumed above, the break-even point on the five-item order is $40. On any five-item order less than $40, management would lose money. If the order were received by mail, the break-even point might be reduced—the extent of the reduction, if any, depending upon the treatment of call costs. If the mail order came in as the result of a salesman's call, there would be no change in the break-even order size, since the call costs would follow the mail order. If no portion of call costs were allocated to the mail orders, the break-even point would be $17.50 rather than $40.

Some rather startling results have been obtained by companies that have analyzed their costs of orders. Lewis H. Bronson of the Bronson and Townsend Company, wholesalers of hardware in southern New England, made an order cost analysis and discovered a cost of $1.96 for the simplest one-item order taken by an outside salesman.[3] If the same order came in by mail, the cost was 96 cents. The break-even point with respect to size of order in that particular business was determined to be $15.00. The most startling revelation was that 50 percent of the orders amounted to less than $15.00, so that the other 50 percent gave the company its profits and paid the losses sustained on the first. When the patronage was evaluated in terms of these findings, 73 percent of the 1,464 accounts were found to be unprofitable. The subsequent change of marketing policy resulted in an increase of net profits that was most gratifying.

Some companies have hoped to protect themselves from selling unprofitable accounts by setting a minimum annual volume of sales per customer. A large furniture manufacturer, for example, sets the minimum amount of sales at $250 annually for each customer. Those customers who buy less than the minimum are considered unprofitable for a salesman's attention and must be served by mail.[4] To the extent that small orders are rather definitely concentrated in small accounts the problem of the unprofitable orders may be handled this way. There is danger, however, in assuming too close correlation between order size and account size. The variables that condition the profitableness of any customer's account are so numerous that no single factor can easily be chosen to represent the others.

[3] Lewis H. Bronson, "Evaluation of Territory of Customers," an address delivered before the 16th annual meeting of the Chamber of Commerce of the United States, May 7, 1928.

[4] Childs, "Methods of Analysis of Sales Records."

CLASSIFICATION BY TERRITORY OR GEOGRAPHICAL AREA

Differences with respect to the number of customers, the volume of their purchases, the type of goods they buy, the distances between towns, and the general topography of the region are among the more important sources of diversity that operate to produce profit in one sales territory and loss in another. To discover the profitable and the unprofitable sections of a company's distribution area is one of the chief purposes of an analysis of sales by territories. Such an analysis has been the starting point for many selective selling programs, as a result of which distribution areas have been trimmed and then cultivated more rigorously and intensively.[5]

For the assignment of territorial sales quotas the sales must, of course, be classified by territories. The classification is essential both for setting the quota and for checking the performance against estimates. Finally, the sales classified by territories may be used by the budget director in building up and checking the total estimated sales for the company. If, for example, the sum of the separate estimates, made more or less independently for each territory, checks closely with the estimate made for the whole company, considerable confidence may be placed in the reasonableness of the forecasts.

CLASSIFICATION BY TERMS OF SALE

Cash, C.O.D., credit, on approval, and so forth are some of the designations employed in classifying sales on the basis of terms of sale. Within the credit category various subdivisions indicating the terms of credit may be used.

The chief purpose of classifying sales on the basis of terms is that of enabling the treasurer to plan his financial requirements. By referring to the record of previous sales, broken down according to terms, he is able to allocate into similar categories the estimated future sales and to draw up a schedule showing estimated cash receipts for the ensuing period.

[5] An excellent example of the effective reduction of a sales area to produce net profit is afforded by the Brockway Company. This company was started in 1855 as a carriage shop and by 1930 had become a large manufacturing enterprise selling motor trucks in 48 states and 65 foreign countries. A series of deficits following 1929 forced the company to retrench. By reducing its sales area to eleven states located in the heart of the motor truck market it has made its operations show a profit.

A second purpose that an analysis of sales by terms might serve is that of appraising a sales policy. The costs incident to the granting of credit can be weighed against its benefits as shown through the volume of credit sales. Each of the various terms of sale might be evaluated in a similar fashion in order to discover which is most profitable.

CLASSIFICATION BY METHODS OF DELIVERY

The mounting costs of delivering goods has become the increasing concern of retail stores. The larger delivery areas, the greater degree of traffic congestion, and the increased tendency of customers to use the delivery service are the more important factors responsible for this problem. A classification of sales on the basis of delivery methods is the starting point for the control of current delivery costs, the making of estimates for the probable requirements of equipment and personnel in the delivery department, and the appraisal of various delivery methods and policies. The fulfillment of these purposes assumes that costs as well as sales are classified by method of delivery. The decision as to whether a particular territory is worth exploiting frequently hinges on the cost of delivery. A knowledge of these costs can aid also in adapting the method of delivery to the location and the volume of business that each territory contains.

CLASSIFICATION BY ADVERTISING COPY AND MEDIA

Most advertising is purchased on the shot-gun principle. A heavy charge of ammunition in the form of a huge advertising appropriation is fired in the general direction of the market in the hope that a few of the shots may find their way to the target. The wastes incident to this policy may arise either from a defective firing piece (poor advertising copy) or from defects in marksmanship (poor selection of space and media). The making of test campaigns and the keying of advertisements are among the devices by which advertisers have endeavored to overcome these respective defects. Both devices assume a classification of sales. The first assumes an analysis of sales by advertising copy, and the second a classification by either or both copy and media.

A cost analysis by copy or by media presents little difficulty, since the expenditure is directly associated with copy or media in the purchase of advertising space. A comparison of media costs with records of analyzed sales provides the advertising manager with an effective instrument of control both in arranging advertising contracts and in estimating advertising expense. Ratios representing the relation of media costs to sales may be developed and applied both as a check on the estimate of advertising expense and as a basis for judging its reasonableness.

CLASSIFICATION AS RELATED TO ALLOCATION

Two complementary processes are involved in most of the applications that have been made of sales and cost analyses. The first of these is classification, and it involves the setting up of categories into which a large number of relatively small items are sorted and accumulated into a series of subtotals. The second process is allocation, and it represents a break-down of some aggregate item into a number of parts applicable to a series of minor subdivisions. Whereas sales analysis is primarily a classification process, cost analysis is largely allocation. Sales are usually made under circumstances that permit recording on the original sales invoice of every item of information that is likely to be significant in the making of any subsequent analysis. Only the direct costs (those definitely associated with specific products, customers, territories, and so forth) can be treated in a similar manner. The joint and overhead costs must be allocated, and the process of allocation presents greater difficulties than those found in classification.

Regarded as problems in methodology, the allocation of costs and the setting of sales quotas exhibit similar characteristics. Both involve the subdivision of totals, and both require the selection of equitable bases. Moreover, the results obtained in each case are estimates and must be interpreted as possessing somewhat less "reality" than either accumulated actual sales or total actual expenditures. These common characteristics seem to warrant treating the two problems in a common setting. Their discussion has therefore been reserved for the concluding chapter, which deals specifically with combination and application of analyses.

CHAPTER IV

Ratio Analysis of Sales and Costs

THE DIVISION of sales and costs into categories determined by some criterion of classification represents analysis in accordance with the usual dictionary definition of the term. This "separation of anything into constituent parts or elements" does not, however, constitute the whole of analysis. There remains an equally important function for which classification represents the preliminary preparation. This second function consists in the establishment of significant relationships of the parts to one another and of the parts to the whole. The dictionary defines this complementary aspect of analysis in the following addenda: "also, an examination of anything to distinguish its component parts separately, or in relation to the whole."

RATIO VERSUS FUNCTIONAL ANALYSIS

Relationships rather than absolute magnitudes are to be emphasized in this chapter and the following chapter. Relationships, however, may take either of two forms. The present chapter deals with ratios indicating the proportion between certain magnitudes selected from the summary statements of a business. Chapter V deals with the less familiar but more refined relationships expressed as algebraic functions. Since a ratio is itself a function of two variables, it also may be represented as an algebraic equation of a specific type. Hence, the functional relationships represent the general category of which ratios constitute a part, but a part so important that it merits separate treatment.

The practice of computing ratios to serve as instruments of managerial control began somewhere around the turn of the century in the elementary analyses of balance sheets and has spread to include the items on the income statement as well. The use of algebraic functions as instruments of managerial control represents a more recent development, having been used first in the study of time relationships and in certain agricultural problems involving the use of correlation technique. The earlier type of analysis has become fairly well known under the designation of "ratio analysis." The more general algebraic method of expressing relationships will be referred to as "functional analysis."

The relationships that are described in this chapter and the following chapter pertain to some specific time period. Consequently, both types of analysis are static rather than dynamic in nature.

RATIO ANALYSIS ILLUSTRATED

The following income statement will serve to illustrate a few of the simple ratios in which the item of net sales appears as the common divisor or base to which other items in the statement are related.

TABLE 4

JOHN SMITH

PROFIT AND LOSS STATEMENT FOR THE YEAR ENDED DECEMBER 31, 1938

Sales			$37,015	
Less: Returns			1,665	
Net sales			35,350	100.0%
Cost of Goods Sold				
Inventory, January 1, 1938	$1,500			
Purchases	26,737	$28,237		
Less: Inventory, December 31, 1938		3,250		
Cost of goods sold			24,987	70.7
Gross profit on sales			10,363	29.3
Selling Expenses				
Salesmen's salaries	3,950			11.2
Rent of sales office	1,500			4.2
Depreciation of salesroom furniture	500			1.4
Total selling expenses		5,950		16.8
Administrative Expenses				
Office salaries	1,800			5.1
Office supplies	205			0.6
Telephone and telegraph	156			0.4
Insurance	85			0.2
Taxes	134			0.4
Depreciation of office furniture	150			0.4
Total administrative expenses		2,530		7.2

Financial Management Expenses				
Sales discount	685			1.9
Bad debts	200			0.6
Total financial management expenses		885		2.5
Total expenses			9,365	26.5
Net profit for the year			$998	2.8

The statement as shown above, with each item expressed as a percentage of sales, indicates the manner in which the average sales dollar is distributed. For example, each dollar of net sales was applied as follows:

TABLE 5

DISTRIBUTION OF THE SALES DOLLAR

	Cents
Cost of goods sold	70.7
Selling expenses	16.8
Administrative expenses	7.2
Financial management expenses	2.5
Net profit	2.8
Total	100.0

Were the analysis to be terminated at this point, it would have little significance. In the first place, there are a number of important relationships involving sales and items closely associated with sales that do not appear upon the income statement. Secondly, a percentage standing alone is no better (and from some points of view much worse) than the absolute magnitudes upon which it is based. The only possible purpose of reducing the profit and loss statement to a percentage basis is that of aiding comparison. Comparison, however, assumes the existence of other similar ratios that may be taken as guides or yardsticks in appraising current condition and performance. Unless these can be found, ratio analysis degenerates into a jumbled series of more or less meaningless percentages.

WHAT RATIOS ARE IMPORTANT

The number of ratios and reciprocals of ratios that may be derived from a statement containing n items is equal to $n^2 - n$. Thus a simple income statement of ten items contains ninety possible ratios and reciprocals of ratios. Consequently, the analyst must select from the possible relationships only those that are most significant and must concentrate his efforts on establishing and maintaining those relationships at levels that indicate a sound and healthy enterprise.

Authorities are not of one mind as regards the relative degree of significance to be attached to the various ratios developed from the summary statements of a business enterprise. One authority, for example, lists nine important ratios and groups them into categories according to the specific business ailment for which each serves as a diagnostic aid.[1] Another authority has prepared a list of fourteen ratios which he considers important and for which he has developed an elaborate table of summary data classified by years and by industries.[2]

Since the purpose of the present study is limited to the treatment of methods appropriate for controlling sales, only those ratios in which net sales are used or which constitute an important adjunct to the control of sales will be discussed. Among the more important ratios in which the item of net sales appears either as divisor or dividend are the following: ratio of net profits to net sales; ratio of net sales to net worth; ratio of net sales to net working capital; ratio of net sales to receivables; ratio of net sales to inventory; and ratio of net sales to fixed assets.

Ratios in which net sales do not appear but which are significant adjuncts in controlling sales are: ratio of current assets to current liabilities, commonly called "current ratio"; ratio of quick assets (cash and receivables) to current liabilities, frequently referred to as the "acid test" of solvency; and ratio of net profits to net worth.

Each of the above named ratios has been designed to meet one or more specific purposes. These can best be discussed by grouping the ratios into three categories, which are as follows: (1) ratios designed to measure the results of operation; (2) ratios designed to indicate weaknesses and defects in current operations; and (3) ratios designed to reveal deficiencies in the financial structure and character of fixed investments.

RATIOS USED TO MEASURE RESULTS OF OPERATION

The desire for profits constitutes the principal motivating force in our present-day economy. The success of a business enterprise is to

[1] Gilman, *Analyzing Financial Statements.*

[2] Foulke, *Behind the Scenes of Business,* and *Signs of the Times.*

be gauged, however, not so much by the absolute amount of profit, but by the relationship of net profits to other magnitudes. The two most frequently used denominators are net sales and net worth. The ratio of net profits to net sales represents the average amount of net profit for each dollar of net sales income, whereas the ratio of net profits to net worth shows the average amount earned on each dollar of capital invested. Since the first ratio is usually much smaller, it has frequently been featured in educational advertising campaigns to demonstrate the reasonableness of the profit earned. The more significant test, however, is provided by the net profits to net worth ratio. The level of current interest rates is usually accepted as representing the minimum value for this ratio. Unless the capital invested in the business enterprise earns at least as much as it would if it were put into good bonds, it provides nothing to compensate for the hazards of the enterprise.

RATIOS DESIGNED TO REVEAL DEFECTS IN CURRENT OPERATIONS

Among the ratios designed to reveal defects in current operations are the following: net sales to net working capital; net sales to inventory; net sales to receivables; current assets to current liabilities; and quick assets to current liabilities. The state of health of the enterprise as gauged by these various ratios is one over which management can exercise a very considerable influence within a relatively brief period of time. In this respect they are distinctly different from the third category of ratios that pertain to the financial structure of a business.

The ratio of net sales to net working capital is referred to as the rate of working capital turnover and is derived by dividing net sales by the difference between current assets and current liabilities. The highest working capital turnover rates are to be found in industries whose products are perishables of relatively small unit cost. The lowest rates are provided by industries selling some durable product of relatively high unit value upon long credit terms. Studies made by Roy A. Foulke,[3] of Dun and Bradstreet, Inc., reveal that during the five-year period 1932–36 the three lines of business having the highest rates of working capital turnover were as follows: fresh fruits and produce (15.55); butter, eggs, and cheese (11.90); and canners of

[3] Foulke, *Signs of the Times.*

fruits and vegetables (11.19). The three lines of business having the lowest rates of working capital turnover during this period were: installment furniture (1.80); industrial machinery (2.35); and installment clothing (2.44). As far as different industries and lines of business are concerned there seems to be no real relationship between the rates of working capital turnover recorded during this period and the net profit percentages on sales. Within any specific industry the relationship might be either direct or inverse depending upon what sales policies were pursued in obtaining the larger turnover rates. If prices were cut as a means of increasing sales, the net profit ratios would tend to decline and the relationship might well be inverse. If, however, the larger turnover rates were secured by means of a more efficient use of working capital, the relationship would tend to be direct.

The ratio of net sales to inventory expresses the logical connection between the selling process and the antecedent condition which is the possession of merchandise. The inventory used as the divisor should be an average over the fiscal period and should be valued at selling price in order that it may agree with the terms of the dividend which is net sales. For the sake of expediency, however, these conditions have frequently been sacrificed. Lacking information as to average inventory, the analyst has employed simply the closing inventory —and this not at sales prices, but at the value as shown by the balance sheet. A ratio which is calculated in this manner is obviously a hybrid and may be quite far from the true merchandise turnover rate. If, however, all merchandise turnover rates within a specific line of business are computed in this manner, all will tend to be exaggerated and the extent of the exaggeration may be about the same. A comparison between ratios is, therefore, legitimate, even though accuracy in the measurement of turnover has been sacrificed.

Since inventory is one of the principal components of working capital, the turnover of merchandise tends to vary directly with the turnover of working capital, the former tending, of course, to range higher in magnitude. A graphic analysis made upon the data provided by Roy A. Foulke [4] revealed only one out of sixty-one lines of business in which the working capital turnover was markedly higher than the merchandise inventory turnover. Being more directly related to sales, the inventory turnover is a more precise and effective tool for sales

[4] Foulke, *Signs of the Times.*

control. It indicates the number of times during the fiscal period that the investment in merchandise has been liquidated through sales and reinvested. Other things being equal, the business unit which has the largest merchandise turnover will make the most profit.

As inventory represents the usual condition antecedent to sales, so accounts receivable represent the usual consequence of sales. The ratio of net sales to accounts receivable is the logical complement to the merchandise turnover ratio, and the two ratios taken together provide a more detailed and specific explanation for either a high or a low turnover of working capital. The magnitude of the sales-receivables ratio is a function of four variables, namely, the credit terms, the value of sales, the proportion of goods sold on credit, and the collection policies of the company.

Assuming a relatively constant rate of sales, all of which are made on credit, the net sales during any fiscal period should bear approximately the same relationship to accounts receivable that the length of the fiscal period bears to the length of the credit period. For example, if the credit period is thirty days, the ratio of annual net sales to accounts receivable should not be less than twelve, since not more than one-twelfth of the annual sales should be outstanding in receivables at any one time.

The assumptions required to give validity to the foregoing relationship of sales to receivables are seldom fulfilled. A considerable proportion of the sales may be made for cash, and the sales curve rarely conforms to the assumption of a uniform horizontal line. Unless correction factors are introduced, one to make allowance for cash sales, and the other to take account of intra-yearly variations in sales, the magnitude of the ratio may be so distorted that nothing of value can be obtained from it.

The last two ratios included in the category of those designed to guide current operations are best considered simultaneously. The "current ratio" (current assets to current liabilities) and the "acid test" ratio (quick assets to current liabilities) are primarily measures of ability to meet current obligations. For years these two ratios constituted practically the only tools used by credit men in passing judgment upon the soundness of a credit risk. They are significant as instruments of sales control primarily because of the part that sales must play in transforming working assets into quick assets. Occasionally the current ratio may indicate a very comfortable margin of current assets over current liabilities, but because of a top-heavy inventory, including possibly a great deal of merchandise which is obsolete and overvalued, the company lacks the ability to pay its current obligations. The "acid test" would, of course, reveal the nature of this weakness, and sales represent the remedial outlet for reducing the investment in merchandise and building up the quick assets of cash and receivables. Thus, the two ratios, if read together, may often provide clues to weaknesses in the merchandising policies and subsequently reflect improvement once remedial measures have been taken.

RATIOS DESIGNED TO REVEAL DEFECTS IN FINANCIAL STRUCTURE

Within this third category of significant relationships fall the two ratios, net sales to net worth and net sales to fixed assets. The first is sometimes referred to as the rate of capital turnover, since it represents the number of times during the course of the fiscal period that the investment in the enterprise has been reclaimed through sales and reinvested. If this ratio is low in comparison to like ratios computed for the industry, it indicates a state of overcapitalization in which the volume of sales is not adequate to support the capital invested in the enterprise. Since the capital, once invested, is not easily retrieved, corrective measures usually lie in obtaining a larger volume of sales—a remedy that is easy to prescribe, but frequently impossible to administer. As a consequence, the deficiency in sales volume may often be the prelude to business failure.

Undercapitalization is the reverse situation. This condition is reflected by a ratio of net sales to net worth that is much higher than it ought to be. It arises out of the ambitious attempt on the part of management to secure a larger volume of sales than the capital structure warrants. The large volume of sales is usually obtained on a small profit margin and can be maintained only by creating heavy liabilities. "Trading on too small equity," "overtrading on the equity," and "overworking the capital" are expressions used to describe the condition. It is one that can lead to failure just as certainly as the opposite condition, that is, not having enough work for the invested capital to do.

The ratio of sales to fixed assets is a more specific relationship designed to show when the investment in assets of the durable type, primarily plant and machinery, gets out of line with the volume of sales. This ratio should usually be read in conjunction with the preceding one of sales to net worth. Over a period of time the ratio of sales to fixed assets should increase somewhat faster than the ratio of sales to net worth. Obviously, this difference in the behavior of the two ratios must be found in the denominators, where the regular charging of depreciation would tend to reduce the values of fixed assets, but the net worth under the normal expansion of business would tend to increase.

STANDARDS AS A NECESSARY POSTULATE

In passing judgment upon the quality of management of any particular business enterprise one must make the postulate that for each of the various ratios derived from the summary statements there is some ideal magnitude that will serve as a standard of comparison. This ideal may be something of a will-o'-the-wisp, which varies from industry to industry, from region to region, from one sales volume to another, from year to year, and even from one season to another within the year. The existence, however, of the ideal, difficult though it may be to locate, cannot be denied without depriving the terms "good" and "poor" of all significance as applied to management. The stubborn reality of business failures would be left in an anomalistic category of events which occur without any causality of prior circumstances.

This postulate of a set of "ideal relationships" for the control of business enterprise may be something of which the individual business manager, especially one engaged in a small enterprise, is wholly unaware. Indifference may characterize his attitude toward the use of any formal set of standard ratios. He may be quite content just to get along and make a reasonable profit. "Getting along," however, implies a certain harmony of relationships, and a "reasonable profit" most assuredly demands some standard of reasonableness.

THE PROBLEM OF OBTAINING STANDARDS

As soon as one grants the pragmatic necessity of having some standards of comparison, the mooted problem how best to secure the standards must be met. That standards must come from experience is granted, but controversy centers in the following problems: what part of experience, whose experience, and by what methods are the standards to be derived?

The first "standards" to be used in the analysis of financial and operating statements were developed without benefit of formal statistical treatment. They were born out of the personal experience of credit men who, in their daily tasks of examining a considerable number of balance sheets, began to perceive a certain regularity and persistency of relationships among the items on the statements examined. These rules of thumb gained wide acceptance, and their popularity has remained even to the present.

One of the earliest and most widely accepted rules of thumb was the "current ratio," which assumes that for every dollar of current liabilities there should be two dollars of current assets. "For years," says one author [5] "this 'two for one' current ratio was the alpha and omega of analyses." Another popular rule of thumb, developed somewhat later as a supplemental guide in appraising the soundness of a credit risk, was the "acid test" relationship of quick assets (cash and receivables) to current debt. Here a dollar-for-dollar relationship was assumed to indicate a safe condition.

The limitations and inadequacies of these early rules of thumb lead to the application of statistical methods in the determination of standard relationships. Here the simplest procedure is that which involves the averaging of the firm's own statements covering several preceding years. The "ideal" relationships for any particular business enterprise are assumed to be those computed from a composite statement whose values are either arithmetic averages or totals of the corresponding values in statements for several years preceding. Let us assume, for illustrative purposes, that the last three annual income statements of the A.B.C. Company showed net sales averaging $240,000. If during this same period of time the balance sheets of the company showed average receivables of $20,000, the standard ratio for sales to receivables would be shown, under these circumstances, as 1,200 percent.

Standard ratios derived in the manner described are identical with those which one would secure were he to compute percentage relationships for each successive year and then summarize by calculating a weighted average—the weights being proportional to the several mag-

[5] Foulke, *Signs of the Times.*

nitudes used as divisors. The number of years chosen for the analysis may vary, though usually it is not less than three nor more than five. For convenience in computation the totals of corresponding items may be substituted for averages. Typical relationships rather than typical magnitudes is what is wanted, and these will be the same in either case.

One of the chief objections to the use of a company's own experience in developing standard ratios is that it tends to perpetuate and to place the stamp of approval upon every undesirable relationship which happens to be current in the balance sheets and profit and loss statements of the company. Any condition of a chronic nature remaining consistently unfavorable over a period of years is carried through into the averages and reflected in the standards. Moreover, there are no possible means by which standards representing an average of experiences over a period of years may exhibit flexibility and allow for major temporal factors such as, for example, changes in the general price level and variations in social and economic conditions.

The second statistical approach to the problem of computing standard ratios seeks to eliminate the possible bias of individual company experience by broadening the base of computation. By including a number of companies engaged in the same line of business the assumption is made that the abnormal relationships in any individual business enterprise will be offset by abnormal relationships of an opposite character in some other company. If this assumption is true, and if no other disturbing elements are present, averages taken of a series of ratios derived from companies engaged in the same line of business would truly represent the standard or normal relationships for the industry.

TIME AS A DISTURBING FACTOR

Much was taken for granted in the earlier statistical analyses from which standard ratios were developed. Pioneers in this field exhibited an overreadiness to ignore the significant influences frequently exerted by the changes in the price level and general business activity. Recognition is gradually being given, however, to the disturbing influence of temporal forces. As the information relative to their impact upon policies of business management accumulates, a greater opportunity is afforded for setting, not a single set of standard ratios to which all firms within an industry are expected to conform, but rather a series of standards that vary both as to homogeneous groups set up within the industry and as to conditions prevailing outside the industry. If standards are to be that which the term itself implies, they must be made flexible enough to take cognizance of the various dynamic forces that are continually modifying business practices and managerial policies.

The ratios which are most likely to be disturbed by temporal factors are those in which either net sales or net profits appear as one of the variables. Balance sheet relationships are somewhat less susceptible to changes over a period of time. Individual items, such as cash, accounts receivables, merchandise inventory, and so forth, may vary considerably because of their very close and direct connection with sales, and yet the relationships involving the larger groups on the balance sheet, such as, for example, the ratio of current assets to current liabilities, may remain relatively stable.

The following are to be considered among the more important classes of temporal factors tending to produce changes in standard relationships:

Changes in the general level of prices.—The prevalence of forward buying on a rising price level as against hand-to-mouth buying on a falling price level (to use but a single illustration) calls for a double standard of all ratios in which inventory is a factor.

Fluctuations in business activity.—If one considers the business cycle to be a characteristic phenomenon of modern industrial economy, consistency would seem to require that its various distinctive phases should be given recognition in establishing standard ratios.

Fluctuations associated with seasons of the year.—Since sales are especially subject to seasonal movements, any ratio in which sales is a factor would tend to exhibit variations of a seasonal character. Because of the heavy seasonal liquidation of merchandise regularly taking place at the end of the year, December 31 ratios involving sales, inventory, accounts receivable, and so forth are likely to be considerably out of line with similar ratios computed at other times during the year.

Fluctuations due to specific changes in managerial policies.—Changes in sales policies that permeate a whole industry such as, for example, the trend toward the establishment of retail outlets by mail-order houses and by certain types of manufacturers, will usually be reflected in the financial and operating ratios. Previously established standards are likely to be so greatly disturbed by these changes that they no longer serve their purpose.

Variations produced by new legislation and changes in governmental policy.—Decisions made by government officials and acts of legislative bodies can be quite as effective in making standard ratios obsolete as the decisions made by management itself. The distribution of corporate surpluses induced by the taxation policies of the Federal Government and the speculative buying sprees of 1936 and early 1937, initiated by the fear of the Government's inflationary policies, are obvious examples of how effective governmental policies can be in disturbing previously established internal relationships.

MEANS FOR OBTAINING CURRENT AND FLEXIBLE STANDARDS

Most students and agencies engaged in establishing standard financial and operating ratios recognize the disturbing influences enumerated above and seek to overcome them by developing their standards from the most recent summary statements. Out of these periodic studies a sequence of standard financial and operating ratios is kept current for each major line of business. Each company within a specific line of business is then able to compare its own ratios with the standards currently developed.

The trend toward currency in ratios is one that might easily lead to the development of seasonal standards for each industry. Logically the justification for intra-yearly standards, especially for industries of a highly seasonal nature, is quite as great as for standards on a yearly basis. The practical difficulties in obtaining a sufficiently large number of monthly or quarterly statements to make the seasonal averages significant might be overcome once the advantages of having more precise and more nearly current standards were demonstrated.

Economists have gone to great lengths in attempting to designate conditions that are characteristic of specific phases of the business cycle. No comparable amount of study has yet been given to differentiate balance sheet and profit and loss relationships during the various cycle phases. The annual studies throw some light upon the problem, but no systematic effort has been made to establish ratios that might be called typical for depression as against those that might characterize prosperity. The obstacles in the way of this type of analysis are even greater than those mentioned in connection with seasonal studies proposed above. If the study were to have validity, each phase of the cycle would call for a considerable number of observations extending back over a term of years. Moreover, comparability of the basic data would require uniform accounting methods within each line of business. Both requirements are difficult to fulfill.

DISTURBING SOURCES OF HETEROGENEITY

Time is not the only major disturbing factor in the establishment of standard financial and operating ratios. If standards are to be derived empirically as averages of a group of ratios, one should avoid the too-common error of mixing "flesh and fowl and good red herring" and treating them as though they were one. Averages are assumed to be restricted to describing homogeneous groups of items, and if the data are in fact heterogeneous, violence is done to this basic assumption. The following are among the more common sources of heterogeneity of which cognizance should be taken before averages are computed.

Geographical location.—Merchandising enterprises, for example, which are close to large wholesale centers, such as New York or Chicago, usually have materially higher inventory turnovers than firms located at such distances that larger orders must be placed and heavier stocks must be carried. Also, labor costs, rents, prices of raw materials, and even interest charges are likely to show significant differences between sections of the country.

Size of the business enterprise.—Not only are the hazards of a large business somewhat different from those of a small enterprise but also the relationships themselves tend toward somewhat different norms or standards. A significant example of the influence of size of enterprise is afforded by the stock-turnover rate of department stores, where the largest stores have an average rate of more than twice that of the smallest stores.[6]

Method of distributing the product.—Some companies may sell to jobbers, whereas others sell directly to the retailer or even operate their own retail store outlets. One could hardly expect the same set of standard ratios to apply throughout an industry within which there

[6] See reports of Bureau of Business Research, Harvard University.

existed these diverse methods of distribution. The rate of inventory turnover and the ratio of sales to receivables would obviously be different.

Terms of sale.—If within the same industry some companies sold exclusively for cash while others sold on credit, any averaging of their sales to receivables would yield a figure quite without meaning as far as serving as a standard is concerned. Moreover, even the firms granting the credit privilege would be lacking in homogeneity unless cognizance were taken of the different credit terms.

Nature of product.—Two business enterprises may fall within the same industrial category and yet have so little in common that a single set of standard ratios would not serve both of them.[7] One may be manufacturing a very high quality product requiring highly skilled labor and sold only within a very select market. The other may specialize in a low-cost product manufactured on a mass production scale and sold upon a wide market. The two could hardly be expected to conform to the same financial and operating standards. Even the articles manufactured may be distinctly different; for example, one paper company may make paper boxes, and another high-grade writing paper; or, one steel company may manufacture steel rails, and another steel pipe. Since the market for these products would be conditioned by different factors, the operating ratios, especially those involving sales, would tend toward different standards.

Type of customer.—Closely related to the nature of the product is the type of customer served. Both sales and accounts receivable are conditioned largely by the amount and variation in customers' purchasing power, which, in turn, is dependent largely on the type of industry dominant in the community. Farmers, for example, create debts during the crop-growing season in anticipation of the harvest, so that sixty to ninety days or even longer terms of credit are not uncommon. Even the social, religious, racial, and educational back-

[7] The great variation in ratios that may be found among companies manufacturing even the same type of product has been studied by John N. Myer, and the results of his analysis appear in his privately printed book *Financial Statement Analysis.* From the financial statements of 40 cotton textile companies and 17 Portland cement companies Myer computed and arrayed three principal ratios. The range in ratios (using the current assets to current liabilities ratio as an example) was from 80 percent to 4,005 percent for the cotton textile manufacturers and 134 percent to 1,684 percent for the cement manufacturers. As Myer points out, such a great variation can hardly be properly described by a single average.

grounds of the customers must be considered insofar as they affect their debt-creating and debt-paying activities.

Size of city or town.—The size of the city or the town in which a business enterprise is located is very likely to exert a significant influence on the financial and operating ratios. This is particularly true of ratios for mercantile establishments. For example, the National Retail Hardware Association classifies ratios for hardware stores into five categories, ranging from ratios for stores in towns of less than 1,000 people to those for stores situated in cities with population of more than 50,000. Selecting the category of stores having approximately the same annual sales volume ($40,000 to $60,000) and tracing the standards for two important ratios (salaries as percentage of sales and profits as percentage of investment), we find the following variation in passing from cities or towns of one size to those of another: [8]

TABLE 6

STANDARD RATIOS SELECTED TO SHOW EFFECT OF SIZE OF TOWN OR CITY

Size of City or Town	*Salaries as Percentage of Sales*	*Net Profits as Percentage of Investment*
Less than 1,000	10.60	7.82
1,000–3,500	11.20	7.54
3,500–10,000	13.38	6.82
10,000–50,000	14.94	4.29
More than 50,000	14.44	3.67

Accounting methods and practice.—No set of financial and operating ratios can possess a degree of either accuracy or uniformity greater than that which is characteristic of the accounting records. Although the American Institute of Accountants, together with such governmental agencies as the Federal Reserve Board, the Interstate Commerce Commission, and, more recently, the Securities and Exchange Commission, have performed yeomen's service in improving the form, terminology, and content of financial and operating statements, there still remain many defects in the manner of recording and presenting accounting information. Sometimes essential information is intentionally obscured, or items are lumped together so that detailed com parative analysis is impossible. Less serious but equally exasperating

[8] The National Cash Register Company, Merchants Service, *Expenses; Margins, Net Profits, Stock-Turns in Retail and Wholesale Business*, Dayton, Ohio, The Service 1935.

is the lack of uniformity in account classification, so that the analyst must recast much of the basic data in order to obtain comparability in the ratios.[9]

MEANS USED TO SECURE HOMOGENEITY

Classification provides the means for reducing heterogeneous data into small groups within which homogeneity may be found. This implies the investigation of each of the various sources of heterogeneity and the use of those that are clearly significant as criteria of classification. Standard ratios may then be compiled for each minor subdivision composed of reasonably homogeneous business units.

The criterion of classification which appears most often in the published studies, such as those prepared by various universities and trade associations, is the size of the business unit. In some instances, size is gauged by capitalization, but more often income is assumed to be the better measure and classes of companies are arranged according to the dollar value of their sales.

The need of carrying the classification of companies beyond the two criteria of type and size of enterprise has not been sufficiently recognized. To be intelligently critical the user of standard financial and operating ratios should be informed upon such significant facts as the number of observations used in establishing the standards, the range or variability of these observations, the precise period of time covered by the analysis, and the methods of averaging that were employed. Too frequently the publishing agency leaves the reader either in the dim light of incomplete supplementary information or in the utter darkness of no information save that represented by the standards themselves. This deficiency is one which will hardly be corrected until users of standard ratios come to appreciate how misleading an average may be if accepted without inquiry into the nature of both the basic data and the methods used in their analysis.

AVERAGE RATIOS VS. STANDARD RATIOS

The justification for using some form of statistical average in deriving standard relationships rests upon the assumption that the optimum value for each ratio lies in a middle ground somewhere between the

[9] For specific defects in financial statements see Myer, *Financial Statement Analysis*, chap. iii.

highest and the lowest values recorded. Defense of this postulate has been conspicuously lacking in the various publications dealing with standard ratios. On the other hand, trenchant criticisms have been made respecting the validity of using any sort of average as a standard. Possibly the best appraisal of the concept and methods may be had by examining a series of possible suppositions.

Starting with the supposition that poor management characterizes every company from which financial and operating results are secured, one can readily see that the mere process of averaging will not improve the quality of the derived ratios. Under such supposed conditions no set of average ratios could be developed that would serve as "standards" according to the intrinsic meaning of that word. At best they would serve as rough guides in ascertaining a company's competitive position in the industry or, at least, from that section of the industry from which the averages of ratios were compiled.

The second supposition, and the one which probably corresponds most closely to current practice, is that within the group of selected companies all degrees of efficiency in management are represented, ranging from the poor to the very best. Under these assumed conditions any set of summary values that one might develop is likely to be nothing more than a triumph for mediocrity. If the averages of ratios representing good, bad, and indifferent managements are to emerge as standards of excellence, one has to assume that poor management is represented by the two distinct ranges upon a scale of values, one of which is among the high ratios and the other among the low, and that both are about equally probable and equally objectionable.

Although much of the current practice in establishing standard ratios indicates a tacit agreement with this assumption, few authorities have critically examined its validity and none have had the boldness to defend it. One writer who has compiled extensive tables of average ratios for a great variety of industries, warns the reader not to accept them as "normal standards," since "the really successful healthy concern in any one of these divisions of industry or commerce would be the business enterprise whose ratios were better than the average." [10] For some relationships "better" means a higher ratio than the average, and for others it represents a lower one. Since the reader is not provided with any measure of variability, he must decide for himself

[10] Foulke, *Signs of the Times.*

how much better any specific set of ratios should be than those provided him by the table. The paucity of information conveyed by a single average of ratios has been partly overcome by the dual system of reporting used by the Harvard Bureau of Business Research which furnishes "goal figures" as well as "common figures." [11]

The third possible procedure for developing "standard" ratios is to confine the analysis to a select group of companies which are considered financially sound and efficiently operated. The virtue of this method is that it provides average ratios that are typical of what has been proven successful by experience. The assumption, of course, is that relationships that have worked for the more profitable companies should continue to work for them as well as for the less profitable ones. In this sense the average ratios are real standards of operation. The merit of this procedure, however, is partly offset by the practical difficulty of finding a sufficiently large number of successfully managed companies to provide significance to the averages. Classification of the selected companies to obtain homogeneous subgroups might easily reduce the number in each category to a point where not only no central tendency of ratios could be found but also real doubt might arise as to whether the experience of the few in a particular class might not be unique and subject neither to duplication nor to imitation.

The foregoing discussion has tended to indicate the impossibility of any ideal solution of the problem of developing standard ratios. If confidence in the magic of large numbers is not to be strained by including a great many heterogeneous companies, then credulity must be given to the potentially typical nature of the relationships found in a few selected companies. No analyst has yet been able to circumvent the horns of this dilemma.

FACTORS IN THE INTERPRETATION OF STANDARD RATIOS

Standard ratios may be interpreted from two points of view. The business executive is interested in standard ratios primarily because they provide him with a yardstick by which he may measure the conditions of his own business. The economist's interest is more general. To him standard ratios provide a factual basis for drawing certain generalizations with regard to trends in business behavior. The inci-

[11] Schmalz, *Operating Results of Department and Specialty Stores in 1936.*

dence of the business cycle, for example, can be quite as effectively gauged by a study of the annual balance sheets and profit and loss statements of an industry as by the analysis of data representing production volumes, stocks of goods, price levels, new capital issues, and similar composite series. The summary statements of individual business enterprises may be regarded as a myriad of tiny springs out of which flows the information that feeds the main streams of economic and business data. Some of the springs of information may be polluted; others may fail to provide the quantity and quality of data desired. These inadequacies and impurities augmented by incomplete, inconsistent, and biased reporting find their way into the main streams from which the information for most economic analyses is drawn.

Preceding topics have indicated a few of the factors that require investigation before applying standard ratios. The following enumeration summarizes and supplements those already given.

Nature of companies included.—An intimate knowledge of the industry is the basic requirement for the intelligent application of any set of standard ratios. The application itself involves: a knowledge of the significant factors producing distinctive differences in the ratios; a classification of companies in which cognizance of these factors has been taken; and, finally, an identification of the specific company with some one of the various homogeneous subgroups for which sets of standard ratios have been compiled.

Number of companies represented.—One can hardly designate any minimum number of companies needed to provide reliable standards. For certain branches of some industries one might take every company and still the number would be inadequate to give much significance to the averages. Standard ratios representing less than a half dozen companies have been published. Necessity is the only acceptable excuse for deriving standards from such limited data.

Recency of data.—The fluctuations in standard ratios from year to year clearly indicate the importance of having standards compiled from recent data. In periods of rapid economic change and severe fluctuations of a cyclical nature, standards even of the preceding year may be completely out of line with current conditions.

Accounting methods and practice.—The virtue of homogeneity in the type of companies analyzed may be lost in a heterogeneity of accounting systems and variety of fiscal periods. Trade associations have done a great deal toward obtaining uniformity in each industry, as regards both accounting methods and the dates upon which statements are prepared.

Type of average employed.—The user of standard ratios is entitled to know what type of average was used in summarizing the individual ratios. Yet some have been published without this information. With five types of averages from which to choose, one writer has felt constrained to devise a sixth—a hybrid sort of thing representing a combination of arithmetic mean, median, and mode.[12] Purely *a priori* reasoning would seem to indicate the mode or the geometric mean as conforming most closely to the nature of the data. The mode, however, is often ruled out because of the limited number of observations, and the geometric mean is very little known outside its small circle of statistical friends.

Significance of a ratio.—Assuming that standard ratios are substantially what their name implies, a comparison of the ratios of an individual company with the standards can be most suggestive. Whereas conformity to the standard in any particular ratio is no guarantee of sound condition, any considerable variance from it is most certainly worthy of investigation. Since a ratio is a function of two variables, consideration must be given to both variables when one is interpreting any specific departure from standard. For example, the ratio of net sales to inventory, so often regarded as a measure of selling efficiency, may quite as reasonably be taken as a measure of buying efficiency. The failure to move obsolete and unsalable merchandise can hardly be charged to the sales force. Again, the ratio of net sales to receivables may be too low, not because the credit department has been indulgent and careless, but because the sales department has been much too eager to achieve a large volume of sales and oversold its customers with goods for which they have had difficulty in paying.

Relative seriousness of variance from standards.—A set of standard ratios provide a sort of fever thermometer for detecting unhealthy conditions in the body of the business enterprise. But, just as a fever thermometer makes no distinction between the abnormal temperature arising from a slight cold and one produced by a tubercular condition of the lungs, so standard ratios give no indication to the business executive how serious a particular abnormal relationship is. Stephen

[12] Wall and Duning, *Ratio Analysis of Financial Statements.*

Gilman [13] has suggested this field as one ripe for research. He points out that in the present state of knowledge common sense is the only criterion, and he lists two business ailments as moderately serious and two as dangerous. Overinvestment in inventories and overinvestment in receivables are conditions quite easily remedied and consequently are only moderately serious. Insufficient capital and overinvestment in fixed assets, however, are conditions that are not easily corrected and consequently are to be interpreted as serious ailments.

STANDARD RATIOS AS RELATED TO BUDGETARY CONTROL

The point of view which dominates most of the published information on the subject of standard ratios tends to emphasize the use of standard ratios as means of appraising the current state of a company's financial health. This emphasis upon the degree of solvency of a business enterprise is quite understandable in the light of what has previously been said concerning the origin and development of standard ratios. A somewhat broader purpose, however, must be invoked if one is to justify the inclusion of standard ratios as one of the methods used in the control of sales.

One can conveniently divide the problem of sales control into two parts; the first is planning and the second is execution. Planning, as expressed through the business budget, is primarily a matter of establishing certain consistencies, some of which relate to factors internal to the business and others to the business unit as influenced by and through environment. First, the sales budget must be consistent with the company's own sales record of current and preceding periods; secondly, it must be in conformity with the potential market for the product; and finally, it must stand in a harmonious relation to all other items appearing upon the summary statements of the specific business enterprise.

Inasmuch as standard ratios presumably represent consistent relationships of items derived from the immediate past, they provide the logical basis for establishing relationships of estimates to guide the immediate future. The comparison of the interrelationships of the budgeted items with the most recent standards for the industry may reveal discrepancies that need correction. Unless the variance is one

[13] Gilman, *Analyzing Financial Statements.*

that can be explained by special circumstances, a revision of the budget would seem to be indicated. If management is willing to make the comparison and accept the burden of explanation for those relationships that are out of line, standard ratios can eventually become powerful prophylactics for the prevention of business ailments, whereas at present they are little more than diagnostic aids.

CHAPTER V

Functional Analysis of Sales and Costs

A REVIEW of the various methods useful for controlling sales and costs reveals at least two broad bases for classification. One centers in the element of time and the part it is assumed to play in making the analysis. The other relates to the mathematical form which the analysis takes. Whereas Chapter IV dealt with ratios as media for expressing sales and cost relationships, this chapter is directed toward the application of more refined methods—graphic devices and algebraic functions.

ILLUSTRATIONS OF STATIC FUNCTIONAL ANALYSIS

Functional relationships of the static type may be grouped into three categories, depending upon the particular variable assumed to be dependent. In order of their size and importance the three categories are: sales, costs, and earnings. The studies discussed in this chapter fall primarily into the first of these three categories, in which sales are expressed as a function of one or more other variables. Functions of the second and third type are to be considered only as they provide a basis for estimating sales and regulating the policies so as to achieve a maximum rate of profit upon the capital invested. Simple two-variable relationships are provided below to illustrate each of the three categories.

In the following illustration sales are expressed as a function of advertising expenditure. The relationship is not intended to be typical, since the particular product is one for which the market demand is almost entirely a function of amount and character of the advertising. The data relate to successive observations made monthly covering a period of sixty months. The observations that are most out of line can be accounted for by particular conditions that tend to distu the normal relationship.

Some of the more distinctive examples of functional cost relationships are to be found in the field of public utility management. R. T. Livingston [1] has employed a least squares straight line in describing the following functional relationship between total operating expenses of a steam-generating plant and different levels of output as recorded

CHART IV. RELATIONSHIP OF MONTHLY SALES TO MONTHLY ADVERTISING EXPENDITURES FOR A WELL-KNOWN DRUG PRODUCT

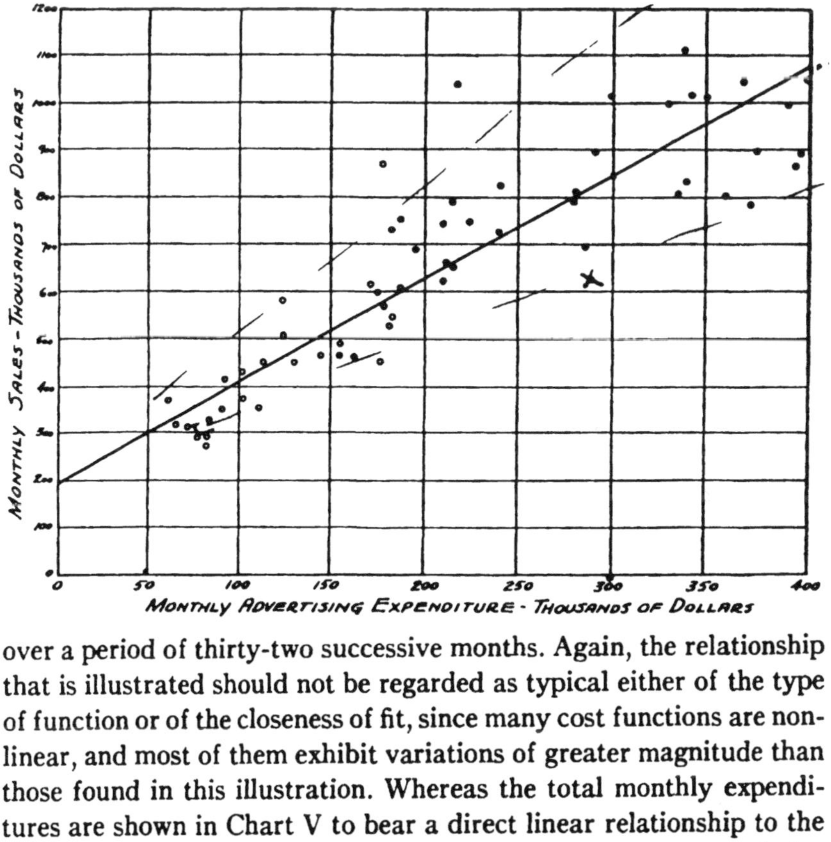

over a period of thirty-two successive months. Again, the relationship that is illustrated should not be regarded as typical either of the type of function or of the closeness of fit, since many cost functions are non-linear, and most of them exhibit variations of greater magnitude than those found in this illustration. Whereas the total monthly expenditures are shown in Chart V to bear a direct linear relationship to the volume of output, unit costs are inversely related to output and plot as a hyperbolic type of function with a lower limit that is gradually approached as the monthly expenditures divided by larger outputs reduces the cost per unit.

The last of the three categories of functional relationships (that in

[1] "Control of Operating Expenses," *Mechanical Engineering*, LIV (Oct., 1932), 711–17.

which earnings serve as a dependent variable) is perhaps the least significant. Earnings are a differential. They may be either a positive or a negative quantity, depending on the relative magnitude of income as against costs. Hence, they are influenced by all the variables that bear upon either of these magnitudes. The number of factors that condition the earnings of most business enterprises is so large

CHART V. RELATIONSHIP OF MONTHLY EXPENSE TO MONTHLY OUTPUT IN A STEAM-GENERATING PLANT

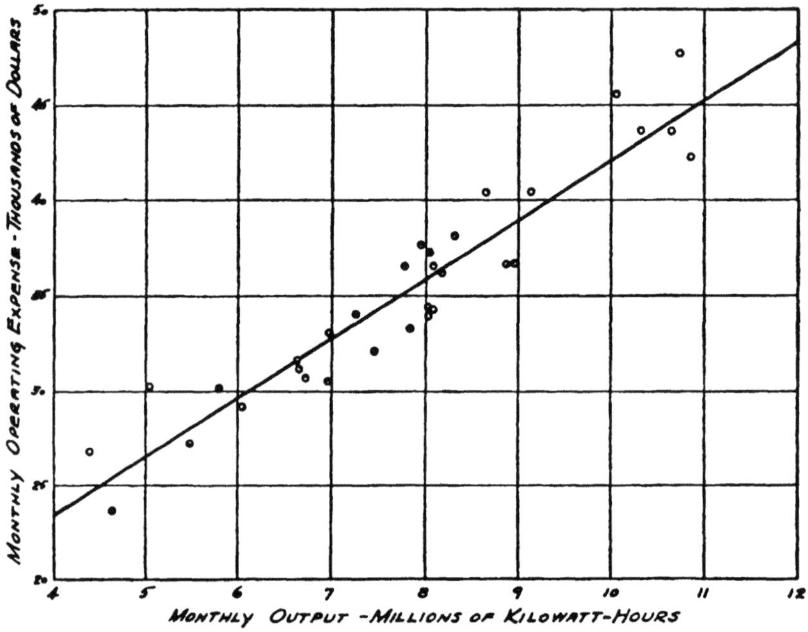

that the problem becomes unwieldy. It can be much more effectively handled by concentrating on the source of earnings. If sales and costs, for example, can be adequately controlled by developing significant relationships, the resulting differential will automatically come under control. Then there is the added advantage of dealing directly with the factors that are most responsible for variations in income and costs. Specific and valid quantitative relationships are much less likely to become blurred through the cancellation of positive relationships by those of a negative character. Also, there is less danger of the real association becoming disturbed by non-commensurable factors such as changes in managerial policies, restrictive legislation, and international disturbances.

Relationships of earnings to output may assume a variety of forms, ranging from the simple straight line to curves of a complex nature. Direct linear association is more likely to be present in companies where selling prices are kept relatively stable. In such companies the income from sales varies in direct proportion to the volume of goods

CHART VI. RELATIONSHIP OF QUARTERLY EARNINGS TO QUARTERLY SHIPMENTS IN THE U.S. STEEL CORPORATION

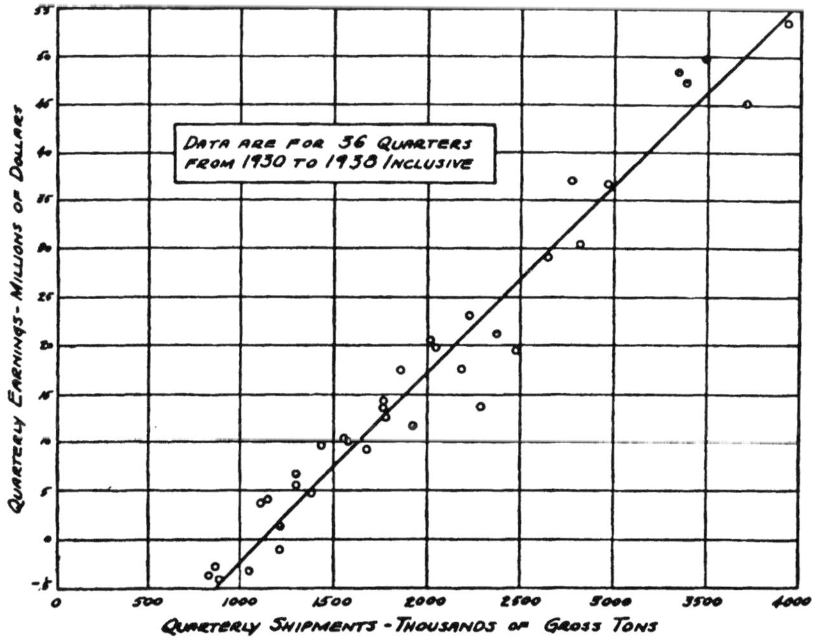

sold. Hence, if expenses can be kept either fixed or increasing proportionately to the volume of sales, earnings will also assume a straight line relationship.

Chart VI will serve to illustrate the third category of functional relationships. The quarterly earnings of the United States Steel Corporation have been plotted against the shipments of the company for the thirty-six quarters beginning January, 1930, and ending December, 1938. It will be observed that over this nine-year period the earnings kept remarkably close to the general linear relationship. By assuming the continuance of this relationship management can estimate earnings in advance from a knowledge of shipments. More important, perhaps, is the opportunity afforded by the analysis to appraise the quarterly earnings and to find reasons for all significant variations.

The relationships that have been illustrated above present static functional analysis in its simplest form. As more variables are introduced, the problem becomes increasingly complex, so that a point is quickly reached beyond which the benefits of analysis fail to compensate for the effort involved.

BREAK-EVEN POINT ANALYSIS ILLUSTRATED

Halfway between the ratio analysis of the preceding chapter and the functional relationships empirically established lies a graphic method of analyzing the interrelationships of sales, costs, and earnings. "Break-even chart," "cross-over chart," "profitograph," and "alignment graph" are among the various appellations that writers have used in discussing this graphic method of analyzing the income statement of a business enterprise.

The technique of constructing a break-even chart requires a minimum of empirical analysis in combination with a maximum of *a priori* reasoning. Costs are first classified according to their degree of responsiveness to changes in output. For the usual application the analyst employs a twofold classification and designates each cost item as either fixed or variable. The fixed costs are assumed to be absolute, and the variable items are represented as directly proportional. As a consequence, sales and costs can be shown as a series of straight lines. The differential between the slope of the sales curve and that of the total-cost curve results in an intersection point whose ordinate is the dollar volume of sales that the business requires in order to break even. Hence, "break-even," "cross-over," "stop-loss," "no-profit," and "profitless" are some of the various terms used to describe this critical sales level.

The abscissa scale of a break-even chart is usually labeled in percentage terms, 100 percent representing either capacity output or something less than capacity, depending upon how management defines its standard. Absolute units may also be used along the abscissa scale. These may be expressed in physical units of output or in the value units of the product sold.

The three hypothetical companies whose income statements were the basis for the triple diagram appearing on page 74 had the same percentage of profit when all were operating at 100 percent of capacity. A study of the diagram should reveal at least three significant points. First, it is obvious that fixed costs are responsible for the break-even point. When all costs are variable the company either makes a profit or suffers a loss on each unit of product beginning with the first. Secondly, the larger the magnitude of fixed costs in relation to sales, the greater the output required in order for a company to break even. Finally, the profit possibilities that lie in the expansion of sales beyond the break-even point are much greater for a company whose fixed costs are high. The rapidly expanding area of profit lying to the right of the break-even point may thus be regarded as a sort of compensation for the greater hazards of loss that lie to the left of that point.

VIRTUES AND LIMITATIONS OF THE BREAK-EVEN CHART ANALYSIS

The chief contribution made by the advocates of break-even chart analysis has not been in the novelty of their technique. The representation of relationships by means of lines and equations has been the common property of mathematicians for a number of generations. Descartes, who was among the first to weld the algebra with the geometry of Euclid, probably deserves specific mention for having laid the foundation.

The break-even chart as an application of Descartes's analytical geometry is worthy of distinction because of the much-needed emphasis it has given to the concept of functional relationships in management. Accountants' efforts to control sales and costs have too frequently been directed solely toward the computation of ratios and averages. Useful though these concepts are, they are very crude devices in comparison to the more precise relationships that it is possible to describe by means of algebraic functions. The advocates of break-even charts have very properly emphasized the flexible nature of costs as a function of the output and have presented the interrelationships of costs, sales, and profits in a manner that has proved both interesting and helpful.

The chief limitations of the break-even chart analysis are to be found in the assumptions usually made by those who apply the tech-

CHART VII. BREAK-EVEN DIAGRAMS ILLUSTRATING EFFECT OF FIXED COSTS UPON "CROSS-OVER" POINT AND PROFITS

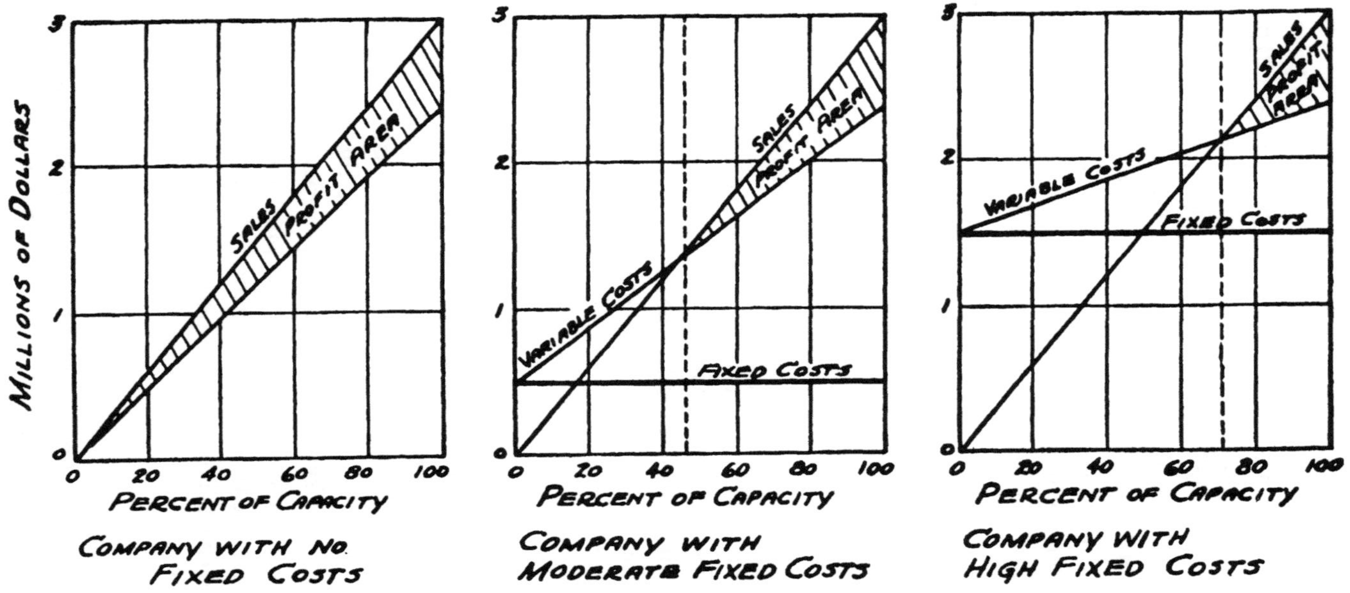

nique. Costs are represented as a function of a single variable, which is output. Although output is probably the most important factor in conditioning costs, there are many others which cannot be easily disregarded.

A second limitation of the break-even analysis lies in the tendency to assume that all costs are either perfectly fixed or proportionately variable. The difficulty of fitting all costs into this dichotomous arrangement has led some break-even chart analysts to create an intermediate category of semivariable costs. Although this tripartite division into fixed, semivariable, and variable provides a more realistic pattern, it makes the analysis considerably more complicated.

A third limitation lies in the assumption of linearity which the analyst usually makes in plotting the total cost curve. Although curvilinear cost functions are not inconsistent with the analysis, and some analysts have introduced them, they add considerably to the complexity of the diagram and tend to lessen its general effectiveness. If one is to become technical in analyzing the interrelationships of sales, costs, and profits, it would seem better to use less of the *a priori* type of analysis and go more deeply into the statistical control of costs. The latter methods are admittedly complex, but they provide a certain empirical foundation for the results against which it is difficult to argue. Although the cost curve might conceivably be modified to allow for a nonlinear relationship, there seems to be no satisfactory method for adjusting the sales curve for curvilinear influences. Drawn as a straight line, the curve assumes the unit selling price constant regardless of output. This is obviously an unreal assumption, except insofar as one might be dealing with a product whose price is subject to a very high degree of control. Some advocates of this type of analysis have said that a new chart with a new sales line can be drawn to meet each new shift in the sales price of the product. This appears to evade the criticism rather than to meet it. The chart, no matter how frequently drawn, represents sales income as increasing in direct proportion to output; and this is an unreal condition, except for the unusual circumstance mentioned above.

A fifth limitation is the assumption that costs are flexible and respond quickly to variations in output—an assumption which is substantially true for increases in cost items, but is certainly not true for decreases in costs. If the output increases, management usually has no difficulty in increasing costs and may frequently advance costs before enlarging output. When output suddenly declines, however, there is no such easy adjustment. The break-even chart does not and cannot make allowances for this troublesome factor of time lag and lead between output and costs.

Finally, the break-even chart, as it is usually applied, assumes the possibility of determining the company's capacity of output. This may be either in units of the product or in dollar value. If capacity is indeterminant, as it usually is in the case of mercantile enterprises, the application of the break-even analysis must be modified to show an indeterminate area extending to the right of the largest recorded sales magnitude.

A general blanket observation that one might make with respect to most of the break-even point analyses is that the technique has been most helpful in illuminating the fundamental nature of costs as a function, but has tended toward oversimplification of a problem which is tremendously complex.

APPLICATION OF BREAK-EVEN CHART ANALYSIS TO BUDGETING

Fortunately, the usefulness of the break-even chart analysis is not conditioned upon the removal of all its limitations. Usually the interest of management is centered in that relatively brief period of time represented by the current fiscal period and the next succeeding period for which plans are being laid. The variations in output which either have been or are likely to be recorded during this time span are usually not so great but that they can be assumed to fall within a relatively limited range along the abscissa scale. As long as one's interest is confined to the values which lie in the immediate vicinity of currently recorded magnitudes, the various assumptions discussed above may be made with a greater degree of validity.

One of the encouraging aspects of the publications appearing in recent years upon the general subject of budgeting has been the general emphasis upon the flexible nature of the budget. One author defines flexibility in a budget as "the facility with which it may be adjusted to different conditions and different volumes of business." [2] The usual procedure for obtaining this desirable quality of flexibility is to ex-

[2] Williams, *The Flexible Budget.*

amine each item of cost for the purpose of ascertaining how it behaves with respect to the volume of business. A schedule of adjustments, called the data sheet, is then prepared to accompany the list of cost items showing how each item is to be modified in the event that the actual volume of business turns out to be either more or less than that which the budget has stipulated.

One of the distinct virtues of the break-even diagram is that management can obtain in one swift glance information that it might spend considerable time and effort in attempting to extract from the detail of the data sheet. It can see, for instance, what volume of business, assuming current cost and selling price conditions, the enterprise must secure in order to pay dividends on the capital invested by the stockholders and the interest on that loaned by the bondholders. Moreover, it has in pictorial form a schedule of the major expense classes as well as of the over-all cost for obtaining the budgeted volume of business. If actual output and sales either exceed or fall short of the budget estimates, the diagram reveals the corresponding adjustments that management should make in costs.

STATISTICAL DETERMINATION OF SALES FUNCTIONS

Statistically determined sales and cost functions differ in two important respects from those assumed by the break-even type of analysis. First, the numerous preconceptions and *a priori* reasoning of the break-even analysis are reduced to a minimum in the statistical approach, and open-minded empiricism is given greater sway. For example, instead of assuming certain types of functions relating sales and costs to output, the statistical analyst seeks first to assemble a body of data and from them to determine what specific type of function seems most appropriate.

The second point of difference between the functional relationships of the break-even chart and those arrived at by statistical analysis lies in the degree to which liberty of choice may be exercised by the analyst. If and when he decides to employ statistical technique, he may choose not only the type of function but also the particular variable or combination of variables that hold promise of being significant. As a consequence, both the range and the variety of problems with which he can deal are increased tremendously. The appreciation of this opportunity, however, has been somewhat tardy.

In general, the sales of a business enterprise are dependent upon just two categories of variables. The first of these is represented by factors and forces that operate largely within the enterprise. Over these management exercises a very considerable degree of control. The second is represented by phenomena that are largely external to the business but which impinge upon and condition its success. There is not much that management can do to control this second group of variables, and as a consequence its principal object is to direct the affairs of the business in conformity to them.

Definiteness may be achieved without serious sacrifice of accuracy, if we lump into the first category all variables associated with the company's efforts to sell goods. The number of salesmen employed, their intelligence and aptitude ratings, the amount of their previous training, the length of their selling experience, the salaries they receive, the manner in which they are paid, the amount and character of the advertising, the frequency and methods of delivery, the channels of distribution, and to a limited extent the price at which the product is sold are among the variables over which management is able to exercise a very large degree of control. With one or two exceptions they represent factors which can be expressed in quantitative terms and made the basis of a series of functional relationships in which sales occupy the role of dependent variable.

The variables over which management has little or no control are the consumptive characteristics of the market and general business conditions. These constitute the common heritage of all business enterprises. Some of these inherited differences conditioning the sale of goods are of a more or less permanent nature. Different geographical and climatic features fall into this category. Other factors conditioning the sale of goods exhibit a certain variability, but the rate of change is not great enough to disturb the relative standing of sales areas except over quite long periods of time. Differences as regards population, wealth, railroad and highway facilities, number of wholesale and retail outlets are a few of the factors that one might list among the semi-stable variables. Finally, there are uncontrollable differences between territories that are in a more-or-less constant state of flux. Vagaries of the weather, differences in the extent of government spending, and variations in the incidence of the general business cycle fall into this third category. These differences require constant and continuous study on the part of management.

The efficiently managed sales organization is one in which the controllable factors represented by all the various efforts to sell goods have been adjusted and coördinated with the various uncontrollable factors that condition the sale of those goods. This adjustment and coördination of effort with opportunity assumes that management is able to approximate the incremental effect upon sales of additional amounts of selling effort applied either successively to the same area or simultaneously to a number of areas representing varying potential markets. The problem is one for which correlation analysis is particularly well adapted, since it enables the analyst to make a simultaneous solution with all the significant variables represented.

Unfortunately, from the viewpoint of achieving practical results the number of variables that exercise a significant influence upon the sales of a company is usually so great that a simultaneous solution of the equations is beyond the powers of the analyst. The routine labor of solving the constants in problems involving no more than four or five variables is sufficient to tax the patience and the endurance of most statisticians. As a consequence, most of the analyses in this field have been restricted to simple two-variable relationships, in which sales (usually on a per capita basis) have been related successively to each of a series of variables.

The coefficients obtained in a series of simple correlation studies represent only very rough approximations to the real underlying influence which each of the various factors exercise upon sales income. Those who have essayed the task of measuring the influence of each of the several factors simultaneously have done so usually with only a partial list of the variables, and these chosen largely from among the uncontrollable factors that are the common property of all analysts.

STATISTICAL DETERMINATION OF COST FUNCTIONS

The first principle for the control of costs is the same as that for the control of sales. Management must recognize that there are two groups of variables, only one of which is amenable to control. The general purpose of the functional analysis of costs is threefold: (1)

to determine the operating variables that condition the magnitude of costs; (2) to measure the relative influence of these various factors; and (3) to establish cost standards on the basis of the analysis so that management will have been made responsible for only those cost variations that are within its control.

The costs that are subjected to functional analysis may be expressed in the form of either total costs or unit costs. If total costs are made a function of output, the ordinates of the fitted curve provide estimates of costs at each of a series of output. From Livingston's data [3] that were shown as a scatter diagram in Chart V the following estimates of the monthly operating costs for a public utility plant have been made.

TABLE 7

ESTIMATES OF OPERATING COSTS BASED ON PLANT OUTPUT

(*Equation of relationship:* $y = 11{,}060 + 3{,}100x$)

Monthly Output (*In millions of kilowatt hours*)	*Estimated Operating Costs*
5	$26.560
6	29,660
7	32,760
8	35.860
9	38.960
10	42,060

The zero ordinate of the cost curve provides an estimate of the fixed costs of operation, and the difference between the zero ordinate and one erected at some specific output is the estimated amount of variable costs. In this illustration the fixed costs are estimated at $11,060, and the variable cost (assuming 5 million kilowatt hours for output) make up the difference of $15,500. Neither of these estimates should ordinarily be accepted for any more than rough approximations unless the observations to which the cost function has been fitted cover the entire range of outputs used in the estimates and the function itself is a relatively good fit.

By taking successive differences between ordinates separated by a unit of output one obtains marginal costs. "Differential" and "incremental" are other terms sometimes used in describing this increase in total costs that is associated with a unit increase in the output. If the

[3] "Control of Operating Expenses," *Mechanical Engineering*, LIV (Oct., 1932), 711–17.

function is linear, the differential is represented by the slope of the curve and is constant for all increments in output. From the estimates of cost shown above it may be seen that the incremental cost associated with each million kilowatt hours is $3,100.

When unit costs replace total costs as the dependent variable, the shape of the cost-output curve is materially changed. Negative relationships replace positive, and the hyperbolic function becomes the characteristic vehicle for describing the underlying tendency. By the use of paper scaled harmonically along the horizontal axis the unit-cost curve may be made to assume linear form.[4]

The ordinates of the unit-cost curve provide estimates of the cost per unit for each of a series of outputs. The following unit costs were secured from the previous series of total costs. They might just as easily have been secured directly from the unit-cost estimating equation. Transformation of a linear total-cost equation into a hyperbolic type descriptive of the unit costs is accomplished by simply dividing through by the independent variable.

TABLE 8

ESTIMATES OF UNIT COSTS BASED ON PLANT OUTPUT

(*Equation of relationship:* $y = .31 + \frac{11.06}{x}$)

Monthly Output (*In millions of kilowatt hours*)	*Estimated Costs per Unit of Output* (*Cents per kilowatt hour*)
5	0.5312
6	0.4943
7	0.4780
8	0.4483
9	0.4329
10	0.4206

The presence of fixed costs distributed over an increasing number of units of output produces a decreasing cost per unit and the characteristic hyperbolic function. If all costs were both fixed and stationary, the hyperbola of unit costs would assume rectangular form and approach infinity along each scale as the other variable approached zero. Since a part of the costs are usually variable, the curve tends to approach infinity along the vertical axis only. Along the horizontal

[4] For an illustration of harmonic scaling see article by Hovey, "Cost Accounting and Budget Making," Taylor Society, *Bulletin,* XVI (No. 3), 100–103.

axis it approaches a constant ordinate, the value of which is an estimate of the variable cost per unit.

Although output has here been assumed to be the independent variable, it is by no means the only factor that conditions the magnitude of costs. In the multiple correlation studies made by Joel Dean, using cost data from a furniture factory, the following six factors were found to be significant: [5] (1) output; (2) size of production order; (3) number of styles; (4) change of output from preceding period; (5) labor turnover; and (6) quality of material. The list is not intended to be typical. Each industry must discover for itself the factors that are most important in determining its costs. To a certain extent each business enterprise constitutes a unique problem, for which the cost variables must be found and appraised.

By including in the correlation analysis the major cost factors, the analyst is able to evaluate the relative significance of each. This rating may be established not only for costs in general but also for each major category of costs and even for specific items. A break-down of the dependent variable in this manner accomplishes at least three purposes. First, it enables management to see the characteristics of each of the various types of cost and how increases in sales and output are reflected in each. Secondly, it enables management to segregate the high incremental cost items from those relatively fixed and to concentrate its attention upon the former when considering its sales budget. Finally, it facilitates the control of the incremental costs by indicating the variables most responsible for them.

ESTABLISHING THE MAXIMUM DIFFERENTIAL BETWEEN SALES AND COSTS

The two variables, sales income and total costs, generate a third, which is the net profit differential. The factors that condition the magnitude of net profits are therefore simply a combination of all the factors that condition the volume of sales and the magnitude of costs. The test of efficient management is its ability to manipulate the controllable elements among these factors so as to make net profits as large as possible. Since the sales of any successfully managed enterprise provide the upper limit for costs, the factors that limit the magnitude of sales are the same as those that ultimately determine the upper

[5] Dean, *Statistical Determination of Costs, with Special Reference to Marginal Costs.*

boundary for costs. Selling constitutes the most vital function of the business enterprise in the sense that it represents the bottle neck through which all other functions must find their outlet. Hence, successful management begins with the ability to manipulate the controllable factors associated with the sale of its goods. These it must harmonize with the uncontrollable factors associated with the market. In making these adjustments, however, attention must be directed continuously toward the operating conditions that determine the costs to manufacture.

The economic principle of diminishing returns gives rise to the problem of distributing economic resources in productive effort. The principle as applied to effort expended in the sale of goods may be stated as follows: equal increments of selling effort tend to beget diminishing increments of sales income. The converse form of this principle is as follows: equal increments of sales income are usually obtained by increasing the increments of selling effort.

This principle is applicable to each type of selling effort, each specific product, each sales area, and each separate group of customers. The operation of the principle within these specific limits leads management to seek variety in its sales efforts, to open up new market areas, to diversify and to extend its line of products, and to search for new groups of customers. Hence, there is developed both an intensive and an extensive margin for the application of sales effort. The intensive margins are created by the successive increments of effort of a specific kind applied to selling a specific product either within a specific area or to a specific group of customers. The extensive margins are created by increments of effort applied simultaneously to all market areas and to all groups of customers. The task of management is to establish an equality of these two margins for each type of sales effort and for each product sold.

A simple illustration may serve to translate the rather abstract and theoretical terms in which the problem has been stated into a more intelligible language of business experience. Advertising in newspapers will be taken as representing one type of selling effort. Equal increments of money spent in advertising a specific product within a specific area and to a specific group of customers do not, of course, yield equal increments of sales income. Sooner or later the sales revenue per dollar of expenditure begins to decline, and the point where these diminishing increments start will vary with the product, the sales area, the group of customers, and the type of advertising. Even the size of the increments by which expenditures are made has its effect upon the point at which diminishing returns begin.

Each separate variable with which management deals in its effort to sell goods introduces its own distinctive pattern of diminishing returns. As a consequence, management deals, not with one curve, but with a host of curves, each of which it seeks to follow to the point where its ordinate is equal to that of every other curve. In terms of our illustration this would mean a distribution of newspaper advertising so effective that the return per dollar of advertising expenditure would be approximately the same, irrespective of the product advertised or of the sales area covered.

The equilibrium of marginal returns established for one type of sales effort must be reproduced for other types of effort. For example, there is no reason to assume that the curve of diminishing returns established for newspaper advertising would apply to radio advertising. Increasing sales effort through the increase in the number of salesmen would likely result in a curve of diminishing returns different from either. The intensive use of all forms of productive effort is reserved for those products carrying the highest profit margins, for territories having the largest sales potentials, and for groups of customers representing the best prospects. These provide the opportunity for the development of the intensive marginal return.

At the extensive margins lie the products, the sales areas, and the customers that yield sales income barely sufficient to cover costs. When the intensive margins and the extensive margins are equated and the whole has been geared to a similar set of equated margins representing effort applied in producing the goods, the entire business enterprise may be regarded as being in a state of equilibrium. Each dollar spent for productive effort, whether it be in the manufacture of the goods or in their distribution, results in approximately the same sales income.

LIMITATIONS IN THE APPLICATION OF THE MARGINAL CONCEPT

When the management of a business enterprise fails to distribute the productive efforts under its control so as to achieve an equilibrium of the extensive and intensive margins of return, there is loss of an economic as well as of a business character. Productive effort may be poorly distributed either among various types of effort or among various opportunities for the application of effort. For example, too much effort may be expended upon processing of the article and not enough on advertising and selling. Again, too much effort may go into a blind attempt to force the sales and not enough into research. Granting that effort is properly allocated as to types, there may still be maldistribution in the application of each type. Certain products, for example, may be requiring far more effort to sell than the income derived from their sale justifies. Certain market areas and certain groups of customers may necessitate expenses which are much in excess of the sales revenue they provide, whereas other areas and other groups may possess sales potentialities so great that additional increments of effort could be applied with profit.

These inequalities in marginal returns arise, not because management fails to recognize the principle involved, but rather because of the practical difficulties which lie in the way of its application. The large number of variables whose marginal returns are to be equated, the difficulty of allocating joint costs, the discrete nature of many of the variables, the limited number of observations, and the lack of familiarity with the technique of measuring net relationships simultaneously are the chief obstacles blocking the way to a more nearly perfect equalization of marginal returns.

CHAPTER VI

Measurement and Prediction of Long-Term Forces Affecting Sales and Costs

An analysis is considered to be dynamic in character if the observations with which it deals are geared to a time sequence and made a function thereof. That the observations have been taken successively through time is not in itself a sufficient condition to make the subsequent analysis dynamic. The sequence in time must be retained and the analysis made to center in it.

GENERAL PURPOSE OF DYNAMIC ANALYSIS

The general purpose of dynamic analysis as applied to sales and costs is the planning of the future course of the business enterprise. Sales and cost records, considered solely as data to be analyzed, are but the "dry bones" of yesterday's business transactions. When the analyst approaches these records, however, with the expectation that a proper analysis of them will assist in planning tomorrow's business activities, the "dry bones" begin to take on the "flesh and blood" of human interest. By observing the effects of previous mistakes and the direction of current trends the manager is in a position to avoid future errors and correct any undesirable tendencies.

Classification, measurement, and projection represent the three major steps by which the general purpose of dynamic analysis is achieved. The first and second steps may be regarded as analysis proper, whereas the third step is in the nature of synthesis.

CLASSIFICATION OF FORCES

Statisticians have classified into four categories the many factors responsible for variations in data that are ordered in time. "Secular trend," "seasonal," "cyclical," and "random" have become standard labels for designating the four general types of movement. Although the meaning and measurement of these several categories can be readily ascertained from statistical reference books, some explanation of each class and its relationship to the specific problem of sales forecasting seems appropriate.

"Secular trend" refers to the gradual long-time movement that is apparent in most chronological series. An industry in a dynamic society is usually either expanding or declining. The same observation holds for a specific business enterprise. Both the character and the rate of growth or decline tend to vary with each industry and with each enterprise. Among the factors responsible for this gradual growth or decline are: the growth of population as well as changes in its composition, improvements in the arts, transformations in the organization of industry, and changes in the habits, tastes, customs, and morals of people.

Seasonal forces are those that are both recurrent and periodic in their influence. The movement of planets, the recurring holidays, the payment of wages and taxes, the transportation of crops, the observance of social customs, and the indulgence of habits are among the many factors that lead to regular repetitious fluctuations in social and economic data. The monthly sales of department stores, mail-order houses, and five-and-ten-cent stores clearly reveal the influence of the seasonal factor. A study of sales at shorter intervals, such as the day or the hour, also shows definitely recurring patterns of fluctuation. If we accept recurrence and periodicity as the characteristics of seasonal fluctuations, then we include as "seasonal" all regular intra-yearly changes whether the pattern of movement is complete within the year or within the day. The problem of analysis is much the same for all such movements, but since confusion might arise on account of the connotation of the words used, possibly the term "seasonal" should describe only the regular recurring fluctuations of the calendar year. The shorter periodic fluctuations might be designated as intra-seasonal movements.

Cyclical variations in the sales of a company arise from the tendency of business to pass alternately back and forth from prosperity to depression. They resemble seasonal movements in that they are recurrent. In all other respects they are quite different. The cyclical fluctuations take place within varying intervals of time, and never is the cycle complete within less than twelve months. Single phases of the cycle will sometimes last for several years. Moreover, the business cycle cannot be regarded as a constant factor. Cyclical fluctuations do not occur with a constant intensity, neither do they conform to any constant and predictable pattern. Their irregularities involving differences in intensity, duration, and incidence have made the role of the business forecaster a most difficult one to play.

"Random fluctuations," as the term itself suggests, are those produced by a large number of unpredictable and incalculable factors whose effects are fortuitous. One can measure, or at least approximate, the influence that previous random or accidental forces have exerted upon the sales of a company by assuming that the favorable and the unfavorable forces are equally probable and therefore will tend to cancel out over a "sufficiently long" period of time. Just what length of time may be regarded as "sufficiently long" is a matter of opinion and judgment. Theoretically the postulate would be strictly true only for an infinite number of observations. In a time series this would represent eternity—an impossible condition.

RELATION OF FORCES TO LENGTH OF SALES FORECAST

The period over which a forecast is to be made bears a direct and specific relationship to the forces that influence a series in time. We shall now examine the nature of this relationship and the bearing it has upon the technique employed in making a dynamic analysis of sales data.

A sales forecast may be made for the ensuing period of a day, a week, a month, a year, or even a decade. For convenience we may classify the various time intervals covered by a forecast into three categories: short-term, medium-term, and long-term. A short-term forecast covers a period of one year or less; a medium-term forecast extends over a period from one to five years; and any forecast made for a period in excess of five years falls into the long-term category.

Secular trend is the most important factor in making long-term forecasts. Present expenditures for durable goods call for a forecast of future needs extending over a considerable number of years. A manufacturer debating the wisdom of a plant extension, a railroad executive planning the construction of a new road bed, a city engineer seeking sources of additional water supply, and others interested, as these persons are, in making long-term commitments of capital and labor would have need for long-range forecasting. The seasonal fluctuations would wisely be considered in planning the construction program, once the decision to build had been made. For the initial task of estimating the volume of a company's sales ten or fifteen years hence, these short-run movements, however, are of little significance. They are like ripples on the long tide swings of time. Cyclical fluctuations have a somewhat better claim for consideration in long-term forecasting. Any company planning a permanent improvement might very well analyze the cycle for the purpose of determining the most opportune time to begin construction and the most economical method of financing. The decision as regards the fundamental question whether to build or not to build, would still depend, however, upon the character and extent of the secular trend.

In medium-term forecasting the business cycle assumes the place of greatest importance. The secular trend is still of great interest, since it provides the basis upon which subsequent analysis of cycles must be built. Like the foundation, however, it ceases to be an object of chief interest as soon as a superstructure is erected. Cyclical fluctuations are, as it were, the superstructure. Only if the trend were very marked and the cyclical fluctuations relatively small could we expect this condition to be reversed.

Most forecasting is done for periods not to exceed one year. Virtually all budget estimates are made for a twelve-month period or less.[1] In this short-term forecasting the seasonal fluctuations tend to become the most important. Cyclical and trend forces tend to become less important as one's future focal point travels backward toward the eyes of the present. In the very short-run period the trend factor can be ignored. Rarely, however, can one safely leave out the cyclical fluctuations. If they happen to be extreme, their influence will be of an importance equal to and possibly greater than that of the seasonal fluctuations even in the short-run period.

The random or accidental fluctuations are last to be considered, but they are by no means least. They are frequently even more important

[1] A survey made in 1930 by the National Industrial Conference Board covering 294 manufacturing companies showed that twelve months was the budget period used most, with quarterly periods next in order of popularity.

than seasonal variations in short-term forecasting. The real difficulty, however, consists in being able to predict them. For example, the automobile manufacturers attempted a few years ago to smooth out their demand by introducing new models about November 1. The theory back of this move was that the characteristic seasonal demand with its high in May and June and its low in November, December, and January could be averaged out by making the high and the low for new-model demand run counter to the seasonal variation. The unusual and accidental factors, however, such as the zero weather in February, 1936, the soldiers' bonus in June, 1936, and strikes in automobile factories early in 1937, put unexpected and unpredictable kinks in their sales forecasts.[2]

RELATION OF LENGTH OF FORECAST TO TECHNIQUE OF ANALYSIS

Just as the forces of chief interest change as one passes from long-term forecasting to short-term, so must the techniques change by which the forecasting is done. Since the secular trend is the basis for long-run forecasting the obvious place at which to terminate the analysis is after the function to the trend has been computed. On the other hand, short-term forecasting (unless it pertains to an extremely short period) requires a complete analysis in which all the factors influencing a series in time are measured.

Both consistency and clarity will be served by explaining the problems of analysis as they are related to the three major classes of forecast. Although the length of the forecast is unquestionably the dominant factor, both in the selection of forces to be analyzed and in the choice of tools to be used, the magnitude of the forces themselves must always be considered. The trend factor, for example, could not be important for any length of forecast unless the particular series exhibited a trend. This observation, obvious though it may seem, must be kept in mind with respect to each of the other categories.

CORRECTING THE RECORD OF SALES FOR PRICE CHANGE

The tremendous fluctuations in the level of prices within recent years have made difficult any comparative analysis of sales data that

[2] Reported by J. W. Scoville in an address before the semiannual meeting, Detroit Michigan, May 17–21, 1937, of the American Society of Mechanical Engineers.

are in terms of value only. Each change in value has to be interpreted as a function of two variables—one of which is the price of merchandise sold, and the other its quantity. For certain purposes the analyst may desire to isolate the effect of price change and to convert the series into dollars of uniform purchasing power as regards the specific merchandise sold. The statistical procedure by which the adjustment is made consists in dividing the sale values by some index that appropriately measures the direction and magnitude of price change during the period. With sales data of the W. T. Grant Company and the United States Bureau of Labor Statistics index of wholesale prices of finished goods as a deflater series, the procedure is illustrated in the table below.

TABLE 9

SALES OF W. T. GRANT CO. CORRECTED FOR PRICE CHANGES

Year	*Average Monthly Sales* (*In thousands of dollars*)	*U.S. Bureau of Labor Index of Wholesale Prices* (*Finished Goods*) *1926 = 100*	*Average Monthly Sales Corrected to Prices of 1926*
1917	370	109.2	339
1918	495	124.7	397
1919	644	130.6	493
1920	845	149.8	564
1921	1,051	103.3	1,017
1922	1,257	96.5	1,303
1923	1,695	99.2	1,709
1924	2,070	96.3	2,150
1925	2,514	100.6	2,499
1926	2,995	100.0	2,995
1927	3,610	95.0	3,800
1928	4,582	95.9	4,778
1929	5,454	94.5	5,771
1930	5,921	88.0	6,728
1931	6,271	77.0	8,144
1932	6,109	70.3	8,690
1933	6,471	70.5	9,179
1934	7,061	78.2	9,029
1935	7,664	82.2	9,324
1936	8,157	82.0	9,948
1937	8,280	87.2	9,495
1938	8,110	82.2	9,866

Whereas the term "deflation" has found wide usage for describing the general procedure of correcting one variable for the influence of a second, it is open to misinterpretation when applied to the procedure that has just been illustrated. If the index used as a deflater series has its base in a year of relatively high prices, the effect is to "inflate" rather than "deflate." To avoid this possible contradiction between the meaning of the word and the result of the procedure, the expression "correction for price change" seems more precise and appropriate. It has the added advantage of eliminating all possible confusion between "deflation" as a statistical process and "deflation" as the economist understands the term.

Whereas correction for price changes unquestionably aids the analyst in appraising the significance of previous fluctuations in sales, there are reasons to doubt its benefits in making a statistical forecast of future sales. If the forecast is made directly from the uncorrected series, no modification is needed to put the estimate into appropriate value terms. If, however, the corrected series be used, the forecast comes out in terms of prices that prevailed in the base year of the divisor series. In the illustration given above this would mean prices as of 1926. A supplementary estimate of price change must then be made and applied before a forecast of sales in terms of value can be had. Whether this estimate would be superior to one derived from the value series directly cannot be answered apart from experience and the nature of the series studied. In general, a correction for price change can yield no advantage to the forecaster unless the corrected series exhibits greater statistical stability than the uncorrected.

CHOICE OF AN APPROPRIATE INDEX

Wherever possible sales should be recorded both in physical quantities and in dollar values. The analysis can then be made of the quantity series, and forecasts can be expressed in physical units of the product. A simple multiplication of expected quantities by expected prices yields the desired dollar volume for use in the sales budget.

Unfortunately the variety of products is usually so great that the value of goods sold provides the only practical basis for recording the sales transactions. The subsequent correction of the value series for price changes requires the selection of an appropriate "deflating" index. Selection requires a knowledge of the specific problem and of the purpose for which correction is to be made. In the illustration given above the purpose was relatively simple. It involved the selection of an index that would show changes in the retail prices of popularly priced merchandise. Since no index of this specific type is currently published, the choice lay between constructing an index to meet the specific purpose and using some currently published index even though it provided something less than personal preference might dictate. The first course of action would have involved difficulties that outweighed its advantages. The United States Bureau of Labor's index of wholesale prices of finished goods was, therefore, used as a rough approximation to what an index of retail prices tailor-made for the specific company might show.

SELECTING THE METHOD OF DETERMINING TREND

Before the analyst begins calculations for the measurement of secular trend either in sales or in costs, he should seek answers to the three following questions: (1) What method of determining trend is most appropriate? (2) What type of function will best describe the trend? (3) What shall be the length as well as the limits of the period to which the trend is to be fitted?

Listing the questions in numerical order does not imply that they present themselves to the investigator in any such consecutive manner. They usually occupy his attention simultaneously. Their consecutive treatment, however, will serve to give coherence to the discussion.

The first of these three questions may best be handled by listing the principal methods of trend determination and then providing a brief exposition of the procedures together with a few of their limitations.[3] The following represent the most important methods for measurement of trend: (1) freehand method; (2) method of selected points; (3) method of moving averages; (4) method of grouped data; and (5) method of least squares.

As the name of the freehand method implies, the line of trend is drawn by observing the general pattern of the plotted points and sketching in a curve so that the areas above and below the line (those irregular segments bounded on one side by the trend and on the other by the plotted series) appear to be equal. The chief advantage of this method lies in its simplicity, whereas its chief limitation is that no two

[3] Examples and a detailed treatment of the procedures for trend fitting are provided by most of the modern texts in statistical methods.

analysts are likely to obtain the same results. Even if the same general type of trend curve be sketched, the subjective differences tend to become more pronounced as the freehand curves are extrapolated for obtaining a sales forecast.

The method of selected points is a step removed from the purely subjective freehand method. Certain points are selected first upon the graph of the plotted sales series. The coördinates of these points substituted in the necessary normal equations provide the basis for a simultaneous solution. Both the number and the location of the points lie in the realm of individual personal judgment, the first of these two factors being conditioned by the type of function desired. Empiricism begins with the solving of the simultaneous equations and extends through to the extrapolation of the resulting trend equation. Assuming, therefore, that an agreement is possible in the type of function and the location of the selected points, any two investigators will arrive at the same sales forecast.

The method of moving averages establishes the trend by taking successive averages based on overlapping time periods of uniform length. Since each average is assumed to be centered at the middle of the period for which it is taken, this method of trend fitting is subject to the serious limitation that the trend must always be one or more years behind the present, the extent of the time lag being dependent upon the length of the average used. Although the procedure is entirely empirical once the length of average has been chosen, the impossibility of extrapolating the results makes the method unsuited for the forecasting of sales.

The procedure involved in fitting a trend curve by grouped data is similar to that required by the method of selected points. It differs only in that the points and their coördinates upon which a simultaneous solution of the trend equation is based are obtained by a grouping of the observations rather than from an *a priori* selection. Since both the number of groups used and the mathematical treatment of them are conditioned by the type of function desired, this last is the only subjective element in the procedure. The empirical character of the method plus the relative ease of its application make it superior for sales forecasting to any that has been previously discussed.

The method of least squares places the trend line in accordance with the well-recognized mathematical criterion, that is, the line of "best fit" is one from which the sum of the squared residuals is a minimum —a residual being the algebraic difference of an observed value from its corresponding trend. As in the preceding method, the choice of function is the only subjective element involved in the procedure. Each observation exercises a direct influence in determining the position of the sales trend, and hence the method is more empirical than any of the others. For the simpler types of function the least-squares technique is perhaps the most satisfactory. For the more complicated types the labor involved in a least-squares fitting is usually great enough to offset this mathematical virtue and to give the advantage to the less precise, but more easily handled, method of grouped data.

SELECTING THE TYPE OF TREND LINE

The number of trend relationships theoretically possible is almost infinite. As a concrete problem of sales analysis and forecasting, however, the best types of function are few. In order to determine what type of trend is most appropriate for describing the secular change in sales one must have some specific sales series in mind. Also, one must be keenly aware of the nature of the relationship that a sales trend is assumed to describe. Plotted upon the horizontal axis of the sales chart is time (usually expressed in years), whereas along the vertical axis appears a scale appropriate to the units and the range of the sales data. A sales trend line superimposed upon such a system of coördinates describes the nature and extent of the change in sales (expressed either in terms of value or in terms of physical quantities) that tends to take place with each unit of change in time. Consequently, the problem of selecting an appropriate type of trend resolves itself into a study of the general nature of the year-to-year changes in sales data and then matching these against the characteristics of the more common trend equations. Table 10 presents some of the more useful types of curve applicable to the dynamic analysis and forecasting of sales.

The various types of trend listed in the table are illustrated in the diagrams shown on pages 98 and 99. Those curve types that have either an upper or a lower asymptote (approaching some value as a limit) are shown on both arithmetic and semi-logarithmic scaling.

TABLE 10

Types of Curve and Their Characteristics

Type of Curve	*Generalized Form of Equation*	*Character of Year-to-Year Changes*	*Presence or Absence of Limiting Values*
Straight line	$y = a + bx$	Increasing or decreasing by a constant amount according as b is positive or negative	No maximum or minimum values
Exponential or compound interest	$y = ab^x$	Increasing or decreasing by a constant percentage according as b is $>$ unity or some positive value $<$ unity	No maximum; zero is approached as a lower asymptote
Modified exponential	$y = a + bc^x$	Increasing or decreasing by amounts that vary in accordance with a constant proportion	No minimum if b is negative; no maximum if b is positive; value of a is asymptote at $x = \infty$
Second degree polynomial	$y = a + bx + cx^2$	Increasing or decreasing by gradually diminishing amounts until maximum or minimum is reached; after maximum or minimum points changes are reversed by gradually increasing amounts	A minimum, but no maximum if c is positive; a maximum, but no minimum if c is negative
Modified polynomial	$y = a + bx^{1/2} + cx$	Same as second degree polynomial, but changes less pronounced resulting in plotted curve showing smaller degree curvature	Same as for second degree polynomial
Second degree logarithmic polynomial	$\log y = a + bx + cx^2$	Increasing or decreasing by gradually diminishing rates until maximum or minimum is reached; changes are reversed by gradually increasing rates after maximum or minimum points	Same as for second degree polynomial
Gompertz	$y = ab^{c^x}$	Increasing at a gradually diminishing rate that approaches zero as a limit	Minimum is zero, and maximum is the value of a; both limits are approached as asymptotes
Pearl-Reed	$\frac{1}{y} = a + bc^x$	Same as for Gompertz equation	Minimum is zero and maximum is the reciprocal value of a; both limits are approached as asymptotes

The selection of the proper curve type is very largely a problem of matching one's knowledge of curve types and their characteristics with the behavior of sales data as shown by graphic forms of presentation. Successive plottings, first upon arithmetic and then upon semi-logarithmic scaling, may occasionally be desirable in this matching process. The actual fitting of several types of curve may even be necessary in order to select the most satisfactory curve type. Throughout the whole process of selection, the analyst should keep in mind the purpose for which the fitted curve is to be used. Occasionally a curve type that is suitable for evaluating current or previous sales (interpolation) gives quite illogical results when projected or extrapolated for forecasting. Moreover, an extrapolated curve may yield results consistent with reason as long as the period of extrapolation is brief, whereas impossible values result as soon as it is extended into the long-term forecast. Curves without limiting values, especially the parabolic curves, are subject to this defect when used for long-term forecasts.

In addition to using graphic representation and observation for selecting the curve type, the analyst may find the computation of differences to be helpful. If the first differences (that is, the year-to-year changes) in the sales are constant or nearly so, he may assume that a straight line fits the data. If the second differences (differences between the year-to-year changes) approach a constant value, a second degree polynomial may be assumed to fit. Similarly, a constant first difference between the logarithms of the yearly sales would indicate the advisability of an exponential curve, whereas a constant second difference would argue for a logarithmic polynomial of the second degree.

Equally important with the knowledge of the curve types is the knowledge of the industry and of the particular company. The sales record of the company provides the quantitative basis for the analysis, but the interpretation and the forecast requires in addition certain qualitative information that can be gained only through familiarity with the company and with the industry. Contemplated changes in sales policies, the introduction of new products, and the perfection of new processes can do much to upset any sales forecast that one might make solely on the basis of some statistical trend line.

Finally, it is well to consider the influence of certain broad economic

CHART VIII. SIMPLE TYPES OF TREND CURVE

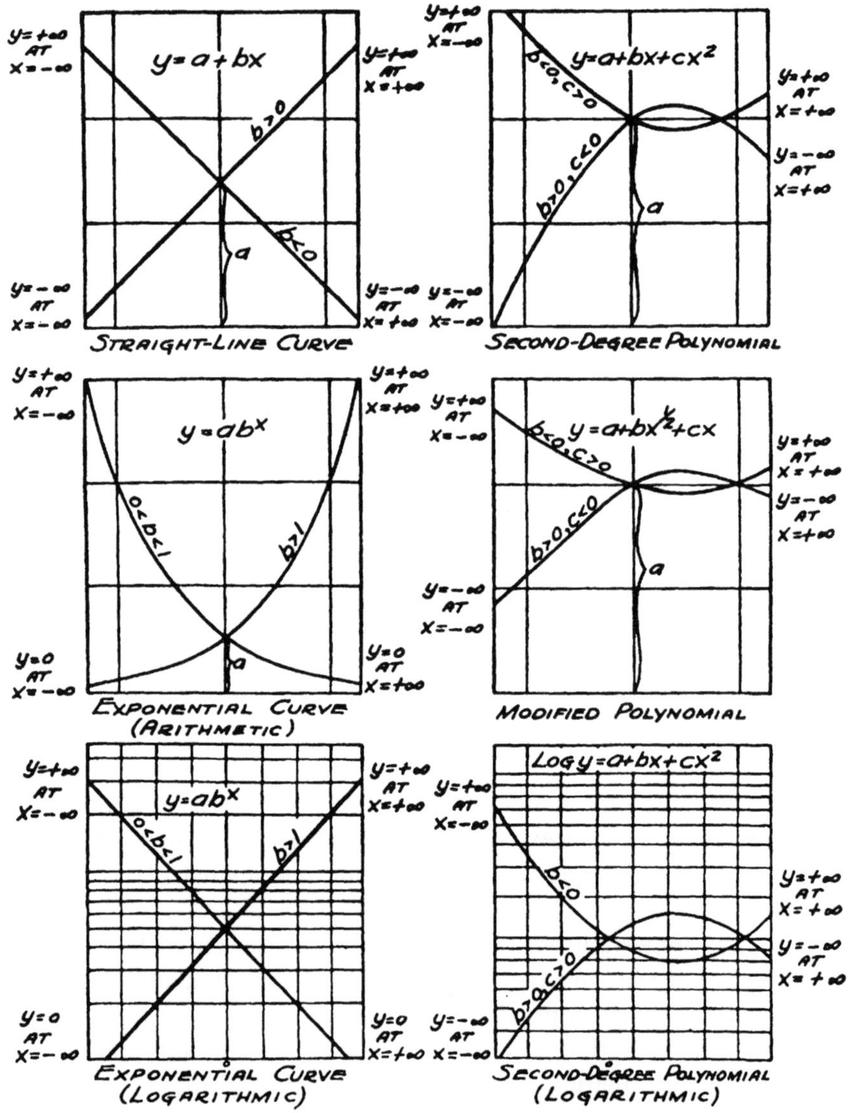

and sociological factors in the making of a sales forecast, especially if the forecast covers a long period. The sales record of a company or of an industry will frequently be found to resemble the growth of population. Since population is one of the basic factors limiting the volume of sales of any product, there is considerable logic in the analogy that

CHART IX. MORE COMPLEX TYPES OF TREND CURVE

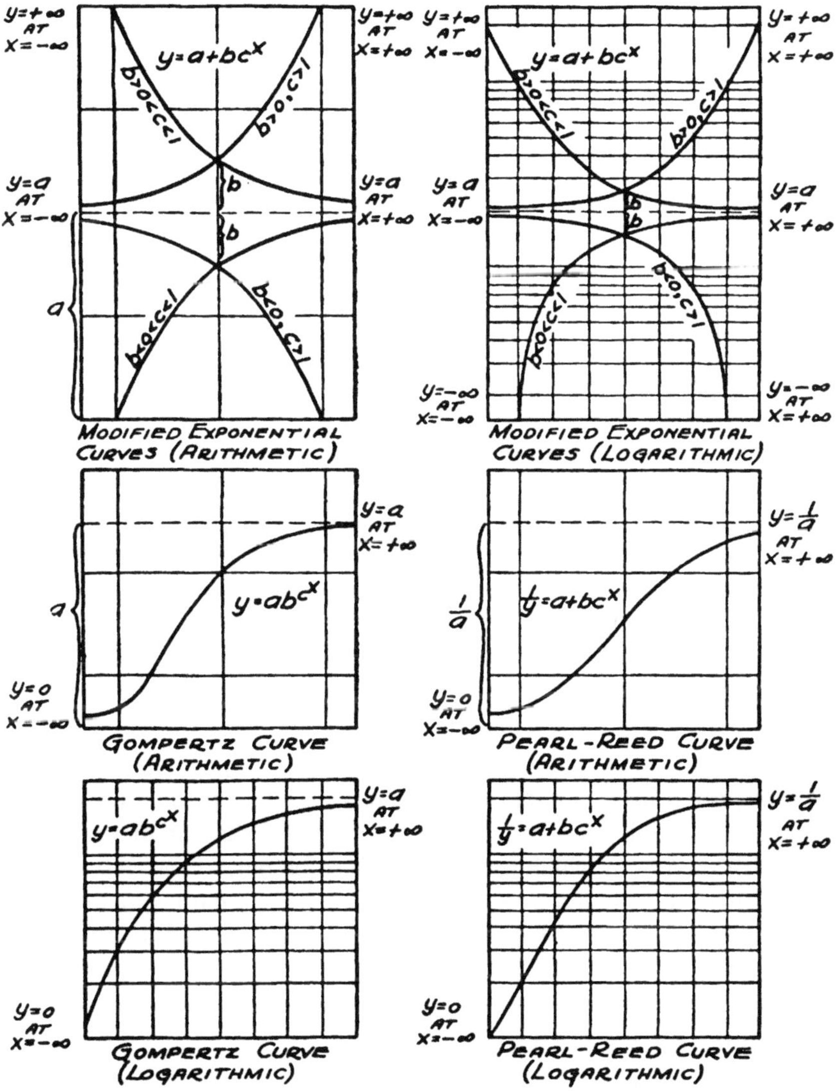

is frequently drawn between the stages of population growth and the stages in the growth of sales. Each industry (so the argument runs) tends to pass through three stages. The first is one of slow movement, during which much effort must be exerted to introduce the product or service and the growth curve rises slowly. The second stage is one of very rapid expansion and development, and the curve assumes a slope that is very steep. The third and final stage begins when the industry approaches the saturation point and the growth curve begins to flatten out to assume a horizontal position. The Gompertz and the Pearl-Reed are perhaps best known among the various S-shape curves used in time-series analysis. Plotted on ratio or semi-logarithmic paper, the S-shape curves assume convex form, indicating growth at a decreasing annual rate.

From what has been said concerning the selection of the proper type of curve, the reader might infer that the answer to the problem rested very largely upon the factors of personal judgment and common sense. Moreover, he might infer, as a corollary, that personal predilections of choosers might lead to the selection of two or more curves as both "reasonable" and "proper" for the description of some specific series. Both inferences are correct. Users of statistical trend equations would do well to remember that the "proper type" of curve to describe a specific series is that which the analyst says is "proper," so that something of the statistician is usually present in every statistical analysis.

As signposts to direct the judgment of the analyst in making a selection of an appropriate trend type, the following general considerations may provide assistance.

1. Of two curve types which afford a satisfactory fit to the data, the simpler one is usually the better. A safe working principle, yet one that has often been honored in the breach, is to keep the analysis as simple as possible, consistent always with the behavior of the data and with the use to which the results are to be put.

2. Whenever possible one should go behind the data and select a type of curve that can be justified on the basis of all the available supplementary information. This precaution is extremely important in fitting a trend to the sales of a company that may be passing through a transition period. Considered quantitatively, these changes in trend become apparent only in retrospect, whereas if they are subjected to the high light of qualitative information they may frequently be recognized at their inception.

3. If the forecast from a trend line differs decidedly from that which seems reasonable from all that is known of a qualitative nature (represented by knowledge of legislative measures, court rulings, com-

pany policies, new inventions, and so forth) the information that is qualitative should be given precedence. Statistical trend lines are simply tools, and as such they need to be kept subordinate to all other information possessed by the sales analyst.

SELECTING THE PERIOD

The definition of "secular trend" as a gradual long-time movement raises the question as to what period of time may be regarded as a "long time." Just how long should the record of sales be in order to justify the fitting of a line of trend? This question, like many another that one might pose with regard to statistical procedure, is incapable of a dogmatic answer. A conditional answer may be made by enumerating the most important factors in the selection of the trend period.

The duration of the company's experience is perhaps the most important factor in deciding the trend period. A rule of thumb states that one should not fit a trend line to any period of less than ten years. However, a nine-year record of sales (if that were all the data which the company possessed) would not be wisely cast aside as inadequate. The analyst might like to have data covering a period of several decades or more, but necessity is usually the mother of his choice, and he must take what she gives him.

The use to which the trend is to be put is another important consideration. A trend that is to be projected for purposes of forecasting should be based on a longer period than one that is to be used solely within the limits of the data. Also, the longer the period of the forecast, the longer should be the period of the trend from which the forecast is made. In this respect a line of secular trend is somewhat like a personal habit or social custom, that is, the longer it persists, the more confidence we have that it will continue.

Another factor to be considered is the degree of fluctuation present in the series. A series exhibiting very wide fluctuations would ordinarily need to be analyzed over a longer period than one that fluctuates within relatively narrow limits. Articles having a relatively elastic demand would tend to belong in the first category. In the second we find necessities, especially those purchased frequently, and articles that are firmly established by habit or custom. This stability in the sales data enables the analyst to fit trends with a greater degree of precision and confidence.

A fourth element influencing the length of trend period is the type of curve that the analyst chooses. If the series is one that can be described by a simple straight-line function, in either arithmetic or logarithmic form, the period may well be shorter than for one requiring a more complicated type of curve. Usually the more constants a trend equation contains, the longer the period should be for its application.

Finally, the homogeneity of the data has to be considered in selecting the period of trend. The entrance of some new factor, such as the addition of a new product, the extension of the plant, a new invention, changes in the marketing policies, and so forth, may frequently modify the underlying trend of sales to such an extent that the period subsequent to the entrance of the new factor must be considered as distinct from the period preceding it. Any compromise trend chosen to describe the underlying secular changes of a nonhomogeneous sales record would very likely fail to be a good description of any particular segment of the experience. Consequently, the only logical procedure in such cases is to fit as many trend lines as there are homogeneous periods in the recorded data. No criterion other than that of personal judgment coupled with an intimate knowledge of the factors responsible for a company's growth can serve to detect homogeneity or the lack of it in a record of sales.

The choice of points at which the calculation of trend shall begin and end is almost as important as the choice of length of period. By a slight shifting of the terminal years it is sometimes possible to show rather contradictory results. A straight line, for instance, that has its beginning in a year of prosperity and its ending in a year of depression will provide an understatement of the annual increase or an overstatement of the decrease if the trend happens to be downward. The reverse, of course, is true when the trend begins in a depression year and ends in a period of prosperity. If the trend has both its extremities in depression years, the slope will be approximately correct, but the line will be constantly below its proper level. All the trend values will be underestimated. The opposite is true when both extremities of the trend lie in years of prosperity. The shorter the period used in fitting the trend the greater this bias of extreme values at the beginning and ending tends to be. To avoid this source of distortion, effort should be made to have the terminal years fall in some intermediate phase of the business cycle.

USE OF TREND FOR LONG-TERM FORECASTING

Long-term forecasting is required for the successful operation of all companies that have large investments in fixed assets of a specialized type. Railroads and public utility companies can be listed as those having greatest need for the making of long-term predictions if they are to avoid unwise commitments of capital and labor in the present and excessive costs of emergency expansion in the future. In general, long-term forecasting is essential under the two following conditions: (1) wherever capital, once invested, becomes irretrievable, except as it is consumed by use over a long period of years; (2) wherever the prerequisites of expansion are covered by various franchise and property rights that cannot be acquired under the pressure of need except at very great expense and trouble.

The following long-term estimates of sales for the W. T. Grant Company have been made from the extrapolated curves [4] of three types of growth functions: the modified exponential, the Gompertz, and the Pearl-Reed. The characteristics of each of these three curves compare favorably with the general trend of the plotted sales. Consequently, the differences in estimates shown by the comparative table are fairly attributable to the influence that the accident of choice can play in selecting the function.

TABLE 11

ESTIMATES OF SALES BASED ON VARIOUS TYPES OF TREND

	TYPE OF FUNCTION EXTRAPOLATED		
Estimate of Sales for	*Modified Exponential*	*Gompertz*	*Pearl-Reed*
1940	$115,263,000	$108,517,000	$ 97,953,000
1945	146,800,000	123,114,000	101,082,000
1950	180,246,000	132,127,000	101,873,000

Such wide discrepancies in extrapolated values as are shown above are not unusual. Differences equally marked have been observed in

[4] Data used in the fitting of the curves covered the period from 1918 to 1938. The equations from which estimates were made follow:

Modified exponential: $y = 448{,}710\ (1.0119)^x - 401{,}925$

Gompertz: $\log y = 5.15976 - 1.61122\ (.89006)^x$

Pearl-Reed: $\frac{10^{10}}{y} = 97{,}914. + 2{,}100{,}720.\ (.753704)^x$

The equations have been fitted to the sales in thousands of dollars and origins are as of 1918 except for the modified exponential in which the origin was taken as of 1928.

the reports submitted by graduate students in statistics who had been asked to make independent statistical forecasts from a common body of sales data. Fortunately, for long-term forecasting there is required less accuracy than is needed in planning operations for the immediate future. Frequently the long-term forecasts may be expressed in terms of maximum and minimum values. The range that may be allowed in long-term forecasts will, of course, be dependent upon the uses to which such forecasts are put.

USE OF TREND FOR MEDIUM-TERM AND SHORT-TERM FORECASTING

Since the sales of any particular time period are a resultant of the interplay of secular trend with all other forces affecting a series in time, cognizance must also be taken of trend when one is forecasting sales for the medium and short terms. The secular change is fundamental in that it provides the basis from which regular and irregular movements are measured. Since the succeeding chapter deals specifically with these medium and short-term variations from trend, the present discussion is limited to the use of extrapolated trend curves as checks upon the reasonableness of budget estimates.

If a uniform system of sales classification has been in use over a period of years, there will have been recorded within each sales category a series of values to which separate trend lines may be fitted. From these various intra-company trends the analyst is able to make an estimate of sales for each of the several divisions and subdivisions into which the total sales income has been separated. Then, by applying the axiom that the whole should equal the sum of its various parts, the analyst can check the estimate made from total sales against the sum of the estimates made from the several subdivisions. Classifications by products and by sales areas have been used most frequently in this manner. The principle, however, is capable of being applied to sales that have been classified according to any of the numerous bases that were discussed in Chapter III.

SUPPLEMENTARY DEVICES FOR CHECKING TREND FORECASTS

When such factors as the youth of the company, the lack of homogeneity in its records, and the erratic fluctuations in its sales either preclude or make difficult the fitting and projection of trend to sales, certain supplementary devices may be invoked to aid in making the prediction. For instance, the record of sales for the industry, if available over a sufficiently long period, can be fitted with a trend for the purpose of projecting a total. Through the application of a percentage representing a reasonable share of the estimated total sales, a forecast may be obtained for the individual company's sales. This procedure has great merit as a checking device upon the accuracy of a company's forecasts even when the record of sales data is sufficiently long and homogeneous to allow for the fitting of a trend equation.

The trend of some related company or industry represents a second supplementary device that may be used either in lieu of or as a check upon the trend of a specific sales series. The projected trend of new automobile registration, for instance, should provide a direct clue to the future trend of those industries that are engaged in the manufacture of automobile accessories.

A third possibility for either a substitute or a supplementary series consists in the sales record of some non-competing company selling the same or some quite similar product or service. Before using the sales trend of Company A as a basis for forecasting the sales of Company B the sales analyst should investigate to see that no unique or unusual condition of operation is present to destroy the validity of the comparison.

Finally, the analyst has available a considerable body of data and information relating to long-term forecasts of population growth. These population growth studies have been made for a number of countries and for many large municipalities. From census data similar growth curves could be developed for forecasting the population of smaller cities and of other geographical divisions in which the sales of any company are made. Public utility companies have relied very largely upon population forecasts for estimates of their future requirements. In fact, any industry that sells a product or service whose distribution is primarily a function of the population would do well to study population growth curves and the various estimates that have been made from them.

The usefulness of the various supplementary devices just discussed is by no means confined to their employment as props to bolster up the projection of an inadequate sales trend line. Even when the record of sales affords an ample base for the extrapolation of a trend there is great need for resorting to every possible supplementary device as checks upon the estimate. Safe forecasting is not such a simple matter as the mere extension of a trend line. Every possible source of information must be tapped which will assist in appraising the reasonableness of the projected curve.

CHAPTER VII

Measurement and Prediction of Medium and Short-Term Forces Affecting Sales and Costs

THE MEASUREMENT and prediction of medium and short-term forces that affect a series in time presupposes an understanding of the significance of the term "normal." As applied to a time series, "normal" represents the average course of the data with various irregularities eliminated. If the original data, for instance, pertained to a record of sales by years, normal sales would correspond to the secular trend of sales, since trend is the only regular force influencing the series. Cyclical and random would presumably account for the irregular departures from trend. On the other hand, if the original data represented monthly sales, all four factors (trend in combination with fluctuations of a seasonal, cyclical, and random nature) would be present, and normal sales would correspond to a combination of the two regular forces, trend and seasonal variation. In general, the sales of any particular year are considered normal when they correspond to the curve of secular growth, whereas the sales for any particular month are normal when they equal the secular trend modified by the average seasonal movement.

METHODS OF APPROXIMATING MONTHLY NORMALS

When the business man says that his sales for a particular month are approximately normal, he usually has in mind some combination of the seasonal and trend concepts, even though he may be quite unfamiliar with the statistical methods by which these two forces are measured. A rough approximation to the normal sales for any month is obtained by adding (or subtracting if the trend is downward) a certain average annual amount of change to the corresponding month of the year preceding. For example, we shall assume that January is the month for which the business man is interested in estimating normal sales. Looking over his record of monthly sales, he observes that his business has enjoyed a fairly constant growth from year to year. He sees that with the exception of several unusual cases (instances that he can account for as "abnormal" variations produced by the "hard times" or the "hard winter") the sales of each January have been consistently better than those of the January preceding. By striking an average of these annual increments and applying it to the sales of the preceding January, the business man obtains an approximation to the normal sales for the coming January. If the preceding January happened to be "abnormal," he might go back two or more years and add the appropriate multiple of the yearly increment.

The procedure just described is admittedly crude, and yet it meets the requirements laid down by the definition of "normal" given in the preceding section. The trend is accounted for by the amount of the increment. The seasonal force is recognized and allowance is made for it in that a corresponding month is used as the base of calculation. Finally, cyclical and random forces are eliminated by omitting the "abnormal" cases in the application of the increment.

A second method of approximating the hypothetical normal sales for any given month involves the concept of a trend line without introducing any statistical technique beyond that of a simple line graph and the computation of an average percentage. Let us assume that a graph of the annual sales is available and that upon this the analyst draws in a line of trend free hand. A projection of this line into the future provides the analyst with an estimate of normal for the following year's total sales. To this estimated total sales the analyst applies an average percentage representing January's quota of the yearly sales. This percentage quota is simply the sum of all sales made during previous Januarys divided by the sum of all sales made during previous years. If we assume a value for the January quota of 7.5 percent and an extrapolated trend reading for the ensuing year of $100,000, the estimated normal sales for the ensuing January would be $7,500. An identical procedure would, of course, be followed in estimating the normal sales for each of the other months of the year.

A third rough and approximate procedure for obtaining an estimate of normal sales for the ensuing period has special application to companies whose experience has been too brief for the fitting of any kind of trend line. Those who employ the procedure call it the "one-percent method." The basis for the designation will become apparent from the following brief exposition of the technique.

The one-percent method is built upon two basic assumptions. First, it assumes that the pattern of this year's sales will follow the pattern of the previous year's sales. Secondly, it takes for granted that the level or order of magnitude of sales for the whole of any given year is set by the magnitude of any portion of that year's sales. Consequently, a forecast can be made with no more than thirteen months of sales experience, the first twelve of which are used to determine the seasonal pattern and the thirteenth of the series to set the order of magnitude.

As an example of the application of the one-percent method, we shall assume that a forecast of sales is being made at the end of February for the second quarterly budget starting with the first of April. Since two months of the calendar year would have elapsed, the sales for these two months can be used to determine the order of magnitude in expected sales for the second quarterly period. The pattern that this order of magnitude will assume is obtained from an analysis of the sales for the preceding year. If 15 percent of the preceding year's sales came in January and February a like percentage is assumed to have taken place in these two months of the current year. Hence, one percent of the sales expected for the current year equals one-fifteenth of the sales recorded during January and February. Assuming $75,000 as the sales for these first two months, one percent of the estimated yearly sales would be $5,000. From this one-percent value and the pattern of the preceding year the estimated sales for any one of or all the remaining ten months can be computed. Using 10, 9, and 7 as the respective percentages of sales made during the three months April, May, and June, the estimated sales for the corresponding months of the current year would be $50,000, $45,000, and $35,000, respectively.

Several modifications of the one-percent method are possible. One of these consists in replacing the sales of the preceding year by data covering several years. The month-to-month pattern of sales is then set by the weighted average percentages determined as in the second approximation method. Chance or non-typical fluctuations in the monthly sales of one year tend to cancel those of other years through the averaging process, so that the month-to-month pattern of sales gains in reliability.

Similarly, the analyst can improve the reliability of his estimate by increasing the number of monthly sales used as the dividend in deriving the one-percent value. Possible random and non-typical variations in the sales of one or two particular months provide a rather unstable barometer by which to gauge the order of magnitude of subsequent monthly sales. If that number is increased to three or four or even more, the one-percent value gains much in stability and accuracy.

FITTING THE TECHNIQUE TO THE PROBLEM

The procedures described above are admittedly rather crude. To those who are familiar with the magnitude and difficulty of the problem no apologies need be given for the use of approximate methods. In the first place, "normal" is a sort of will-o'-the-wisp concept. As a means of conveying an idea of the state of business or of the magnitude of a company's sales it is decidedly helpful, but it is not nearly so precise as some of the more technical methods of measurement would seem to indicate. In the second place, the presence of various intangible and, as yet, incommensurable factors that might easily render inaccurate any forecast of sales tends to make the application of the more involved methods appear somewhat superfluous. Finally, the presence of a "loaded" or biased error of an unknown magnitude in the original data may often be so large as to make the application of very refined statistical procedures deceptive and out of place.

The application of statistical methods to a specific problem may be viewed as a series of adaptations in which the following four elements are present: materials, concept, audience, and purpose. Each element conditions the choice of techniques and of the language through which exposition is made. Alfred T. Falk has appraised the value of statistical methods to the marketing research man in the following words:

> In some instances, it is folly to apply advanced methods of statistical research and in other cases it is a great mistake not to use such methods. It takes good judgment to determine just the right amount of exactness in method to make the most of a given body of data without wasting effort on the one hand or risking misleading conclusions on the other.[1]

---

[1] American Marketing Society, Committee on Marketing Research Technique, *The Technique of Marketing Research,* chap. xix.

OPPORTUNITIES FOR THE APPLICATION OF MORE PRECISE METHODS

Occasionally the original sales data warrant the application of statistical techniques somewhat more precise than those that have thus far been explained. Among the conditions pertinent to the application are: a fairly long record of sales; a fairly homogeneous period for analysis; a rather marked seasonal variation; and no very decided cyclical or random movements. An appreciation of the importance of these conditions rests upon an understanding of the concept that is being measured.

Normal sales for any particular month have been defined as the result of two forces in combination, namely, secular trend and seasonal variation. Therefore, the precision with which normal sales can be measured rests upon the degree of reliability that may be attained in the measurement of these two concepts. Both are constant elements that lend themselves readily to prediction provided the conditions set forth above have been fulfilled. With a long and homogeneous record of sales to analyze, little difficulty is likely to be experienced in fitting and projecting a trend line. Similarly, if the seasonal movement is pronounced and there are few cyclical and accidental fluctuations to distort its influence, significant and reliable indexes of seasonal variation may be developed. A combination of the trend with the indexes of seasonal movement yields a series of hypothetical normal sales that possess an unusual degree of precision. Consistency requires that the methods of analysis also be precise in order that they may be in keeping with the data and the nature of the problem.

PRELIMINARY ADJUSTMENTS IN MONTHLY SALES DATA

Prior to the application of some of the more precise methods of measuring the influence of the seasonal factor, the analyst may desire to make corrections in the original sales data for the disturbing influence of the varying number of working days per month. February, for example, is shown in the sales records of many industries as a month of low activity, yet if allowance be made for February's initial handicap in having only twenty-eight days (except when leap year gives it twenty-nine) and for the additional disadvantage of having somewhat more than its proportionate share of Sundays and holidays, a quite different situation might be found. Sales reduced to a working-day basis might frequently show February leading, whereas on the basis of total sales it might be lagging. The question whether or not the monthly sales should be adjusted for the varying length of the month as well as for the varying number of working days per month cannot be answered unequivocally. The following considerations bear upon the problem, and the answer must rest with the conditions surrounding the specific series being analyzed.

If one desires the index of seasonal variation to show the relative efficiency or degree of activity within the selling organization during various months of the year, the proper approach is to put the monthly sales on a comparable daily basis. If, however, the seasonal indexes are to be used in estimating future sales for budgetary purposes one should deal with the monthly totals as given. Estimates made in this form will then correspond to the actual monthly sales as recorded by the accounting department.

One of the major requirements of any system of budgetary control is that the estimates should be made in such form as to facilitate comparison with subsequent performances. If it is the practice of the accounting department, for instance, to divide the year into thirteen months of twenty-eight days each, this same time division should be used in constructing the seasonal indexes. Since most accounting records, however, are kept on the usual calendar-month basis, consistent budgetary control requires that indexes of seasonal variation be on the same basis. The fact that February has only twenty-eight days, whereas January has thirty-one, need cause no concern as long as the estimates are being made upon those terms and performances are being appraised accordingly.

The question whether Sundays and holidays should be considered in constructing seasonal indexes for budgetary purposes cannot be answered quite so definitely. For instance, if February always had twenty-two working days and January twenty-five, Sundays and holidays would not be a problem. Even though the total sales for these two successive months would never be comparable as measures of selling efficiency, they could still be compared with respect to the total sales made in the corresponding months of all the years preceding. This comparison is obviously the important thing in constructing indexes of seasonal variation when the purpose is that of making budgetary estimates.

Perhaps even before the purpose of the analysis is considered, one should make inquiry to determine whether or not the presence of Sundays and holidays really makes any appreciable difference in the total volume of sales during the month. In some businesses Sundays and holidays are not recognized, and business goes on much the same as on any other day. Obviously, no adjustment would be required for enterprises falling in this category. Neither would any adjustment need be made in those businesses that observe Sundays and holidays but in which the sales both prior to and after the period of recess are sufficiently larger to make up for the time that was taken out. Department stores, for instance, would hardly sell more goods by operating seven days a week, yet restaurants and soda fountains must count each day as lost during which their doors remain locked. Only by a critical examination can one determine in just which category a particular type of business falls.

METHODS OF ADJUSTING FOR THE INFLUENCE OF SUNDAYS AND HOLIDAYS

If we assume that the number of Sundays and holidays does make an appreciable difference in the total volume of sales recorded, just how shall we make the adjustment? The most satisfactory method is to adjust the final index of seasonal variation rather than the monthly data from which the index is computed. The former procedure permits the indexes of seasonal variation to be computed in the ordinary manner from the record of monthly sales. The index for each month can then be assumed to be based on the average number of Sundays and holidays contained in each calendar month. Since no month has less than four Sundays nor more than five, the average number is always somewhere between four and five. For instance, January (in common with all other months of thirty-one days) has an average of 4.43 Sundays. After deducting these and the one holiday (New Year's Day), January is left with an average of 25.57 working days. In a similar manner the average number of working days in other months may be determined.

The twelve monthly indexes of seasonal variation derived from the uncorrected monthly sales can be assumed to relate to months containing the average number of working days. Thus, if the seasonal index for January should be 75, one can assume it relates to a month having 25.57 working days. For the purpose of estimating the normal for any particular January one must modify this index to take account of the specific number of working days. If the particular January for which sales normal is being estimated has only four Sundays, its actual number of working days is 26, or 1.7 percent greater than this estimate. Conversely, if the particular January has five Sundays, there are only 25 working days and a proportional reduction is made in the estimate.[2]

METHODS OF MEASURING SEASONAL VARIATION IN SALES

After the necessary preliminary adjustments have been made in the monthly sales data, the analyst may apply one of the several standard methods for measuring seasonal variation. The four principal methods of computing seasonal indexes are: method of monthly averages; ratio-to-trend method; twelve-month moving average method; and link-relative method.

Since each of the above methods is explained in detail in the various statistical reference books, no attempt is made here to explain or to illustrate the detailed statistical procedure. The results obtained through the application of the various methods are pertinent, however, and these are shown in the table on page 115. The sales data which served as the basis for their computation appear in Appendix A.

An examination of data in Table 12 shows that the methods do not provide identical answers. The indexes of seasonal fluctuations are to be regarded, not as exact measures of a precise concept, but rather as approximations or estimates of the magnitude of an influence that is likely to change even while it is being measured. Whereas methods are available for measuring a shifting seasonal pattern the usual assumption is that of a constant variation which at best can be nothing more than a mathematical idealization in the shadow of which the "real"

[2] All the calculations used in this illustration have been made on the assumption that the analysis has been of such length as to permit the average number of Sundays in any month to hold. A somewhat more exact procedure would be to make an actual count of all Sundays and holidays that fall in each of the twelve months over the period of years being analyzed and strike the average on this basis. When the period of years is seven or any multiple of seven, the actual count will yield the same average as used above. For any intermediate number of years the average will be slightly different.

TABLE 12

INDEXES OF SEASONAL VARIATION IN THE SALES OF W. T. GRANT COMPANY FOR 1923–38

Month	(1) *Monthly Averages Method*	(2) *Ratio-to-Trend Method* [a]	(3) *Twelve-Month Moving Average Method* [b]	(4) *Link-Relative Method* [c]
Jan.	68.4	69.8	69.7	68.4
Feb.	70.5	72.9	71.7	70.8
March	87.7	88.7	88.3	86.4
April	94.2	94.6	95.2	94.6
May	99.1	99.2	99.2	99.3
June	98.0	97.4	97.3	98.3
July	82.8	82.0	81.6	82.7
Aug.	84.1	84.2	83.9	84.8
Sept.	90.0	89.9	90.0	91.4
Oct.	112.6	113.6	114.4	115.1
Nov.	107.3	109.1	109.9	110.2
Dec.	205.3	198.6	198.8	198.0

[a] Secular trend was measured by the Gompertz curve, and the arithmetic mean was employed for averaging the relatives.

[b] Indexes based on arithmetic means of relatives.

[c] Medians of the link-relatives were taken and adjusted geometrically for the influence of trend.

situation is probably lurking. Therefore, the most one can hope to find in any set of seasonal indexes is a refined estimate of that which would prevail month by month throughout the year if cyclical and random forces were not continually distorting the picture.

The will-o'-the-wisp character of the seasonal concept is accentuated by the variety of methods used in its measurement and the diversity of interpretations that accompany these methods. Without knowledge of the procedure by which a given set of seasonal indexes has been computed, the analyst is in no position to interpret them. The tabular arrangement on page 116 presents the meaning of each set of seasonal indexes in terms consistent with the methods employed in their computation.

In the first and fourth methods the seasonal indexes are expressed in terms of a fixed base, whereas in the second and third the base is constantly shifting. Recognition of such differences is important to anyone who is seeking mathematical consistency in the interpretation and application of the seasonal indexes.

TABLE 13

MEANING OF SEASONAL INDEXES

Method Used in Computation of Seasonal Indexes	*Base to Which Index Shows the Typical Seasonal Position*
Method of monthly averages	The average monthly sales trend of the calendar year
Ratio-to-trend method	The secular trend of sales for the specific month
Twelve-month moving average method	The average monthly sales for the year that is centered at the specific month
Link-relative method	The average monthly sales trend of the calendar year

APPLICATION OF SEASONAL INDEXES FOR FORECASTING

The manner in which seasonal indexes are employed to estimate normal sales for future months is determined by the method used in their computation. Assuming that the monthly average method was used in compiling the indexes of seasonal variation, one may arrive at the estimated normal sales for each month of the ensuing year by the following successive steps: project the trend of sales and compute the average monthly sales trend for the ensuing year; introduce the seasonal factor by multiplying the average thus obtained by each index of seasonal; finally, correct each monthly estimate thus obtained for the influence of the intra-yearly trend. This correction is accomplished by adding algebraically the deviation of the trend of the particular month from the average of the twelve monthly trend values over the year.

The operations outlined above have been performed upon the specific sales series from which the various sets of seasonal indexes were derived. The resulting estimates of normal sales for the twelve months of 1939 appear in column 1 of the comparative table (see Table 14).

When the seasonal indexes have been derived by the method of ratio-to-trend, the steps required to obtain estimated normal sales for each month of the ensuing year are as follows: project the trend of sales to obtain estimated monthly trend values for each of the twelve months; introduce the seasonal factor by multiplying each monthly trend value by its corresponding seasonal index, the twelve products obtained being the normal monthly sales for the ensuing year (see column 2 of Table 14).

Seasonal indexes derived by the twelve-month moving average method are assumed to indicate the typical position of each of the twelve months of the year with respect to a twelve-month moving average centered at the middle of each respective month. A first condition for the application of the indexes in forecasting normal sales would ordinarily be an extension of the moving average into the future. Since, however, a moving average cannot be projected, strict mathematical logic must give way to expediency, and some substitute base must be used. Estimates of monthly normal sales have been prepared first, using a fixed base with the intra-yearly trend reintroduced as in the first method outlined above and, secondly, using a variable trend base as in the ratio-to-trend method. Both sets of estimated normal sales appear in the comparative table below (see columns 3 and 4 of Table 14).

Strict consistency in applying the seasonal indexes obtained by the link-relative method would require the reversal of the analytical steps used in the computation of the indexes. This would involve working backward from the indexes with their average as base to a series of relatives with January as base and thence to a series of link relatives with the element of trend reinserted. The chaining of the link relatives in chronological order to the last month of the year for which a record of sales is available would then provide a series of estimated normals for each month of the ensuing year. Expediency and simplicity, however, may be served without sacrifice of substantial accuracy if the indexes are applied directly to an average of the projected monthly trend values and a correction made for the intra-yearly trend as in the first method outlined above (see column 5 of Table 14).

Table 14 on page 118 presents forecasts of normal sales estimated in accordance with each of the various methods of computing seasonal indexes. There is need for the accumulation of statistical evidence to determine the relative accuracy of these various methods of estimating normal sales. The presence of the personal element in all work of sales forecasting, as well as the individual differences in companies, makes the collection of reliable data upon this problem extremely difficult.

Any study made for the purpose of appraising the relative accuracy of the procedures would need to cover a considerable period of time and involve a variety of companies.

TABLE 14

NORMAL SALES FOR 1939 ESTIMATED BY VARIOUS METHODS

(In thousands of dollars)

Month	(1) *Monthly Averages Method*	(2) *Ratio-to-Trend Method*	(3) *Twelve-Month Moving Average Method (Fixed Base)*	(4) *Twelve-Month Moving Average Method (Variable Base)*	(5) *Link-Relative Method*
Jan.	$5,816	$5,984	$5,929	$5,975	$5,816
Feb.	6,027	6,270	6,132	6,167	6,053
March	7,557	7,655	7,609	7,620	7,443
April	8,152	8,190	8,239	8,242	8,187
May	8,607	8,617	8,616	8,617	8,625
June	8,541	8,488	8,479	8,480	8,567
July	7,240	7,168	7,136	7,133	7,232
Aug.	7,380	7,382	7,362	7,356	7,441
Sept.	7,921	7,905	7,921	7,914	8,043
Oct.	9,918	10,018	10,075	10,089	10,136
Nov.	9,482	9,650	9,709	9,721	9,735
Dec.	18,059	17,620	17,492	17,638	17,423

THE DIFFICULTY OF FORECASTING CYCLICAL AND RANDOM FORCES

If the task of the sales forecaster were limited to that of determining and predicting normal sales, his position would be relatively secure. Unfortunately for the forecaster, the term "normal," as applied either to the state of general business or to the sales of a specific business enterprise, is something of a contradiction. Instead of representing the usual state, it refers more often to a point of intersection, a fleeting condition in a stage of transition as the curve of general business or of the sales of a company crosses the line on its upward swing in the stage of revival, or again, when coming down during the stage of recession.

The nature of the pull that is exerted by cyclical and random forces becomes more apparent when one plots these deviations from normal as a frequency distribution. If normal were what the word itself connotes, a central tendency would emerge with zero as a mode of a fairly symmetrical bell-shaped distribution. Instead, the distribution of cyclical and random residuals approaches a U-shape frequency, with the value of normal at the base of the U, the most abnormal position of the distribution. From this it would tend to follow that the really difficult part of forecasting begins where the concept of normal leaves off and that the sales forecaster who refuses to venture further is about as secure in his estimate as the coin tosser who lays a wager that the coin will come to rest standing on edge.

Whereas the prediction of normal sales was seen to follow along certain well-recognized statistical paths, the trails which lead into the rough and mountainous terrain of the business cycle are less well marked. Although upward of two hundred hypotheses have been advanced to explain the recurrence of this phenomenon of our industrial economy, no principle of uniformity has yet been discovered that will provide a safe guide in predicting its gyrations. Perhaps eventually the resources that have been and are being consumed in the description of previous cyclical fluctuations and in the investigation of their causes will begin to bear fruit in more effective and more intelligent forecasting of future cycles. This would seem to represent a natural development—one for which the general public will probably call with increasing persistence.

From numerous analyses of previous cycles certain general observations may be drawn respecting the nature of the difficulties in cycle forecasting. The first of these observations is that "the business cycle" does not exist in the sense that there is one and only one cyclical movement to which all businesses conform. There are, in fact, many cyclical movements, all of which are related and interdependent. In order that prediction may be successful, each business enterprise must seek to discover how its particular cycle is related to the others. Within such interrelationships of cycles the forecaster frequently finds his most fruitful leads for predicting the cyclical movements of a specific business.

The second observation that may be made from the results of previous analyses is that cyclical fluctuations vary in both dimensions —duration and amplitude. Although some investigators have discovered what they call an "average cycle," they have had difficulty in agreeing upon the length of that average. Even granting that an agreement upon the average length of cycle were possible, the sales forecaster would do well to remember that individual cycles might vary considerably from the "average cycle." Whereas secular trend and seasonal movements are most conveniently handled as constant factors, experience justifies the suspicion with which similar attempts to handle cyclical variations are regarded. The latter can be dealt with most effectively if they are treated as irregular and recurring movements so interrelated that the cyclical fluctuations in one industry provide a clue to the cyclical fluctuations of other industries and the seeds that fall to earth in any specific cycle or phase of cycle simply germinate and bear fruit in some subsequent cyclical period.

METHODS OF FORECASTING CYCLICAL AND RANDOM FORCES

Sales forecasters have made use of a considerable variety of methods in their attempts to predict the influence of cyclical and random forces upon the sales of a business enterprise. No generally accepted basis for classifying these methods has yet been found. A suggested classification based upon the relative emphasis that each method gives to statistical technique will serve as a convenient framework upon which rather widely divergent viewpoints can be represented and possibly made to harmonize.

The three general categories that will be discussed under separate sections are: (1) methods emphasizing the non-statistical or the qualitative aspects of the specific business situation; (2) methods employing the concept of the average and other statistical devices to establish typical relationships; (3) analytical methods representing a combination of the qualitative and the quantitative approaches and in which both points of view are merged and integrated.

NON-STATISTICAL METHODS OF FORECASTING

Perhaps the least technical of all methods of forecasting sales is the pooling of a series of opinions and deriving a sort of composite estimate upon which a majority of those offering opinions can agree. This "round table" method (sometimes called the method of "integrated opinions") involves more than a compromise of guesses. Each department head whose opinion of the probable future sales is presented must have reason for the faith that lies within him and be able to defend his prediction in the presence of his peers.

The chief advantage of this non-technical method lies in the various points of view that it brings to bear upon a common problem. It forces each department head to study the conditions affecting the whole industry and broadens his horizon through the personal contacts which he makes in the round table conferences. The accuracy of the method as a means of forecasting is conditioned by the general level of knowledge and ability which the members of the round table possess. Where the membership is limited to those in the sales department there is a tendency for the estimates to be too high. The over-optimistic viewpoint of persons in the sales organization is too well known to require comment.

A second non-technical approach to the problem of forecasting cyclical swings is that which is known as specific historical analogy. The method consists in comparing the current business or sales cycle with some specific cycle in previous experience to which the current situation shows the greatest resemblance. Although statistical technique may be used in segregating and measuring the cyclical fluctuations, the method is essentially non-statistical in that it rests upon the study of a single parallel cycle rather than upon any series or combination of cycles. The assumption underlying the method is that things resembling each other in part will continue to exhibit a resemblance throughout. Thus, if the current sales position is similar to a cycle phase occupied by the company at some previous period in its history, the subsequent behavior of the sales curve in the earlier period can be taken as a guide in predicting the future course of the current cycle.

FORECASTING CYCLICAL FLUCTUATIONS BY THE AVERAGE CYCLE

One of the more common statistical concepts used in the forecasting of cycle changes is that of the average. The method of the average cycle assumes that any individual cycle approaches the average of all the cycles so that a tendency toward periodicity is regarded as appropriate in describing the cyclical fluctuations of any sales series. The procedure assumes a variety of forms, but the concept of the average figures in all of them.

One form of the average-cycle method consists in determining from a study of previous experience in a particular company the average over-all length of the cycles. By applying this average to the current sales cycle the forecaster can hazard a prediction as to the probable future influence of the cyclical factor.

A second form of the average-cycle method involves a more detailed analysis of previous cycles. By breaking each cycle into its component parts an average is computed for each phase. The application of these average phases to the current cycle position provides the basis for the forecast.

Still a third variant of the average-cycle method involves a combination of numerical and graphical analyses. The procedure employed by the Dennison Manufacturing Company will serve as an illustration.[3] Since data on monthly billings of this company extend back to 1868, the analyst has an unusually fine opportunity for the study of cyclical fluctuations. After the series has been smoothed with a twelve-month moving average to eliminate the seasonal factor, the cyclical fluctuations are analyzed in terms of the peak years which are made the base for expressing all intermediate values in percentage terms. With the sales of each cycle plotted as relatives, with the preceding cycle peak as base or 100, it is possible to superimpose the cycles and to chart the general cyclical pattern. The forecaster can then superimpose this pattern upon the path of the current cycle and make his prediction.

The application of any of the various forms of the average-cycle method assumes an unusual degree of regularity in cyclical fluctuations. Although this assumption is more likely to be fulfilled in a specific sales series than in the curve of general business, the danger of placing too great confidence in the average is always present. Too often the average cycle is not the typical cycle. The great variety of cycle lengths may preclude the possibility of obtaining an average that fulfills the definition of the typical.

FORECASTING CYCLICAL MOVEMENTS BY AVERAGE LAGS AND LEADS

A second general application of the average concept is to be found in the so-called barometric approach to sales forecasting. In this method, effort is directed toward establishing certain average and related sequences in the cyclical fluctuations of business. If the cyclical

[3] Blake and Davis, "Methods of Forecasting Sales Used in New England Industries."

fluctuations in the sales of a particular company are found to follow or to lag behind the cyclical fluctuations of some related series, the latter can be used as a mechanical barometer or forecaster.

The first task of the analyst in using this barometric method is to find an appropriate leading series. Sometimes one of the various published indices of business activity will serve this purpose. Preference, however, leans toward a more specific series, such as the sales of a related industry.

One of the most conspicuous examples of sales forecasting by the barometric method is that of the Walworth Company, manufacturers of pipe valve fittings. The highly speculative demand for the company's products made it difficult to find any external series sufficiently sensitive to serve as a barometer of the company's sales. Joseph H. Barber, the company's statistician, decided to investigate the possibilities that were contained in the company's own records. By segregating information with respect to orders from that pertaining to shipments, Mr. Barber was able to construct an index of the former that consistently preceded cyclical variations in the sales of the company. The extreme sensitivity derived from the speculative buying habits of the jobbers plus the broad sample of sixteen separate series used in its construction gave to the Walworth Valve and Fittings Index a significance that extended beyond the experiences of the individual company.

Assuming that the analyst is successful in finding some appropriate leading series, the second task involves the determination of the average length of period by which the barometer leads the specific sales series. This problem may be approached through the simple graphic device of superimposing the graphs of the two series over a lighted glass and making horizontal adjustments so that the cyclical fluctuations of the two series will approximately coincide. Comparative time readings taken at any point on the horizontal axis will then serve to give the approximate period by which the barometric series is leading.

A more precise method of measuring the average lead is that which makes use of correlation technique. By a process of successive pairing the cyclical fluctuations in monthly sales are correlated with the cyclical fluctuations in the barometer, the latter leading first one month, then two months, three months, and so forth, until a maximum value for the coefficient of correlation has been found. The lead that provides the highest coefficient is assumed to represent the average period of time separating the two cycle curves.

LIMITATIONS OF THE LAG-AND-LEAD PROCEDURE

The method of average sequence has long been practiced in the field of general business forecasting. The problem of searching out and establishing average lags and leads seems to hold a certain fascination for the statistically minded forecaster. Possibly the method possesses too great charm. Many of the errors in forecasting can be traced to the forecaster who has become so wedded to a particular procedure that he either fails to see or refuses to see its limitations. A listing of some of the limitations of the lag-and-lead procedure may prove salutary.

The most fundamental weaknesses of the method pertain to the hypothesis upon which it is based. First, it assumes that the period used in determining the sequence and in establishing the average lag and lead is in the nature of a random sample from a homogeneous universe. This assumption is open to criticism on grounds both *a priori* and empirical. Significant changes may take place in the length of either lag or lead as well as in the order of sequence itself. In view of these possible shifts in relationship, forecasting by the method of average lag or lead is a hazardous undertaking.

A second weakness of the hypothesis consists in the emphasis that it places upon the typical. It assumes that the average lag or lead is likewise the typical lag or lead. Actually the average may be nothing more than a composite of a great variety of lags and leads that exhibit no clear-cut central tendency. Without a central tendency, the concept of a typical sequence is invalid and unreliable.

Weaknesses in the lag-and-lead procedure of forecasting sales are not confined to the underlying hypothesis. There are at least two limitations of the statistical technique by which the relationships are studied and average lags and leads established. Correlation analysis, for example, gives the same weight to lags and leads at intermediate points in the cycle as to those at the turning points. Yet to the forecaster engaged in predicting the sales of a business enterprise and to management interested in adjusting its policies in accord with the forecast, the turning points are those which have the greatest significance. As long as the cycle of sales is in one of its intermediate stages of recession or revival, forecasting is relatively easy, and management has little need to modify its policies. When, however, a turn in the tide of sales is predicted, management generally moves to modify its policies. Expansion gives way to retrenchment or retrenchment gives way to expansion, depending on the direction of the predicted turn.

The same lack of precision in treatment that lumps intermediate phases of the cycle with its turning points extends to the treatment of the turning points themselves. Correlation technique groups the differences in time on the upturn with those on the downturn, and if these happen to be distinctly different, as they often are, the average lag fails to be descriptive of either.

The deficiencies of the correlation technique as an instrument for measuring lags and leads justifies the supplementary device of computing the average differences in time between the turning points of two series. If the average time between peaks and between low points is accompanied by measures of variation, a rather precise picture of these significant phases of the cycle is obtained.

FORECASTING CYCLICAL MOVEMENTS BY CRITICAL LEVELS

In the field of general business forecasting any unstable condition is regarded as a critical level. From the record of previous cyclical movements the analyst determines the symptoms that ordinarily precede each major turning point. Averages of certain significant values are then computed, and critical levels are set up. These may be expressed either in absolute or in relative terms. In the absolute form they relate to certain definitive volumes or values for such items as sales, production, unfilled orders, stocks on hand, accounts receivable, accounts payable, delinquent accounts, and so forth. In relative form the critical levels are represented as certain maximum or minimum ratios derived from a study of previous relationships existing both inside and outside the business enterprise.

Within the business enterprise the balance sheet and the profit and loss statement provide the data from which the analyst may derive most of the significant and critical ratios. Unfortunately from the forecaster's point of view, most of the analyses that have been made of financial and operating ratios have dealt with the static problem rather than the dynamic. The analyst has usually eliminated the disturbing influence of the business cycle by the simple expedient of including within the study a sufficient number of years to allow the highs and lows of the cycle to average out. Information of significance to the forecaster is often lost in this averaging process.

The present need, insofar as the analysis of financial and operating ratios is concerned, is for a more detailed and specific analysis for each business enterprise. Significant differences, both in cycle phases and in the conditions of management and operation, make many standard ratios of the static type of doubtful validity when applied to a specific enterprise. As the static analysis gives way to dynamic, the business cycle and its effect upon the financial and operating ratios of a specific enterprise occupy the attention of the analyst. He seeks to relate each ratio to the cycle phase in which it was recorded in order that he may study and measure the effect of the cyclical swings upon the magnitude of such ratios. The results of the analysis emerge, not as a single set of standard ratios, but as a whole series of ratios and their critical levels.

For significant ratios and critical levels outside the business enterprise, the analyst must turn to the literature dealing with such general relationships as the ratio of bank loans to bank deposits, reserves to deposits, brokers' loans to commercial loans, debts to income, stock prices to stock earnings, production in relationship to plant capacities, wages to output, and so forth throughout a rather formidable list to which forecasters continue to add.

FORECASTING CYCLICAL MOVEMENTS BY EQUAL AREAS

The position of a company's sales within the cycle has sometimes been determined and a forecast has been made by comparing the areas above and below the normal line. This method, as applied to general business forecasting, has long been associated with Roger Babson, who borrowed the concept from the physicists. If one assumes that the cyclical factor exerts its influence in accordance with the Newtonian principle that for every action there exists an equal and opposite reaction, the probable duration of each period of abnormal sales can be gauged by reference to the area enclosed between the cyclical and the normal line in the preceding period of abnormality.

Both the length and the intensity of each departure from normal is considered in applying the equal-areas concept. A departure of moderate proportions may be assumed to continue for a longer period than one of the extreme type, since equal areas must be circumscribed and any deficiency in one dimension of the cycle (its intensity) must be made up by the other (its duration).

THE ANALYTICAL APPROACH TO CYCLE FORECASTING

The analytical approach to the problem of forecasting cyclical movements represents a combination of the two general groups of methods discussed above. It borrows from the non-statistical methods whatever it may find useful, and at the same time it does not hesitate to employ any or all of the various devices suggested in the statistical approaches. Thus, it is not to be confined to any particular basis of forecasting, since it regards any fixed system as dangerous. It recognizes that there are merits in every system of forecasting which has been devised, and consequently it seeks to use the methods very much as a mechanic would employ a set of tools, taking first one and then another until a method is found which lends itself most readily to the particular problem.

In forecasting the cyclical fluctuations in the sales of a particular company, the analytical approach involves the study of what is frequently referred to as "the statistical position" of the company's sales. Competing industries, complementary industries, and feeder-customer industries provide a convenient threefold division of the industries whose trend of growth and present cyclical position have an important bearing upon the prospect of sales for a specific business enterprise.

The sales forecaster who does not possess knowledge of the trend of growth and relative position of competing industries can hardly be familiar with his own industry. The person who would undertake to forecast the sale of silk could hardly afford to be ignorant of rayon. If steel were his product, he would need to study copper, wood, and even the plastics. Rare, indeed, is that product or service which is free from competition, either actual or potential. The study of these competing products and services represents an important phase of the analytical approach to sales forecasting.

An analysis of industries and facilities that are complementary to the sale of a product or service will often repay the forecaster with helpful information. The secular trend of sales, perhaps more than the cyclical movement, will be conditioned by the growth and development of closely related products and services. Improved highways and automobiles, automobiles and camping equipment, cycle paths and bicycles, trailer camps and auto trailers, swimming pools and swim suits—these represent a few random examples of complementary relationships. The most important limiting factor upon the sales of a company has frequently been found among relationships no less obvious than those mentioned.

The third category of industries whose growth and cyclical position are to be studied in the analytical approach to forecasting is composed of those whose productive activities serve either as feeders or as consumers of the industry in question. Steel and glass in the manufacture of the automobile, livestock as a basis for the meat-packing industry, grain as grist for the milling industry, and steel cans and bottles as containers for the products of breweries, canneries, and distilleries constitute a few of the common feeder-customer relationships in industry. The forecaster cannot hope to appraise properly the prospect of sales for a particular company without first studying the position that the company or the industry occupies with respect to those industries whose activities are linked with its own in the chain of industrial fabrication and marketing.

The chief disadvantage of the analytical approach to forecasting lies in the difficulty of its application. No specific formula can be given, since the procedure is not to be confined within the limits of any mechanistic concept. The conditions of its application, however, would seem to be clear. The knowledge which is required is of the following threefold character: first, specific information with respect to the industry; secondly, a good grasp of statistical tools; and finally, familiarity with general economic principles and the industrial system which these principles seek to explain. If these requirements seem to represent "a large order," the task of forecasting sales, even under the most favored conditions, represents nothing less than that.

CHAPTER VIII

Purpose and Scope of Market Analysis

THE FINAL ESTIMATE of sales that enters into the sales budget is best visualized as a compromise. Within the business enterprise the daily activities of buying and selling represent a body of experience upon which the analyst draws in the making of sales and cost analyses. Outside the business enterprise are persons and business units from whom it buys and to whom it sells. As a buyer, the business enterprise identifies itself as a part of some market. As a seller, it is distinct from the market, and although its sales are the counterpart of some segment of the market, they usually constitute a relatively small proportion of the total and are frequently quite unrepresentative of both the present and the potential sales of the product. Hence, a minute and critical examination of the nature, extent, and peculiarities of the market is an essential complement of the analysis of sales and of costs. The progress that management makes in bringing its sales into line with market potentialities provides one of the best possible gauges of its selling efficiency.

MARKET ANALYSIS AS RELATED TO SALES ANALYSIS

The confusion in thought that has led to the identification of distribution cost analysis as a subdivision of sales analysis has been sufficiently contagious to cause some to use the term "sales analysis" as a synonym for "market analysis." The fact that the three types of analyses are frequently conducted simultaneously has tended to blur their fine points of distinction. If every business enterprise were a monopoly and all had attained that stage of efficiency in which sales were in conformity with the nature, extent, and peculiarities of the potential market, any sales analysis would also be a market analysis.

The customers of any business unit would constitute both the present and the potential market for the sale of its product, and whatever was to be learned about the market could be ascertained through an analysis of the internal sales records of the company. In our competitive society, however, most sales data are regarded as confidential information. The analyst of one business enterprise can only guess what is in the files of a competitor. Consequently, if he limits his study to the sales and costs of his own enterprise, he is overlooking two vast areas of significant information—one represented by those segments of the market to which his competitors have laid claim, and the other the unsettled regions of the potential market which only the pioneers of marketing have the vision and temerity to enter and possess.

MARKET ANALYSIS AS RELATED TO MARKETING RESEARCH

To many persons, especially those not engaged in the distribution side of business, the terms "market analysis" and "marketing research" are often interpreted to mean the same thing. Even writers upon marketing problems have been guilty of using the terms in a manner that would lead the reader to assume that they were virtually synonymous. Marketing research, however, is the broader and more inclusive term. As defined by the Terminology Committee of the American Marketing Society,[1] it is "the study of all problems relating to the transfer and sale of goods and services from producer to consumer." The Committee on Marketing Research Technique has given the following convenient fourfold classification into which most marketing problems may be analyzed. The four categories used by the committee are: [2] (1) problems of policy; (2) problems connected with the product; (3) problems concerning the market; and (4) problems involving methods and means.

The reader will observe that the categories listed above cover the mechanism and the process by which goods and service are distributed. No less than the whole of distribution is embraced by the concept of marketing research. Sales analysis, distribution cost analysis, market

[1] "Consolidated Report of the Committee on Definitions," *National Marketing Review*, I (1935), 457.

[2] American Marketing Society, Committee on Marketing Research Technique, *The Technique of Marketing Research*.

analysis, and advertising research are subdivisions of activities within the broad field of marketing research.

When one comes to delimit the field and scope of market analysis he can do no better than to follow the literal meaning of the words. To analyze means "to examine minutely or critically." Hence, market analysis is simply the process of examining minutely or critically the nature, extent, and peculiarities of the market. The field of inquiry usually relates to some specific product or service. This, however, is not a necessary condition. Certain studies have been undertaken for the purpose of measuring the characteristics of the market for goods and services in general. The analyses incident to the construction of general market indexes are typical of this latter type of market studies.

The first condition for establishing limits of meaning and differentiating market analysis from the broader term marketing research is the recognition that the market serves a dual capacity in research activities. It is an object of study as well as a source or vehicle through which information is obtainable. As long as one thinks of the market solely as something about which to get information market analysis may be identified as comprising the third of the four categories mentioned above. If, however, we view the market also as a source from which the analyst can learn much regarding policies, product, and methods, then we must admit to market analysis the same variety of problems that we find covered by marketing research. The difference arises in the source and manner of gathering the information. In market analysis the information must either relate to the market or have arisen out of a study of the market. In marketing research there is no limit either as to the form of the study or the area from which the information is obtained. The systematic study of marketing problems ranges from the field investigations conducted by personal interviewers among consumers to the technical experiments made by chemists, engineers, and physicists working in the testing laboratories of large retail department stores.

The multiple nature of the general distribution problem has created on the one hand unprecedented opportunities for research workers of varied interests and backgrounds of experience, and on the other it has provided the setting for a too-easy acceptance of terms into the vocabulary of marketing research. A great many expressions have been allowed to creep into the vocabularies of research workers without being submitted to rigorous definition. "Commercial research," "marketing research," "advertising research," "market analysis," and "sales analysis" are among the expressions denoting often the same thing under different labels.

To help resolve this confusion of terms the American Marketing Society appointed a Terminology Committee, with Professor R. S. Alexander, of Columbia University, as chairman. The efforts of this committee toward standardizing definitions have already resulted in a marked improvement and a general increase in the recognition of the importance of precise definitions. Usage and logic, however, do not always make amiable companions, and it is no small task that the committee has faced in attempting to establish a common meeting ground that is equally acceptable to the practitioner and to the logician.

STATIC ANALYSIS AS RELATED TO THE DYNAMIC

The two-dimensional analysis that was applied to sales records is applicable with certain minor modification to the analysis of the market. One may, for instance, examine the characteristics of a market as of some particular point in time, a point being any period ranging from a day to a year or more, depending upon the time needed to collect, tabulate, and analyze the data. The picture is nonetheless static. Like a snapshot it shows details and relationships, but no motion. It reveals such things as the present and potential consumption of product A as compared with product B, of brand A as compared with brand B, and the sales potential of territory A as compared with that of territory B.

These static relationships provide only one-half the significant information. The other half consists in following these relationships over a period of time in order to discover market trends and tendencies. Consumer choice is a fickle thing, and time can work tremendous changes in the consumer's order of preference. Products that stand at the apex of popularity today may be on the down grade toward oblivion tomorrow. Even the genius of Henry Ford could not have saved this wizard of the motor car from ultimate commercial annihilation had he not somewhat belatedly acquiesced to the consumer desire for style. Rapid technological changes and highly competitive selling have increased the tempo at which shifts in consumer demand take place. The need for dynamic analysis of the market has grown apace.

The relationship between the static and the dynamic types of market analyses may be illustrated by the following hypothetical case. A manufacturer of a nationally known drug product determines from a sample survey of drug stores that 75 percent of the buyers of the product ask for his particular brand. If the nearest competing brand were receiving only 10 percent of the total preferences, this static cross-section view of the market would indicate a most favorable condition for the leader. If, however, a similar survey conducted a year later should show the relative standing of the leader and nearest competitor to be 60 percent and 25 percent, respectively, there would be little comfort for the dominant brand in such a challenging trend.

Heretofore the need for frequent and current collection and analysis of market data has not been sufficiently recognized. Too great confidence has often been placed in the results of a single cross-section study. Dynamic market analysis assumes a series of static or cross-section studies at intervals of time sufficiently brief to reveal changes which, if unheeded, are likely to prove dangerous and possibly disastrous. The appropriate length of the time interval between successive cross-section studies depends upon such factors as the age of the industry, the degree of control exercised over the market, and the age and strength of competition. A certain amount of change is inherent in any form of economic organization. The more rapid this change becomes, the greater is the need for frequent cross-section studies of the market.

PURPOSES ASSOCIATED WITH AN ESTABLISHED PRODUCT

A market analysis may serve one or more of a great variety of purposes. For convenience of treatment these have been grouped under several major headings of which that given above is the first.

To determine what particular physical features, either of the product or of its container, are most desired by the buyer.—The successful marketing of articles such as perfumes and candy is conditioned largely by the style of container. Sometimes the features of a product that business men emphasize in their sales and advertising campaigns are not those in which the buyers are most interested.

To determine to what uses the product is being put and what new uses, if any, can be found.—Since the maker or distributor of a product is frequently unaware of some of the uses to which his product is put, a census of users may often reveal information that he can employ effectively in sales and advertising campaigns. This is especially true in the field of industrial marketing, where new uses for products are continually being discovered.

To discover ways of improving either the product itself or its container.—Often some such trivial and superficial characteristic as the shape of a radiator on a motor car will interfere with the sale of an otherwise meritorious product. But the maker and distributor cannot afford to wait for customers to suggest improvements. Neither can he afford to follow his competitors. Widespread consumer acceptance is the reward for leadership in matters of style, color, size, price, and quality of product. It is at this point that market analysis can be applied to determine before labor and capital have been committed whether or not new ideas about existing products are likely to "click."

PURPOSES ASSOCIATED WITH EITHER A NEW PRODUCT OR A NEW BRAND

To determine new functions that may provide the basis for a new product.—Necessity has sometimes been called the mother of invention yet a rather inarticulate mother as experience has shown. The persons for whom new products are created have seldom been the ones to suggest them. Systematic study of other persons directed toward finding easier and more effective means for performing the common place activities has been the source from which most of the ideas for new products have sprung.

To search out new brands of some product already on the market.—New brands of highly standardized products are likely to be very similar to those already on the market and little is to be gained through research. If, however, the product is subject to considerable variety as to size, style, price, color, quality, service, etc., very useful information may be secured by searching out the drift of consumer preference on these points.

To search out products to supplement a line.—Both manufacturers and distributors have need at times to add products to their line. Their purpose may be either to serve their customers more completely or to stabilize their operations. Fluctuations in the activities of a company may frequently be compensated by the wise choice of products having movements of an inverse character. Compensation may be either commercial or technical, depending upon whether the reduction in fluctuations relates to the sales or to the production. An example of the first is afforded by a dealer selling refrigerators and radios. Both show decided seasonal variations, but of an inverse character. Again, a dealer in building materials sells coal in winter. Examples of technical compensation are somewhat more difficult to find, since its advantages are lost if the capital equipment must be changed. A factory making skates prior to the winter season and chisels the rest of the year, a furniture manufacturer making lawn furniture prior to the summer season and sleds for the winter trade, and a factory alternating between the making of dyes and antifreezing substances illustrate the technical type of compensation.[3]

PURPOSES ASSOCIATED WITH POLICIES AND METHODS

To determine consumer and dealer attitudes toward one's present sales and merchandising policies.—Policies governing the sale of a product are often so closely associated with the article itself that buyers will sometimes condemn an otherwise high quality product because of some defect in the sales policies. This is especially true of technical products that require installation and repair services. Other sales and merchandising policies that may sometimes influence the sale of a product for either the benefit or the damage of the seller are those connected with the granting of credit, the making of deliveries, the acceptance of returned merchandise, the allowances made on "trade-ins," and the form and character of advertising.

To discover ways of improving present sales and merchandising policies.—The appraisal of policies is usually preliminary to the tak-

[3] For an excellent discussion of the general problem of compensation as concerns the seasonality in the income and expenses of a business see the paper presented by J. G. Stridiron, "Some Recent Developments of the Problem of Seasonal Variations in Sales and Sales Results," in International Congress for Scientific Management, 7th, Washington, D. C., 1938, Distribution Papers, pp. 23–28.

ing of steps for their improvement. The appraisal represents effort directed toward control, whereas improvement represents a phase of planning. The study of reading habits, the testing of types of sales arguments and advertising appeals, the search for appropriate trademarks, trade names, and selling slogans are examples of studies made for the latter purpose.

To analyze present channels of distribution and to discover ways by which short cuts and economies may be effected.—Within recent years there has been a decided tendency to short cut the channels of distribution. The manufacturer seeks to make more direct contact with the retailer on the one hand and with his sources of raw material on the other. Functions that were formerly performed by separate business enterprises tend now to be performed under one management through the process of vertical combination. Market research and analysis should reveal the advantages and disadvantages connected with any present or proposed channel for distributing goods.

To determine the best type of dealer, and to discover ways of assisting dealers in selling a larger volume of goods.—An intelligent approach to the two closely related problems, dealer selection and dealer helps, requires information that cuts across two broad areas. On the one hand, we have the dealers and their various characteristics; whereas on the other, we find the consumers and their purchasing habits. Both, however, constitute fields of study much wider than that of the specific purpose here discussed.

PURPOSES ASSOCIATED WITH PRESENT AND POTENTIAL DEMAND

To determine the size of the total market, present and potential, for an existing product.—The present market of a product or a group of products is measured by present sales. The difficulties in determining the total present market are therefore not nearly so great as those that face the analyst in determining the potential market. The essential idea conveyed by the word "potential" is that of futurity. Hence, any potential market is a future market—an untapped source of income for the business enterprise. This opportunity for increased sales may lie with either or both margins of selling. Perhaps more intensive selling would result in profitable sales to groups of persons residing within the present market areas, whereas extensive selling implies the application of selling effort to market areas not yet covered. One of the purposes of market analysis is to find and to measure the relative importance of these two general sources of increased income. To measure a potential market, the analyst must piece together information pertaining to present and previous consumption of the product with that pertaining to current and prospective needs, abilities to buy, and capacities of the product to satisfy the needs.

To determine the size of the total market for a new product.—The problem of estimating the potential market for a new product is more difficult because there is no record of previous sales by which the analyst can appraise the reasonableness of his estimate. He must build entirely from the bits of evidence he can gather concerning the needs of buyers, their ability to buy, and the characteristics of the product that would make it adaptable to these needs and abilities.

To measure and evaluate the component parts of the market, both present and potential, for either an old or a new product.—A market may be subdivided in ways almost as numerous as those that characterize the classification of sales. First in importance is the division by geographical units. The laying out of new territories, the location and correction of weak spots in existing areas, the setting of sales quotas, the distribution of advertising appropriations, the assignment of salesmen to territories, and the correction of the entire distribution area are among the more important purposes served by territorial market analysis. Occasionally, as in selling an industrial product, salesmen are assigned to industries rather than to territories, and advertising is allocated to publications along industrial rather than geographical lines. In such instances the industrial type of market analysis takes precedence over the territorial and may be used for the same purpose.

Most of the minor bases for classifying the market pertain to characteristics of the ultimate consumer and are of interest primarily to the maker and distributor of consumer goods. Factors such as age, sex, nationality, religion, and occupation might be mentioned as sometimes affording significant bases for subdividing the market.

To determine the proportion of the total market that at present belongs to, or in the future may be obtained by, a particular brand or by a particular company.—A company's relative position in the industry is often more important than the absolute magnitude of its operations. Sales, for example, may be increasing, but if the company is getting a smaller proportion of the total market the condition is hardly favorable. On the other hand, sales may be declining, but if the market is diminishing at a faster rate the company's competitive position has improved.

Since advertising is an accepted means for improving a company's competitive standing, changes taking place in the latter have sometimes been interpreted as indicating the effectiveness of the former. There is danger, however, in gauging the effect of advertising this way, unless other significant factors have remained constant in the meantime. Variables such as the quality of the product, the package design, the territory covered, the training of the sales force, helps to the dealers, and so forth may account for a considerable portion of any improvement in sales if these factors are allowed to change while the effect of advertising is being measured.

To determine the reasons why people prefer certain products or certain brands.—The problem of finding out what people do is relatively easy compared to that of finding out why they do it. The first is simply a matter of inspection; the second involves introspection. It is the thesis of modern psychology "that the most reliable measure of peoples' thoughts, feelings, and preferences are the overt acts in which they express themselves; and that asking people why they have bought certain articles is about the least reliable method of discovering the true reasons." [4]

Fortunately the market analyst need not choose between the overt acts of buying and the reasons people give in explanation of their overt acts. There is room for both bodies of information. One of the distinctive contributions to marketing research techniques of recent years has been the studies made by Dr. Paul Lazarsfeld, who has attempted to make use of the reasons people give for their actions by applying what has become known as "the psychological interpretation of market data." [5] This emphasis on the interpretation of subjective information is not contradictory but complementary to the statistical analysis and interpretation of the more objective type of data. Both aspects of marketing research are worthy of careful study by all students of distribution problems.

[4] Link, *The New Psychology of Selling and Advertising.*

[5] See Paul F. Lazarsfeld, "The Psychological Aspect of Market Research," *Harvard Business Review,* XIII (October, 1934), 54–71.

RELATIVE IMPORTANCE OF MARKET AND SALES ANALYSES IN THE DETERMINATION OF THE SALES BUDGET

The preceding discussion has attempted to show the great variety of purposes for which both sales and markets may be analyzed. The interrelationship between purposes and techniques makes it necessary to eliminate from subsequent discussion those purposes that have no direct connection with sales planning and the setting up of the sales budget. The reader should not, however, interpret this emphasis on budgetary control to indicate any lack of importance of the other functions that may be served by market and sales analyses. Moreover, he should not assume that sales and market data are necessarily of equal importance in establishing the estimate of future sales. There are occasions when the time and effort spent in estimating potential sales from an analysis of the market might be more profitably employed in other directions. Some of the factors influencing the importance of a market analysis as compared to that of a sales analysis are discussed below.

Frequency of purchase.—The less frequently a product is purchased, the more desirable a market analysis tends to become as a means for estimating future sales. Conversely, a sales analysis is likely to prove more helpful in estimating sales when the product is one of very general use and of such small unit cost that it is purchased frequently and widely by the great mass of consumers. Distribution of products in this category becomes primarily a problem of keeping present customers satisfied and pulling new ones from competitors by means of advertising and sales effort. Typical of the goods in this class are groceries, tobacco products, cosmetics, and other general consumer goods.

For products in which the advantage is with an analysis of the market for estimating future sales we must look to the durable consumer goods category, where we find pianos, period furniture, fine jewelry, home sites, prefabricated houses, and other objects in the purchase of which the consumer is put out of the market for an indefinite period of time—sometimes for a number of years and occasionally for life. Except insofar as the current sale acts as an entering wedge for introducing the product to other customers, it bears little relationship to future sales. Consequently, an analysis of records would provide little assistance in establishing a dependable sales estimate.

Selectivity of the market.—The larger the number of factors limiting and conditioning the sale of a product, the greater the need for a market analysis. Industrial machinery, especially if it is highly specialized, affords one of the best opportunities for the application of market analysis. The demand is usually one that is capable of being ascertained with a high degree of accuracy. Like the more durable consumers' goods, the unit values tend to be high and the number of customers limited. In addition, the users' requirements and ability to buy are capable of being determined with a relatively high degree of accuracy. Frequently the customers are concentrated within a small geographical region.

Style factor of the market.—The more susceptible a market is to style changes, the greater is the need for an analysis of present and potential demand. The sales of a single company may often constitute such a small section of the total market that they may fail to reflect the general style trend. A market analysis extends the area of observation so that changes may be observed during the incipient stages of the style cycle while there is yet time in which to take advantage of its upward swing.

Elasticity of demand.—The more elastic the demand for a product, the greater the need for a market analysis tends to be. When the quantity of a product sold is highly responsive to changes in price, a great deal depends upon the pricing policy. A mistake can easily mean the difference between success and failure. The importance of the problem has induced a variety of approaches. From the cost side have come the cost accountants and the industrial engineers; into the theoretical aspects have delved the economists with prolific pens and a proverbial penchant for deriving supply and demand curves deductively; finally, from the inductive side have come the statisticians with their techniques for fitting supply and demand curves empirically. To the business man who is wrestling with the problem of what price to charge for his product, something seems to be missing in all these approaches. If the economist is too theoretical, the statistician is too technical. There is need for an approach that borrows something from each of these various specialists, but seeks to determine from both present and potential buyers what change is likely to occur in the volume of the company's sales as a result of a given change in the price of the article. This represents the viewpoint of the market analyst.

Proximity of seller to consumer.—The more removed the seller is from the ultimate consumer, the greater is the need for a market analysis. Roundabout production and specialization have increased the number of points where estimates must be made on the basis of other people's behavior. The errors in making estimates at various stages of the distributive process tend to be cumulative rather than of a random sort, and a small miscalculation on the part of some middleman may become grossly exaggerated by the time it reaches the manufacturer. A market analysis can serve to place the seller in more nearly direct communication with his ultimate market and save him from becoming too greatly influenced by the currents of overoptimism and overpessimism that are alternately generated by our highly specialized and interdependent economic order.

Size of the market.—The more extensive the market, the greater is the need for surveys to reveal conditions influencing demand. As long as markets were primarily local, the memory of the seller was sufficient to provide an intimate and personal account of the buying habits of each of the few dozen patrons. National and international markets have made obsolete such personal means of keeping in touch with the buyers. Formal market analyses provide the substitute.

TECHNIQUE OF MAKING A MARKET ANALYSIS

No critical consideration of the factors affecting the desirability of a market analysis would be complete without the most careful estimate of probable cost. Money and effort spent in marketing research do not automatically pay dividends to the sponsors. Only by the formulation of a systematic working plan in which the essential issues are evaluated, the scope of the investigation outlined, the methods of gathering the data indicated, and an estimate of its total cost in time and money prepared, can much useless "research" be avoided.

The steps in the actual market investigation represent an application and expansion of the scientific method. The following outline provides a typical sequence.

Definition of the problem.—In the absence of a precise definition of the problem the investigator is prone to lose sight of the objective and to dissipate his energies in seeking solutions and collecting data that subsequently have little or no use. One of the most effective procedures for making the problem definite consists in the listing of specific questions to which answers are to be sought. Several standard classified lists of questions and points of information have been published and are available to persons desiring to make a selection of the appropriate items of investigation. These checklists embrace practically every phase of distribution including policies, product, market, and methods and means for reaching the market.[6]

In addition to the checklists of questions, a number of outlines suitable for making market surveys have been made public.[7] Such standard set-ups are unusually inclusive, and when modified to fit the specific situation they provide against the omission of significant facts.

Formulation of the working plan.—What the blueprint is to the construction engineer, the working plan is to the research worker. It involves: (1) a statement of the purpose or purposes for which the investigation is undertaken; (2) the setting down of the specific items upon which information is to be gathered; (3) the methods to be used in collection of the data; (4) the sources of the information; (5) a tentative outline of the final report; (6) an estimate of the cost of making the survey; (7) finally, an approval of the working plan as the official sanction for the analysis to proceed.

Collection of the information.—Considered from the point of view of both the cost and the accuracy of the results, this step is by far the most crucial one in the investigation. If the original data are not reliable, all the refinement of subsequent statistical analysis will not serve to give accurate results. Lack of information is usually better than wrong information, especially if important decisions are at stake.

The six most important methods for the collection of market information are: (1) bibliographical survey, (2) observation, (3) experiment, (4) personal interview, (5) mail questionnaire, and (6)

[6] Examples of important check lists used in marketing research are to be found in the following publications: Giles, *The Sales Expansion Question Book;* Larrabee and Marks, *Check Lists of Advertising, Selling and Merchandising Essentials;* R. O. Eastman, Incorporated, *Eastman Marketing Seminar.* Among separate chart sheets, two examples are worthy of mention, namely, *Balzari Check-Chart,* published by McGraw-Hill Book Company, and *The Crossindex,* used by the Crossley Company.

[7] See Reed, *Planned Marketing,* chap. xi, and Smith, *An Outline for Market Surveys,* as examples of custom-made outlines.

telephone inquiry. The first-named method provides secondary data, whereas each of the others results in primary data. Selection of the appropriate method for any particular study implies a familiarity with the various advantages and disadvantages associated with each. These constitute the subject of the following chapter in which the general subject of the collection of market data is discussed.

Analysis of the data.—This step is second only to the collection of data in the importance that it bears to the final results. Reliable data may be analyzed to give grossly inaccurate results simply because of ineptitude or false reasoning on the part of the analyst.

Preparation of the report.—The report is the vehicle that conveys the results to those who are responsible for applying them. A favorable impression is so conditioned by matters of form, language, and illustration that effort spent in consulting some of the standard texts upon report writing is likely to be well repaid.

Application of results.—The responsibility of the one who performs the analysis often extends to the application of the results. The entire value of the research is, of course, lost unless the recommendations are put into use. In some respects the results are worse than lost, since the failure tends to discredit all future attempts to study the market in any systematic way. Lack of attention given to the report, inertia of the management, and internal dissension among the officers are some of the various factors that can cause failure in this last step. As in most situations demanding administrative and executive talents, the application is hardly amenable to rules of procedure. However, a certain amount of "missionary work" among the officers of the company, proper attention to report form, and particular care in timing the report can do much to pave the way for a successful application of results.

CHAPTER IX

Methods of Collecting Market Information

THE SOCIAL OBJECTIVE toward which market studies in general should tend is the elimination of waste in the distribution of goods and services. Effort directed toward this goal has often been frustrated. The obstacle perhaps most frequently interposed has been the general unwillingness to divulge information of a "confidential" nature.

DIFFICULTIES CREATED BY COMPETITIVE SELLING

In our competitive economic order certain rather anomalous situations are to be found. One of these relates to the distinctions drawn by business organizations in reporting sales information. Some report current sales under pressure of fiscal and regulatory legislation. Others make public their sales data as a matter of policy. Most firms, however, regard their records of sales as confidential, and the maintenance of this wall of secrecy has been expensive in terms both of the quality of market data and of the money expended for its collection. Much of the information, for example, that is currently gathered through various types of market surveys could be obtained almost as a gratuity if business men were to divulge their sales data. Instead, they have chosen the devious and expensive methods of estimating their own and their competitors' positions in the industry through dealer and consumer inquiries. The front door to complete and highly accurate sales information is ajar, but so long as most sections of the business community keep their sales ledgers in the privacy of inviolate secrecy business men will have need of such back-door methods as the mail questionnaire, the pantry-shelf count, the retail inventory, and the personal interview in obtaining approximate knowledge of what competitors are doing. The pooling of important statistical data relative to plant capacities, unfilled orders, sales, shipments, stocks on hand, billings, and payments would seem to constitute a first step toward economy of effort in the study of markets.

TYPES OF INFORMATION

The wise mechanic chooses his tools to fit his job. The market analyst also has tools and a job to perform. His tools are the methods and techniques for the collection and analysis of market data. His job is represented by the type and source of these data. In general, they belong in three categories: (1) basic statistical data, (2) economic analyses, and (3) explanatory and descriptive material.

Basic statistical data are obviously the most important, since all quantitative studies of the market must be grounded upon information of this type. They are compiled both within and without the enterprise. Most of the external data of value to the market analyst are prepared by the Federal Government and by trade associations.

The economic analyses are one step removed from the basic statistical data. The market analyst must draw his information from a great variety of sources and in choosing to use some materials that have been prefabricated, as it were, in the shops of other analysts he may serve his purpose quite as effectively and certainly with greater economy. Typical of the economic analyses that find ready use in market studies are those providing indexes of prices, production, volume of trade, wages, and general purchasing power.

Explanatory and descriptive information is found principally in textbooks and magazine articles. The former usually contain the statements of general principle, whereas the latter provide a wealth of case material that often proves helpful in solving specific marketing problems. Facts regarding policies, personalities, and marketing processes tend to accumulate in the mind of the market analyst, often without his knowing their particular source. These abstract and intangible bits of information "arise as a sort of aura—sometimes, indeed, as a miasma—found enveloping the executive and marketing departments of a business." [1]

[1] American Marketing Society, Committee on Marketing Research Technique, *The Technique of Marketing Research.*

BIBLIOGRAPHICAL METHOD OF COLLECTING MARKET INFORMATION

The bibliographical method (use of published sources) belongs first in the sequence by which information upon any subject is usually sought. Without first exploring what others have written upon a problem, one runs the grave risk of spending much effort and money in obtaining information that may have been secured gratis from some public library. Since the responsibility for the collection of information obtained from a library was that of some person other than the user, such data are known as secondary. By implication the data are primary when the investigator collects them first hand. These terms are suggestive of a difference in the quality of the information, as though the user of secondary information were willing to sacrifice accuracy for expediency. There seems to be little to justify this inference. Modern research in the social sciences places such emphasis on the collection and analysis of vast quantities of statistical data that the free lance with a flare for the inductive approach may wisely begin with statistical reports of governments and research organizations. By no amount of individual effort can the person dependent on his own resources hope to match in scope and accuracy data that have been compiled by the well-trained staffs of field workers employed by governments and endowed associations.

AIDS TO BIBLIOGRAPHICAL RESEARCH

The difficulty experienced by most college students in finding data relative to some specific topic seems to be symptomatic of a general deficiency in the educational program. Certainly the search for published information seems to present a problem quite as real as the collection of primary data. Only a few of the obvious aids to bibliographical sources, however, can here be given.

Familiarity with all the various library indexes constitutes a first condition for tapping sources of secondary information. In the realm of books the *United States Catalogue* provides a list of all those published in the United States and obtainable from publishers since 1912. The list is supplemented monthly by the *Cumulative Book Index*. In the field of periodical literature the following are deserving of special mention: *Reader's Guide, Industrial Arts Index, Agricultural Index,* and *Public Affairs Information Service*. If news items are the center of interest one may consult one of a number of newspaper indexes, of which the *New York Times Index* is perhaps the best known and most widely used. For a current listing of the publications of the Federal Government the *Monthly Catalogue of the United States Public Documents* may be consulted. All of the above-mentioned indexes are, of course, in addition to the regular library card catalogue with which any person who frequents a library is familiar.

TESTING SECONDARY DATA

The person using secondary data has a more limited responsibility than one who gathers data first hand. The inaccuracies in the sources of his information are not of his making, and he can, if he wishes, disclaim responsibility beyond that of accuracy in reporting. His disclaimer is likely to afford small comfort, however, if he has employed data or used the results of research that fail to conform to what reasonably prudent investigators would require. The following constitute a few of the generally recognized precautions for dealing with secondary information.

In the first place, published information, like an old wives' tale, may be far removed from its origin. The passing of information from one publication to another gives rise to various possible inaccuracies, such as incompleteness in reporting, errors in transcription, misinterpretation of data, and misapplication as regards the original purpose of the information. Reasonable caution dictates the use of publications in which responsibility for collecting the information is united with the responsibility for its publication. Such publications are known as primary sources.[2]

Inquiry into the motive of authorship constitutes a second reasonable precaution. A great deal that carries the label "market research" has been prepared by private organizations intent not so much in seeking truth as in presenting a case. The specific sources of error deserving mention are: misstatements of facts, misuses of concepts, and erroneous conclusions drawn from otherwise correct data.

[2] Confusion has often arisen because of the use of "primary" and "secondary" as terms describing both data and sources. Data, however, are always secondary if taken from a published source, whereas the publication itself may be either a primary or a secondary source. It is the latter only if the responsibility for the collection of the data belongs elsewhere than with the agency responsible for their publication.

The methods of collection are a third factor that requires careful checking. If the data were compiled from a sample, information should be sought on the method of sampling. If questionnaires were used, the nature of questions asked should be scrutinized for sources of bias. In general, the standards set up for gauging the reliability of secondary data are the same as those that pertain to primary data. To know, for instance, what to avoid when collecting data first hand is to be forewarned against sources of error when inspecting data gathered by others.

A check list of questions for appraising market and advertising research has been prepared by the Committee on Research of the American Association of Advertising Agencies. Because of their completeness and general applicability the questions are listed in detail below.[3]

1. Who made the survey?
2. Does the title indicate exactly the scope of the survey?
3. Does the report contain all pertinent data as to how, when and where the survey was made?
4. Is the sample a representative cross section?
5. Is the sample large enough?
6. Are percentages figured for groups or classes that contain too small a number of instances?
7. Are percentages of increase figured on ample bases?
8. Was information obtained by mailed questionnaires?
9. Is causal relationship attributed to one single factor, when other contributing factors are present?
10. If questionnaires were used, were questions such as to yield fair and adequate answers?
11. Was information gathered of such a nature that the memories of the people interviewed might have resulted in inaccuracies as to fact?
12. Can type of information obtained (either by interview or by mail) be relied on as accurate?
13. Have any original or unique statistical devices been employed?
14. Are charts misleading?

SOME DEFICIENCIES IN THE STOCK OF STATISTICAL DATA

The difficulties faced by those who use secondary data are really of two types. The first relates to the misinterpretations, errors of tran-

[3] From *Domestic Commerce*, United States Bureau of Foreign and Domestic Commerce, Washington, D. C., Jan. 20, 1939.

scription, forms of bias, and so forth that were the subject of the foregoing section. The second relates to certain wide gaps in the stock of statistical data. These latter are in the nature of sins of omission rather than commission. A few of the more important gaps are here enumerated:

Need of a finer division both in income and age data.—Since the great bulk of the consuming public fall within the lower-income brackets ($2,000 or less), a finer grouping, consisting perhaps of $100 class intervals, among those with incomes less than $2,000 would enable the market analyst to appraise their buying power with greater precision.

Similarly, the publications of the Census Bureau pertaining to the number of persons within various age groups would have greater usefulness to the market analyst if the classifications were modified toward a finer grouping of persons under fourteen years of age. The swiftly moving kaleidoscope of youth may reveal changes within a year comparable to those of a decade in later life. For the measurement of the juvenile market common sense dictates a subdivision of the present five-year intervals into classes more nearly commensurate with the rate of change in the human organism.

Need of specific information on family incomes.—Most of the data published by the Bureau of Internal Revenue relate to individual incomes. To the market analyst, however, the individual income is secondary to the family income. For many consumer goods, especially those of the durable type, the family is the buying unit and when there are two or three "breadwinners" within the same household the income of each may be low but their combined buying power is such that most of the comforts and possibly some of the luxuries may be purchased. Sample studies of family incomes and of family budgets are gradually filling in the gaps left in the basic statistical compilation of income data.

Need of more information on the dynamics of consumption.—Social and economic changes are continually affecting consuming habits. For those who have things to sell these changes may spell either a golden opportunity or ultimate ruin. Some of the more important elements in the dynamics of consumption are: the retardation in the rate of population growth, the migration from rural to urban centers, the counter migration represented by the decentralization of congested urban areas, changes in the stream of immigration, the decline in both the birth rate and the death rate, the increase in tenancy, the decline of industries in the home, the increase in apartment-house living, the growing emphasis on education, and the increase in occupations of sedentary nature. Greater knowledge of these dynamic forces would help many to realize their opportunities, whereas those less fortunately placed might avoid the slow and gradual economic ruin that awaits them in their present ignorance and apparent helplessness.

Need of more information with respect to people's spending habits.—Information concerning people's power to buy is considerably greater than that concerning their willingness to buy, yet it is the latter that is the more important in the measurement of markets. The assumption that willingness to buy varies directly in a fixed manner with purchasing power is unsafe, especially as applied to consumer goods. Moreover, the same absolute increase in spendable income will be employed in widely different ways depending upon the income level, the nationality, the occupational interests, and the general cultural background of the recipients. If the market analyst aspires to forecast the probable path that a given amount of distributed purchasing power will take, he must accumulate first the basic statistical material from studies made of small and relatively homogeneous groups of consumers. A good beginning has been made in this direction, but much more data are needed regarding purchasing habits as conditioned by income levels, professional and occupational interests, nationality, education, religion, geographical location, climatic conditions, and so forth. Within this realm of human behavior there are problems galore for the person whose interest is in group psychology.

Need of specific information regarding the trading habits of people.—After the amount and the character of people's expenditures have been ascertained the question remains, where do they do their trading? The place of purchase is quite as important as the amount and character of the buying. Whereas the census of distribution contains very helpful sales data for cities and towns and furnishes break-downs by types of retail outlets, the field of study represented by trading areas for specific articles and for classes of merchandise is as yet virgin territory. Practically all the published trading-area maps are of the so-called "standard" type, that is, they purport to show by a single design the purchasing proclivities of persons in search of anything from peanuts or a paper of pins to pianos or printing presses. Helpful though such studies are in indicating the boundaries of the typical zones for the centripetal pull of various major and minor trading centers, they cannot reveal the many significant points of difference in the trading habits of people as regards specific articles of merchandise. Such specific studies are possibly best developed as local projects serving primarily local needs. A promising start has been made along these lines.

COLLECTION OF DATA BY OBSERVATION

The collection of data by observation is sometimes called the method of uncontrolled experiment. It is experimental in the sense that the observer is either testing some hypothesis or seeking an answer to some question. It is uncontrolled in the sense that the factors influencing the result are for the most part beyond the power of the investigator to change. For example, a chain-store organization will send an investigator to count the number of people passing a certain street corner that is being considered as a possible location for a retail outlet. Again, the fashion analyst will attend a social function for the purpose of noting the materials and styles of dress that are in public favor. In both illustrations the investigator plays a purely passive role. He simply reports what he sees.

The type of problem to which the method of observation is most suited has already been indicated. The principal difficulty of the method lies in the limitation of the investigator's power of observation and judgment. Any schoolboy can stand on the street corner and count the number of pedestrians passing within the hour, but an appraisal of their combined purchasing power would call for the services of a soothsayer. And to predict the direction in which such purchasing power would flow would require nothing short of a gift for divination. A small photoelectric cell can count with absolute accuracy the number of people who stop to gaze in upon a store window, but who can say to what extent their subsequent purchases have been influenced by what they saw? Yet it is the ultimate selling power of the display that really counts, not its attention-attracting power.

The criticism of behavior measurements is not to be confined to the information gathered through observation. The whole of statistical analysis rests upon the ability of people to count or measure the things in which they are interested. And the things that people count and measure are seldom, if ever, identical with the things in which they are fundamentally interested. For instance, the vast body of quantitative information that comes under the heading "vital statistics" is vital only in the sense that human beings have presumed to read their individual weal or woe in fluctuations of such numerical data. The heavier one can draw the line separating the shadow of statistical measurements from the substance that is being measured, the fewer chances there are for drawing unwarranted conclusions regarding the latter.

COLLECTING DATA BY MEANS OF EXPERIMENT

The process of experimentation implies an ability on the part of the investigator to control the factors that influence the outcome. Control, however, need not mean manipulation. Rarely does the social scientist possess this power over the forces affecting the outcome of his experiments. He has, nevertheless, achieved control over these forces when he has planned his tests so that these variables are made to exert their influence in a uniform manner. For example, an advertising agency desiring to measure the relative sales-getting power of two advertisements may remove the disturbing influence of the weather factor by inserting the copies simultaneously in the local papers of two similar towns. Weather can then be assumed to influence the two results in the same manner. Even minor differences in the experimental towns could be made to cancel through the statistical device of increasing the number of towns and taking an average of the findings.

Again, a manufacturer might adopt the experimental technique for discovering ways and means of getting a larger degree of dealer cooperation in the display of the manufacturer's goods and in pushing them before the public. To this end the company may acquire one or more retail stores in which to carry on experiments with window displays, store arrangements, special advertising, and sales arguments. The Dennison Manufacturing Company and Butler Brothers may be cited as companies that operate such "laboratory stores."

A second purpose of "laboratory stores" might be to gather information by observation. Using the sales counter as a point of observation and a cash-register code for recording the data, such characteristics as age and sex of customers, type of goods sold, and the value of the sale might be continuously recorded.

The experiments in distribution described above will serve to illustrate the sort of "control" that the social scientist is forced to employ. His manipulation of the various factors influencing his results may often seem crude and bungling in comparison with the precise experimental technique of the physical scientist. When direct control or manipulation of a factor is out of the question, the social investigator may resort to the more devious method of selecting his experimental subjects so that the troublesome factor can be considered to influence each subject in the same manner. At other times the investigator may increase the number of his experimental subjects to the point where he is justified in taking an average. The variations induced by the troublesome factor are then assumed to cancel.

The field of distribution is as yet virgin soil for experimentation in the sense that this term is understood by the social scientist. The pretesting of products, advertisements, distribution channels, and so forth is a growing practice that augurs well for lower costs and the elimination of waste in the marketing of goods and services.

The chief disadvantage of the experimental method of gathering information is the time element involved. Most experiments, especially those which deal with human behavior, require the lapse of a considerable period of time for their completion. Many business executives become impatient with such delays. They prefer to take a gambler's chance upon immediate action rather than await the knowledge that is prerequisite to a safe commitment. When the stakes involved are not excessive and timeliness is the essence of gain, their attitude is quite justified.

COLLECTING INFORMATION BY MEANS OF PERSONAL AND TELEPHONE INTERVIEWS

Interviews may be conducted either in person or by telephone. In the absence of any modifying adjective, the method of interview may be interpreted to mean that the interviews were made by interrogators calling in person upon those who had information to give. While this is the older and more common method, the telephone has played a significant and increasing part in the gathering of information which requires only a few brief and simple questions answerable either by "yes" or "no" or by some other equally short and categorical reply. Telephone interviews are more frequently resorted to in making radio-listener surveys. By proper organization hundreds of interviews may be completed within the hour or the fraction thereof during which a radio program is on the air. Thus, its timeliness and relative cheapness are its chief virtues. The cost per interview seldom exceeds the cost per return from mail questionnaires, and it may be very much less. Moreover, the telephone has sometimes been the means of reaching people whose position in the business, the professional, or the social world would tend to preclude, or at least to make difficult, gaining an audience with them.

Offsetting these advantages and merits of the telephone interview method, one can cite limitations in the quantity of information as well as in its quality. The absence of any visual check, either upon the correspondent himself or upon the conditions surrounding him, makes the information distinctly less reliable than that obtained by the personal interview. There is no opportunity for "spotting the interviews" (arranging them according to certain significant factors, such as age, nationality, education, income, and so forth), except insofar as the type of neighborhood itself is correlated with these factors. Perhaps the chief limitation, however, is that the sample of persons from whom the information is gathered is automatically limited to those who are telephone subscribers.

The flexibility of direct conversation makes the personal interview the most desirable means of securing information concerning attitudes and in conducting technical surveys in which either the questions or the answers are in need of supplementary explanation. Moreover, the things that the observing interviewer sees may be quite as important as the things that he is told. Finally, people will sometimes tell in person what they will not talk about over the telephone, much less write about in answer to a mail inquiry. For all these reasons the method of personal interview in the hands of those who are skilled in the art frequently proves successful in getting information that is more extensive, more reliable, and occasionally more personal than that which one might hope to obtain by other methods.

One of the disadvantages of this method of personal interview is that the person interviewed will sometimes bend his answers to suit the investigator. As a rule people like to please, and unless the utmost care is exercised the investigator may find himself asking questions and suggesting the answers by some subtle means such as wording of the question or the intonation of the voice. To guard against the first contingency, the form of all questions asked should be carefully worked out in advance.

Again, the person interviewed may frequently be impatient. In his desire to be rid of the interviewer he may give his answers in a hasty off-hand manner, so that much of the information may be inexact. The skilled and careful interviewer will, however, be quick to observe the moods and manners of the persons interrogated. He will seek either to correct or to eliminate the answers which in his judgment represent less than the truth.

If the survey is made to obtain consumer opinion, the information will quite likely be inordinately weighted by the opinions of housewives. They are usually the only ones at home when the interviewer calls. The assumption that the housewife can speak for the whole family may or may not be valid, depending on the nature of the questions asked. If the assumption seems unsafe, arrangements should be made for the interviewer to call at hours when the members of the family who are gainfully employed will be present.

Formerly the method of personal interview was considered both expensive and tedious. For those who must assemble their own staff of trained field investigators and personally supervise the collection of the information the method is undoubtedly slow and costly, especially for extensive surveys. Specialization, however, has been applied to marketing research in recent years, and business enterprises that do not possess the facilities can engage the services of one of the various organizations that maintain a staff and corps of field workers for market-research purposes. For a stipulated price per interview (depending upon the number of interviews, their length, and the type of information desired) these market research specialists will take an assignment and deliver the information in almost any form desired, ranging from the untabulated and unanalyzed returns to the final report. The economies that have been achieved in the technique of sampling plus those associated with specialization itself have enabled the market research organizations to perform these services more cheaply than a business enterprise could unless it maintained its own permanent market-research staff. In many instances the cost is less and the information superior to what would have been obtained had the mail questionnaire been used.

MAIL QUESTIONNAIRE AS A MEANS OF GATHERING DATA

The mail questionnaire is the shotgun method of getting information as contrasted with the rifle method of personal interview. A few dozen or a million or more questionnaires may be "shot out," as it were, through the mails to a corresponding number of persons, from whom it is hoped a fair measure of response will be secured—one at any rate that will serve as an adequate and reliable sample of the population that is being studied. Investigators have used a variety of approaches and forms of appeal to induce a larger percentage of response. At one end of the scale is the plea for help or the frank request for a favor. At the opposite end is the use of authority or devices suggestive of authority in commanding compliance with the request. Between these extremes we find various *quid pro quod* arrangements in which the receiver of the questionnaire is offered something in return for his coöperation such as, for example, the promise of the results or the offer of some premium or prize. If a letter accompanies the questionnaire, it will usually contain the offer of inducements together with whatever explanations may be needed.

Very rarely will the number of replies to a mail questionnaire exceed 20 percent of the total number of questionnaires posted, and if as many as 10 percent of the addresses respond, the analyst can consider the response was equal to and perhaps even above the average for this method of collecting data. Since the proportion of replies and the reliability of the results are conditioned by the wording of the questions, the form of the questionnaire, and even by such apparently insignificant factors as the color of the paper, there is obvious need for meticulous attention to details in the framing and sending of questionnaires. For the mechanics and principles dealing with the preparation, testing, sending, and editing of mail questionnaires the reader is referred to Appendix B.

ADVANTAGES AND DISADVANTAGES OF THE MAIL QUESTIONNAIRE

Some of the advantages and disadvantages of the mail questionnaire have already been suggested. One of its chief advantages lies in the complete standardization of the questions. The investigator can be sure that every person has been asked the same set of questions in the same way. Personal interviewers are likely to vary the wording of their questions in spite of specific instructions to the contrary.

A second advantage lies in the large number of persons from whom information may be secured. Hence, the method is best suited for making extensive rather than intensive surveys. The information, however, should usually be of a rather impersonal nature and should require a limited number of specific questions.

In addition to the advantages named above, several conditional points favor the use of the mail questionnaire. If comparison is made with the personal-interview method as applied by business enterprises lacking their own well-trained staff of research workers, the mail-questionnaire method has the advantage of being easy to organize and to supervise. After the questionnaire has been written and tested, the sending and tabulation can be performed by a clerk with very little guidance and supervision on the part of the investigator. A second conditional advantage is the greater speed with which returns may be obtained from mail questionnaires when both methods "start from scratch," as it were, without benefit of any previous organization. Economy is likewise on the side of the mail questionnaire under these assumed conditions. Such conditional advantages, it must be emphasized, have now been challenged by specialization in personal-interview technique and organization. Granting the existence of a permanent staff of field workers and analysts well trained in the methods of collecting and organizing data, the advantages of speed, accuracy, and economy are quite definitely on the side of the personal-interview method.

Some of the disadvantages of the mail questionnaire have been implied in the discussion of its conditional advantages. The difficulty experienced in getting people to answer a mailed questionnaire is its most obvious limitation. The method must be used sparingly, since the more questionnaires a person receives, the more likely he is to throw the next one into the wastebasket. If the sender of the mail questionnaire is able to use some legal, social, or moral pressure to induce answers, the point of diminishing returns may be delayed, but not for long.

Less obvious, but equally, if not more, serious, are the limitations in quantity and quality of information obtainable by the mail-questionnaire technique. The answers are usually limited to a categorical "yes" or "no," and rarely is more information obtained than is requested. On the other hand, a personal interviewer may uncover information that was not known to exist. The quality of the information suffers perhaps even greater handicaps than does its quantity. We may eliminate from our consideration the erroneous answers given by practical jokesters. The more serious type of unreliability is the uncontrollable bias that is likely to creep into the results because of the selective process in answering. The mailing list may constitute a group as thoroughly representative of the market as any careful study could devise, and yet the small percentage that choose to answer may be so unlike the silent majority that the results cannot be considered representative. Means for detecting and correcting this type of bias will be discussed in connection with the general principles of sampling that are the subject of the next chapter.

As the need for market surveys has increased, the personal-interview method of gathering market data has gradually grown in favor at the expense of the mail questionnaire. As evidence of this trend one can cite the increasing number of research organizations specializing in the conduct of market studies of various kinds. The reduction in the cost of personal-interview surveys that has accompanied this specialization has been made possible by the combination of such favorable factors as: staff of efficient machine operators, an assortment of equipment specialized for handling masses of statistical data, and a volume of research projects sufficient to keep the organization busy.

CHAPTER X

The Theory of Sampling as Applied To Market Data

RARELY DOES THE MARKET analyst gather complete information. He draws his conclusions usually from the study of a sample. What he finds to be true of the sample he assumes to be true of the larger group from which the sample came and of which it is presumed to be typical. Unless the sampling procedure is sound, the data and all the analyses performed upon them may be worse than useless.

THE THEORY OF SAMPLING

The proper technique for gathering samples and for testing the reliability of measures derived from them requires that the market analyst possess a knowledge that is twofold. First, he must be fully cognizant of the limitations of the data in the field. Secondly, he must have knowledge of statistical methods, since they are tools that lend precision to his work.

In resorting to the sampling procedure the market analyst is in excellent company. Research workers in practically every branch of science have employed the technique of sampling to advance the field of knowledge. Justification for the technique rests upon the principle of uniformity that is presumed to be operative throughout the universe. This principle takes for granted the existence of variability among units of a population, but it assumes that the differences between members will be confined within certain ascertainable limits. Small differences are assumed to be much more numerous and more likely to occur than are large ones. Moreover, the probability of obtaining differences of increasing magnitude becomes progressively less, so that a limit is very quickly reached beyond which, for all practical purposes, a difference is not likely to be found. Everyday experience bears testimony to the reasonableness of these assumptions, and scientific progress has demonstrated their validity.

THE THEORY OF PROBABILITIES

Certainty represents an unattainable ideal for those who employ the sampling procedure. Each numerical result obtained by the inductive approach must be interpreted as an approximation to the true answer. A simple example will serve to illustrate the nature of these sampling errors and the statistical methods invoked to estimate their order of magnitude. We may assume one hundred random interviews to have been made among the housewives of a certain market area to ascertain the relative popularity of different brands of laundry soap. If twenty of the one hundred housewives are found to be using Brand X soap, the analyst might conclude that 20 percent of the families within the entire market area were using this brand. His conclusion, however, would obviously be only an approximation, and its accuracy requires testing by statistical technique.

Statisticians have demonstrated that the sampling errors of a relative frequency (called the standard error of a percentage) may be determined from the relationship[1] $\sigma = \sqrt{\frac{pq}{N}}$, where p is the percentage of cases in the universe possessing a certain characteristic, q is the complement, or $100 - p$, and N the number of observations in the sample. Since the value of p for the universe is usually unknown, expediency requires the use of the percentage obtained in the sample. Substituting this along with other appropriate values and solving, the standard error of the percentage in this hypothetical problem is found to be 4 percent.

For an interpretation of the standard error statisticians are indebted to the gaming table and man's proclivity for gambling. Out of these grew the concept of the normal curve and the calculus for its analysis, so that for data that are normally distributed the analyst is able to read from the table of the probability integral the chances of obtaining values within any stated limits.[2] Using one standard error

[1] For the mathematical development of the standard error formula the reader is referred to A. L. Bowley's *Elements of Statistics*.

[2] For a detailed and lucid exposition of the normal curve and the table of areas see Waugh, *Elements of Statistical Method*, chap. vi.

as a convenient yardstick and applying it to the sample value of 20 percent, the table of areas enables us to quote the chances of sixty-eight (more precisely 68.26) out of one hundred that the true percentage of housewives using Brand X laundry soap in the total market area will not differ from 20 by more than 4.

SOME LIMITATIONS TO THE USE OF STATISTICAL TECHNIQUES

Many seasoned practitioners in marketing research reject the statistical approach to sampling for some simple rule-of-thumb procedure that they consider has provided them with "reasonably" satisfactory results. The only safe generalization on method is that each situation calls for specific study. Choice of approach must rest in each instance upon such factors as the purpose of the analysis, the accuracy of the observations, and the assumptions underlying the proposed statistical techniques.

When statistical techniques are made appropriate to the purpose of the analysis, the application of some of the extreme refinements becomes superfluous. Henry G. Weaver has expressed this idea in words so colorful as to merit quotation.

> Even though it were possible to get results accurate down to the last decimal place, it is difficult to conceive how the action based on such results could ever be reduced to such hairsplitting fineness. For example, whether the consumer's vote indicates 75 percent or 95 percent preference, the action taken would, at best, be more or less arbitrary and probably the same in either case.[3]

Hence the purpose of the analysis is one of the most important factors determining the margin of permissible error in the results and the extent to which refinements of methods are warranted.

The second factor limiting the use of statistical techniques in marketing research is the accuracy of the original data. Errors of observation occur in all measurements and in most enumerations, but such errors tend to compensate in relatively large samples so that refined statistical treatment is justified in dealing with the data. To the extent that the errors in the data are of this type most of the statistical measures will possess a degree of accuracy greater than

[3] Henry G. Weaver, "Consumer Questionnaire Technique," *The American Marketing Journal,* I (No. 3, July, 1934), 116.

their standard errors indicate. Unfortunately the errors that creep into marketing research data are frequently non-compensating, and no amount of refined statistical treatment can remove a biased or "loaded" error.

There are a number of sources from which "loaded" errors in market data may arise, and the most important of these will be discussed in connection with the sampling procedure. The purpose of the present section is to emphasize the folly of attempting to reduce sampling errors of the results to some small fraction of a percent, when there may be present in the data various "loaded" errors amounting to 15 or 20 percent. The way in which the questions are asked, the manner in which the sample was chosen, or some psychological tendency on the part of the respondents may serve to introduce consistent errors many times the magnitude of the sampling errors.

Possibly the most deceptive and unwarranted refinements in methodology are to be found in the analysis of secondary data. There the analyst is frequently unaware of any "loaded" error in the information. Uncritical acceptance of the data is more probable if the analyst's training and experience have been largely with methods of analysis rather than with methods of collection. Hence field work provides the veteran of market research with a sense of proportion that precludes his covering crudities of information with too many habiliments of refined statistical procedure.

Occasionally both the purpose of the study and the accuracy of the data warrant the use of rather precise methods of analysis, but the assumptions upon which the methods rest are not present. Back of most statistical formulas lie certain postulates that may or may not be fulfilled in the situation out of which the data arose. For example, the formula given in the preceding section assumes that the sample of one hundred interviews was taken at random from an infinite universe of independent events in which p, the probability of a housewife using Brand X laundry soap, is a constant element. The mere statement of these assumptions is sufficient to raise doubts about the application. Yet perfect agreement between assumptions and conditions is usually more than one can hope for in any given situation. The analyst will have exercised reasonable care provided he first makes inquiry about the assumptions underlying the formula and then satisfies himself that the conditions found in the problem come sufficiently close to these in order that no fundamental error is committed through the application.

MEANING OF HOMOGENEITY

Homogeneity plays such an important part in the sampling procedure that a definition of the term seems desirable. Unless the analyst is able to designate the population under inquiry as being either homogeneous or heterogeneous, he is in no position to set the conditions for a representative sample. If he elects to call every population heterogeneous, no harm is done except that he needlessly sacrifices time and effort in elaborating the sampling procedure. Serious difficulties in obtaining representative samples develop, however, when populations that are heterogeneous are treated as though they were homogeneous. Hence, a distinction in the meaning and use of these terms is imperative.

The particular label that the analyst may apply to a population is significant only as he relates the term to some specific attribute of the phenomena. For example, the persons comprising some definite geographical area might well be considered homogeneous as respects their consumption of bread, but quite heterogeneous in regard to their consumption of cheese. Again, the persons comprising a particular occupational universe may be homogeneous as regards the amount and character of their income, but very heterogeneous in their manner of spending it.

This concept of relativity carries over into the meaning of the terms themselves. Complete homogeneity in the sense of absolute sameness in the underlying phenomena has probably never existed. If it did exist there would seem to be little need for statistical analysis. On the other hand, complete heterogeneity (meaning the absence of any finite limits to the unlikeness of things) is equally improbable. In general, the major universe of inquiry is considered heterogeneous when the analyst can divide it into rational subgroups that are significantly more homogeneous than the total. In slightly different language, the population is assumed to be homogeneous when no rational basis of classification can be found that yields significant differences between classes. Hence, the distinction finally resolves into a statistical problem of deciding what order of magnitude must differences among subgroups of the population assume before we can safely attribute them to factors other than chance.

Chance is itself a rather vague concept. In a statistical sense it is the net resultant of the interplay of a large and constant number of small forces equal in magnitude and independent and diverse in their influence. When the values of a variable are conditioned by chance, they are assumed to be distributed in accordance with the normal probability curve. Repeated experiments with the so-called "games of chance" bear out the essential validity of this assumption. A reversal of the postulate provides us with the less tenable proposition that normally distributed variables are conditioned by the laws of chance.

In applying various statistical tests to determine the homogeneity of a population the analyst pursues an analogous line of reasoning. He regards the differences among the subgroups of his sample as indicative of a heterogeneous parent population when these subgroup differences (or certain measures derived from them) exceed an order of magnitude that can reasonably be accounted for in terms of the laws of chance. Conversely, the population is assumed to be homogeneous when the subgroup differences are no greater than those obtainable from a series of samples randomly selected from a population known to be homogeneous.

THE SAMPLING PROCEDURE AS RELATED TO THE NATURE OF THE POPULATION

The problem of sampling is to obtain a picture in miniature of the total population from which the sample is drawn. Resolved into question form, the problem is twofold. First, how can the analyst make reasonably sure that the sample is free from bias? Secondly, how can he determine when the sample is large enough to provide a reliable estimate of the universe from which it was drawn? Unless the first of these questions can be satisfactorily answered there is little point to answering the second. If important sections of the market are being omitted in the sample, or if the method of gathering the data results in a distorted view, no amount of increase in the size of the sample can overcome this distortion. In fact, if biased, large samples are worse than small ones, because the deception that lurks within the bias gains in potency with each increase in the size. A million straw ballots distributed in a manner to slight whole sections of the voting population are much more deceptive than a mere thousand would be with an equal percentage error.

Bias is generally assumed to be eliminated from the sample when the analyst's idiosyncrasies are ruled out and pure chance is allowed to dominate the selection. This is the principle of random sampling. Since the sampling procedure is independent of the characteristics of the sampled universe, each member is assumed to have an equal chance of being included. Textbooks usually illustrate the principle by a series of neatly chosen examples such as the drawing of balls from an urn, the flipping of coins, and the rolling of dice. These physical examples are easy to visualize, and they fit the definition admirably. They are quite inadequate, however, for the market analyst who must deal with a body of forces intangible and highly heterogeneous in character. Such factors as race, nationality, sex, age, occupation, income, social customs, place of residence, and so forth, are continually influencing consumer habits relative to specific articles of merchandise. Consequently, the market analyst's major universe (that body of consumers, manufacturers, or middlemen to which his conclusions are to apply) is usually composed of a series of minor universes (smaller groups and subdivisions that exhibit significant differences as regards some specific characteristic). These islands representing distinctive consumer behavior are rarely amenable to the principle of random selection.

Possibly in the purchase of some common necessity, for example, salt, one could expect people to be quite homogeneous, and a selection of persons at random would yield a sample of results typical of the universe of consumers. Closer inspection, however, indicates that even here the population is far from homogeneous. Urban dwellers buy salt almost exclusively in package form for use on the table, whereas rural residents purchase it in packages, in barrels, in sacks, and in blocks for use in a great variety of ways, but mostly for livestock and as a meat preservative. The sampling procedure would be defective if it failed to provide for this distinctive difference in the per capita use of the product.

Heterogeneity in a universe of some physical substance is usually overcome by the simple process of mixing. Gradually the diverse elements are homogenized into one uniform constituency, and a sample taken at random will be representative. But, as Lyndon O. Brown [4] has aptly stated, "people cannot be mixed up as cream can be stirred so that one can 'dip out' the first 400 or 5000 at hand." To be sure one might apply the mixing principle to a system of counters whose units correspond to real persons in the market universe. This, however, is more of a theoretical possibility than a practical substitute. It assumes that the universe under investigation has already been card indexed and catalogued, a condition that is not often found in marketing research.

The obstacles that preclude the application of strictly random selection for getting a representative sample have led to the development of other sampling procedures. In some instances they replace randomness, whereas in others they simply supplement and make effective the earlier principle of selection. Experienced investigators in marketing have frequently employed these techniques, but often without using any of the terms that have become current among statisticians.

A SUGGESTED CLASSIFICATION OF SAMPLING PROCEDURES

Statisticians have used a variety of terms to describe the different sampling procedures, but as yet no standard nomenclature has emerged. Egon S. Pearson,[5] for instance, employs the terms "random" and "representative" for a twofold classification of sampling methods. Yule and Kendall [6] use a threefold classification consisting of random, purposive, and mixed, the last being a combination of the first and second. This threefold division has been followed in setting up the major headings of the following classification:

Random sampling: (1) Unstratified; (2) Stratified
Purposive sampling: (1) Unstratified; (2) Stratified
Mixed sampling: (1) Unstratified; (2) Stratified

"Random," "purposive," and "mixed" are terms descriptive of sampling techniques *per se*. Each may be applied to a population in either

[4] *Market Research and Analysis.*

[5] "Sampling Problems in Industry," *Journal of the Royal Society,* Supplement, Vol. 1 (No. 2, 1934).

[6] *An Introduction to the Theory of Statistics,* pp. 336–48.

its stratified or unstratified form. Hence, stratification is best regarded as a preliminary step to the actual taking of the sample. Presumably it applies only to a heterogeneous population and consists in subdividing the field of inquiry into lesser areas that are assumed to be more homogeneous than the population as a whole. According to Sarle,[7] effective stratification benefits the sampling procedure in two ways: (1) it increases the statistical stability assuming a given size sample; and (2) it improves the representativeness of a sample.

For populations that are truly homogeneous (those whose subdivisions exhibit dispersion equal to that of the whole) the stratified sample is equivalent to the unstratified, and these benefits do not emerge. Since nothing is lost by stratification (save the effort involved), analysts occasionally resort to it simply as a safeguard in case the population is something less than homogeneous.

Random and purposive sampling are contrasting principles of selection that may be applied to populations that are either stratified or unstratified. "Randomness" has been identified with the play of impartial chance in the selective process. Purposive selection implies the substitution of the analyst's judgment for the play of chance. No example from marketing research could serve to illustrate so clearly these contrasting principles as the case of the turnip sampler cited by Yule and Kendall.[8] First, we shall assume that the observer draws two or three turnips from a cartload by shutting his eyes and drawing at random. Since chance rules his selection, he might draw several very large or several very small turnips, even though the probabilities are much against his doing so. Secondly, we shall allow the sampler to run his eyes over the load and choose. Now by substituting his judgment for the play of chance he would most likely take average turnips, that is, turnips that seem to him typical in size, shape, color, or whatever other characteristic is the object of study.

From the illustration it would seem evident that for very small samples a purposive selection has an advantage over the random drawing. It is more likely to give the observer what he is really looking for, namely, something that is typical of the universe. In the field investigations of marketing research the sample is usually composed

[7] Sarle, "Statistical Problems of an Annual Census of American Agriculture," in Conference on Statistical Methods of Sampling Agricultural Data, *Proceedings*.

[8] *An Introduction to the Theory of Statistics*, p. 346.

of a relatively small number of cities and towns, all of which have been purposely chosen for their representative character. An equal number of towns and cities selected at random might provide something quite unrepresentative of the universe, and to increase the drawing to the point at which statistical stability and representativeness emerges would be needlessly expensive.

Mixed sampling is a hybrid of randomness and purposiveness, these two contrasting principles being employed usually at different levels of selection. We may imagine the universe of turnips in Yule's example as being enlarged to contain a considerable number of cartloads, the produce of an entire field of turnips. If, then, the observer were to select a whole cartload at random and purposively draw from the load those turnips that seemed typical of those in the field, his drawing would be a mixed sample. The same would be true of a sample obtained by selecting some specific cartload for its representative appearance and then drawing from it at random.

The illustration may easily be pushed into the realm of stratified mixed sampling by assuming the field of turnips to have been divided into strips representing a variety of conditions as to land, fertilization, and cultivation. If then a cartload were to be selected by design from each strip or section of the field, the resulting purposive sample might be made the basis for a second series of drawings with randomness characterizing the selection from each representative load. The turnips selected in the manner described would constitute a stratified mixed sample. Were personal judgment to dominate the choice at every stage of the selective process, the result would be a stratified purposive sample to which randomness and the laws of chance would have little, if any, application.

TECHNIQUES OF STRATIFICATION

The techniques employed in stratifying a population incident to the sampling process may be classified as equal, proportional, or weighted. Equal stratification expresses the concept of a multidivisioned universe in its simplest form. It may be illustrated by a consumer survey in which interviews are made at one out of every ten houses along each street within the town. In such an equally stratified sample the streets are the strata that are assumed to possess a homogeneity greater than that of the town as a whole. If no statistical evidence can be found in the sample to support this assumption, the town is probably homogeneous as respects the sampled characteristic, and a strictly random selection would have provided an equally representative sample.

When a proportionately stratified sample is to be taken, the diverse elements of the sampled population must either be known or capable of being ascertained. The relative importance of each stratum predetermines the proportion that it shall have in the sample. If income, for instance, were considered significant in determining the consumer preference for a certain brand of breakfast food, the market analyst would first need to determine income distribution within the sampled universe and then make certain that the proportions by income classes were maintained in the taking of the sample. Within each strata the selection might be random, purposive, or some combination of these two. The final result would be a proportionately stratified sample, irrespective of the method of selection used.

The difficulty frequently encountered in getting persons within certain strata of the population to coöperate in providing the information has resulted in a modification of the strictly proportional type of stratified sampling. By weighting the subsamples in proportion to the importance of their respective minor universes it is possible to arrive at a weighted composite result that is an estimate of what would have been secured from a sample that had been stratified along strictly proportional lines. The accuracy of this weighted estimate depends upon the size of the various subsamples. If the smallest of these is still large enough to provide a reliable estimate of its particular minor universe, the weighting procedure is quite justified; otherwise the result is likely to contain a cumulative error, its amount being dependent upon the possible sampling errors in the subdivisions and the weights that are applied in obtaining the composite.

SAMPLING TECHNIQUES ILLUSTRATED

Unstratified random selection may be illustrated by a survey made by *Modern Magazines*.[9] The purpose of the investigation was to determine brand preferences among the readers of the three magazines, *Modern Screen, Radio Stars,* and *Modern Romances*. Subscriber lists were unavailable, since the distribution of these magazines is entirely

[9] See *Buying Begins at $20,* Dell Publishing Company, 1936.

through news dealers. To obtain a random placement of questionnaires, it was decided that every twenty-fifth copy of the magazine should contain a schedule of questions and a return envelope. Response was encouraged by the offer of a premium, but to insure against a possible bias in the returns, great care had to be exercised. Several suggested premiums were rejected because of the possible influence each would have exerted upon the character of the returns. The premium finally chosen was a free copy of the next issue of the magazine.

Major College Publications [10] has modified the technique of a strictly random selection by stratifying the major universe from which its sample is drawn. In this instance the major universe comprised the student population of nineteen important colleges in various sections of the United States. Using the college directories as the basis of its selection, it drew every tenth name and arranged for personal interviews with the persons so selected. The random drawing continued until the proportions of each class and each sex in the sample agreed with those of the entire student population. The result was a proportionately stratified random sample.

A study made by Time Incorporated provides one of the best examples of purposive selection in marketing research. In the summer of 1931 this company undertook to discover how families on different income levels spend their money. Many distributors guess that their best prospects fall within certain income brackets. *Time* wanted the facts. A sample had to be taken, and the people chosen had to be fairly typical and to live in one specific locality.

So *Time* sought a single city—the largest that could be conveniently surveyed. For this purpose a population of about 25,000 seemed best. To find such a city was not easy. Research directors of several large advertising agencies advised *Time* to stay away from the East where cities were too near together, dependent on each other. The Pacific Coast was impractical—too far away. The South, they said, is hardly representative, with its large negro population to unbalance the picture. The Middle West they recommended as the logical choice. There were in Indiana, Illinois, Wisconsin and Michigan several cities that would fit *Time's* requirements, but Wisconsin, with its liberal income tax laws, made it possible for *Time* to do away with all guesswork, all estimating of incomes on a rental or occupational basis. . . . Of all cities in Wisconsin, Appleton was the ultimate choice.[11]

[10] See *The Major College Market*, Major College Publications, A. J. Norris Hill Company, New York, 1936.

[11] *Markets by Incomes*, New York, Time, Inc., 1932, Vol. I.

Here we have purposive selection described in its unstratified form as applied to a market survey. The managers of Time, Inc., knew pretty definitely what they wanted. They desired an independent market, located in an agricultural community containing a variety of manufactures, having a diversity of retail and wholesale trade, and large enough to afford persons in each income bracket, yet small enough to contain no slums and no Peacock Alley. In short, they wanted a "normal" city, and Appleton, Wisconsin, seemed to fulfill their requirements.

In 1935–36 the United States Bureau of Labor Statistics, working jointly with the Bureau of Home Economics, conducted a nationwide survey of consumer purchases. The study was a project of the Works Progress Administration in which the National Resources Committee [12] and the Central Statistical Board coöperated. The sample included approximately 300,000 families living in cities and villages and on farms in 30 different states. The number of cities required to give a properly proportioned sample was obviously small. Fifty-one cities were included. To have selected this small number of cities at random would probably have yielded something far short of the desired geographical distribution. Moreover, the metropolitan areas might not have been represented at all if randomness had been the criterion for drawing the 51 cities. Consequently, a purposive selection had to be made, the country having been stratified both as to geographical sections and as to size of city within each section. Randomness of selection, however, began at this point and was employed in the larger cities and metropolitan communities for selecting the families whose incomes and expenditures were the subject of study. Hence, we have randomness supplementing purposiveness to form mixed sampling of the stratified variety.

ADVANTAGES AND DISADVANTAGES OF STRATIFIED SAMPLING

To a large and increasing extent market analysts are turning to stratified sampling as a means of reducing the size of sample and improving its representativeness. The complexity of forces that condition the sale of any specific product tends to introduce diverse elements

[12] See *Consumer Expenditures in the United States—Estimate 1935–36,* Washington, D. C., Government Printing Office.

into the market. Strictly speaking, these diverse elements could be represented by an undifferentiated random selection, provided we assume a very large universe and a random drawing that is long-continued. Gradually the play of chance forces would result in a sample containing the same elements as the population and in about the same proportions. Unfortunately the universe with which the analyst deals is not always large. Moreover, the need for speed and economy is so urgent that even for an infinite universe the method of unstratified random selection is rapidly being replaced by the more efficient procedure of stratification. The operation of the laws of large numbers upon which unstratified random selection relies is a process painfully slow, and market analysts can seldom wait for it to reveal the shape and form of all the diverse elements within a particular market universe.

The economy of stratification arises from the fact that it enables the analyst to eliminate sampling errors among strata. Having confined the errors of sampling within strata, a point of statistical stability is reached with a smaller number of observations. For example, the standard deviation of the sampling errors for p, the proportion of cases in the major universe having any particular characteristic, has previously been given as $\sqrt{\frac{pq}{N}}$. By stratifying the universe and choosing the sample proportionately from the various strata, the standard deviation of the sampling errors reduces to $\sqrt{\frac{pq - \sigma_p^2}{N}}$, in which σ_p^2 is the weighted mean square of the proportions in the several strata about their own weighted average.[13] Hence, for any heterogeneous population (one containing minor universes with characteristics distinctly different from their weighted composite average) stratification provides greater reliability than one can obtain from an unstratified selection of equal size.

Partially offsetting the advantage of increased accuracy of results from a stratified sample is the labor involved in setting up the various minor universes and establishing their importance relative to the total field of inquiry. Successful stratification requires, first, an ability to identify the various minor universes and, secondly, a knowledge of their relative importance. Concrete suggestions dealing with the prob-

[13] Formula is from Bowley, *Elements of Statistics*, 6th ed., p. 333.

lem of defining the major and minor universes are presented in the concluding sections of this chapter.

ADVANTAGES AND DISADVANTAGES OF PURPOSIVE SELECTION

Choice between purposiveness and randomness of selection is primarily a problem of fitting the sampling technique to the physical conditions that govern the accumulation of market data. The samples used in consumer and dealer surveys usually relate to certain specific cities or territories. The individuals that comprise the sample are, therefore, seldom independent of one another. They are usually influenced by a set of common causes, such as regional topography, climate, racial inheritances, local customs, and industries, that make them more homogeneous than the general population. Moreover, these local influences of environment tend to create markets of distinctly different characteristics. A product that can be sold with ease in one locality may frequently fail to win favor in another.

Again, the samples used in distribution studies are frequently limited to single test markets or, at most, to a small group of test markets geographically distributed. If these test markets were to be selected at random certain communities might be chosen that were decidedly non-typical. To insure the selection of a representative sample the analyst draws upon his knowledge of peculiar local conditions and purposely chooses the specific section of the market from which the data are to be compiled. To assume that pure chance would yield a fair sample under the conditions described would be to tempt fate beyond any reasonable limit.

A third obstacle to random sampling is the difficulty of setting up the major universe into concrete miniature form from which drawings at random may be taken. Some physical counterpart of the universe, such as a card index or a collection of numbered chips, is essential, since human beings cannot themselves be labeled, shuffled, and drawn at random. Moreover, every unit of the total population must be identified in the physical set-up by some name, number, letter, and so forth, so that any drawing from the randomized miniature may be readily traced to the actual market units. Since the major universe shifts for each new market study and since the number of persons in the population sometimes runs into the millions, one can easily see that the construction of the physical counterpart would be difficult and the establishment of each person's identity practically an impossibility.

The obstacles to random sampling are the best arguments for the use of the opposite principle of purposive selection. Its greater economy of time and effort has already been stressed. There is also a gain in representativeness if the sample is relatively small and concentrated at definite geographical points. It must be assumed here, however, that the purpose of the sample is to approach the typical among market units rather than to estimate their variability. Test markets, for instance, are excellent examples of purposive samples. They are chosen to reflect typical demand conditions as opposed to the extreme and heterogeneous forces that condition the sale of a product.

The disadvantages of purposive selection are best presented as advantages of randomness. If we can assume that the conditions for random selection are present and that no specific limits are placed on the size of the sample, we can rely upon chance to provide a more nearly representative drawing. Yule and Kendall [14] point out "that as the sample becomes larger the random sample becomes more and more representative of the parent whereas, owing to bias, the purposive sample in general does not."

Also, if the items in a sample are randomly selected, they are likely to provide a better estimate of the variability in the universe than an equal number of cases deliberately selected. Again, we must assume that the conditions for a random selection are present and that our sample is relatively large. A few cases might be deliberately chosen along a scale of magnitudes so as to approximate the variance in the entire universe, but to deal with any considerable number in this manner would be most impractical.

Perhaps the most serious limitation of purposive selection is the inability of the analyst to assess the accuracy of his estimates. The sampling errors of a random selection are due to the fluctuations of chance, whereas the uncertainties of purposive selection arise chiefly out of the personal equation, to which there is usually an indeterminate bias.

Finally, there is the difficulty of applying purposive selection when there is very little known about the universe under inquiry. For in-

[14] *An Introduction to the Theory of Statistics,* p. 347.

stance, if it were decided that a certain sample should contain only home owners having an "average income" and living in urban communities of "average size," it would be necessary to establish, at least approximately, some quantitative measure of both income and size of city. The statistical information compiled by the Bureau of the Census provides the market analyst with most of the control factors that he follows in purposive selection.

FREQUENT CAUSES OF FAILURE IN MARKET SAMPLING

When the sample fails to represent the population from which it has been drawn, the difficulty may usually be traced to one or more of the following causes: (1) failure to define the major universe precisely; (2) failure to identify the minor universes and appraise their relative importance; (3) oversight of some selective influence lurking within the type of information requested; (4) non-recognition of a possible bias in the method of collecting the data; and (5) insufficient collection of data resulting in an inadequate sample.

Failure to define the real major universe may lead either to the inclusion of observations foreign to the study or to the exclusion of others that are pertinent. A random drawing of names from the telephone directory, for example, would arbitrarily exclude persons without phones and some whose phones are listed under the names of relatives or under apartment-house numbers.

Failure to identify and to define the minor universes leads to a badly proportioned sample. The all-time high for this sort of error was probably set in 1936 by the ill-starred *Literary Digest* poll on the outcome of the presidential election of that year. The returns were definitely overloaded with the political opinions of persons from the middle and upper income brackets.

The type of information requested will occasionally produce a biased sample. For instance, if family expenditures were being investigated, the results would tend to be overweighted by returns from those who meticulously keep expenditure records. A similar sorting of the responses may take place because of the method of gathering the data. A mail questionnaire, for instance, may be sent to a fair cross section of the major universe, but the replies may come largely from either the enthusiastic or the disgruntled persons. In general, those who do not feel strongly one way or the other are unresponsive. A factor less subtle, but often prejudicial, is the tendency of those on the lowest income levels to ignore mail questionnaires. The seriousness of this limitation varies with the purpose of the study. For the *Literary Digest* poll of political sentiments it proved disastrous, but for the numerous surveys made by General Motors concerning buyers' opinions on automobile styles it has been of little or no importance. In the latter case the heavily weighted responses from the middle and upper income brackets has happened to coincide with the actual market for automobiles.

To guard against the sort of bias described above, sample checks should be taken by skilled personal interviewers working from certain sections of the mailing list. But even the personal-interview method is subject to certain subtle tendencies that may bias the returns. Some interviewers, for instance, may center their attention on the more attractive sections of a city. Others may concentrate their interviews within those nationality groups that they find congenial. Occasionally even the knowledge of the origin and the purpose of a study will produce a subtle bias in the interviewer's attitude. Rigorous conditions regarding the spotting of interviews and frequent inspection by the field supervisor may meet the first two situations. To handle the third, one research organization has kept its field workers from knowing the origin and purpose of the survey in which they participate.

A final important cause of failure in the sampling procedure is the inadequacy in the number of observations. Since Chapter XII deals specifically with methods of testing the adequacy of market samples, the present purpose has been served by simply emphasizing the importance of the topic.

CHAPTER XI

Statistical Methods of Testing the Significance Of Market Factors

THE PROBLEM of sampling is conveniently regarded as twofold. The first task of the analyst is to set the conditions for the taking of the sample so that each member of the population stands a reasonable chance of being included. The second task is to insure a sample large enough to make the results statistically significant.

STEPS IN THE SAMPLING PROCEDURE

Although it is difficult to resolve the sampling procedure into any formula or set of rules, an enumeration of the steps can assist in establishing the logical sequence ordinarily followed in the solution of a sampling problem. The following steps are assumed to apply to a heterogeneous body of data such as one usually finds in analyzing a market: (1) definition of the major universe; (2) identification of the various minor universes; (3) measurement of the relative importance of each minor universe and setting the proportions for taking the sample; and (4) testing the adequacy of the sample.

The importance of these steps has already been indicated by the discussion of causes of failure in market sampling. The present chapter deals more specifically with statistical techniques appropriate for carrying the steps into effect.

DEFINING THE MAJOR UNIVERSE

In every study involving the taking of a sample there must be a universe or larger group from which the sample was drawn and to which the results presumably apply—always, of course, within certain limits of sampling error. The setting of the boundary lines to the major universe is the initial task of the market analyst in the sampling procedure. The boundary lines may be geographic, as, for example, in a consumer survey that embraces the total population of some definite geographical region. Occasionally the limits of the investigation are established in terms of some social characteristic, such as age, sex, religion, or nationality. More often, however, economic characteristics in combination with the geographic furnish the means for defining the specific market from which the gross sample is to be taken.

The statement of limits for the alleged universe is relatively simple. If it were proposed, for instance, to study the characteristics of the college market, there could be little difference of opinion respecting the boundary lines of the field of investigation. The real problem consists in gathering the information so that neither more nor less will find representation in the sample than the definition of the universe implies. As was seen in the preceding chapter, the lack of coincidence between the alleged universe and the universe of the sample constitutes one of the frequent causes of failure in the sampling procedure.

IDENTIFICATION OF THE MINOR UNIVERSES

Personal experience and general knowledge are usually sufficient to identify the important minor universes. For instance, sex would be regarded as a dominant factor conditioning the brand preferences for toilet soap. Hence, the analyst would make a twofold division into men users and women users. A second division into manual workers and office workers might prove illuminating, since the former are likely to prefer a gritty type of soap. In a survey of the demand for laundry soap the major universe of housewives might be subdivided by geographical areas and grouped according to the hardness or the softness of the water in each region. Thus, for any particular product and its market reasoning of this *a priori* type must be the starting point in identifying the minor universes. It involves setting down all factors that might possibly exert a major influence upon the willingness to buy.

Once the list of factors conditioning the market has been made reasonably complete, the analyst checks those that he is quite certain require recognition in the sampling procedure. Others he may eliminate as being either unworthy of attention or incapable of measurement. The doubtful factors provide problems for the use of some of the most refined statistical tools. Certain of these techniques apply when one is testing the significance of differences in frequencies or things counted. Others apply exclusively to differences in quantities or things measured. A few apply to either. All have been appropriately labeled as statistical tests for determining the significance of differences.

MEANING OF SIGNIFICANCE

The careful research worker is continually sifting his results through statistical sieves in order to separate the results that might easily occur as a result of chance from those that are due in all probability to certain dominant underlying forces. When a difference is found to be too great to be attributed to chance, it is said to be significant.

The market analyst has particular need for methods that will enable him to separate the valid and significant differences from those produced by chance or, at least, from those that are no greater than chance alone might give. Since the most improbable results (such as obtaining one hundred heads in one hundred tosses of a coin) are not wholly impossible, practical research workers must set up some arbitrary limit beyond which they are willing to accept the results as indicating the operation of something besides chance. The proper location for this level of significance, as it is frequently called, is subject to considerable difference of opinion. There is no argument, however, as to its pragmatic necessity. Without it practical research would bog down into a statistical mire and never arrive at a definite conclusion.

If conservatism be accepted as a statistical virtue, there is no occasion to allow the same range of tolerance to errors of sampling under any and all circumstances. The breaking point for significance will be made to depend upon whether or not the investigator is seeking to establish or to discredit a particular hypothesis. In most statistical tests for significant differences the analyst employs the logic of a double negative to make a positive. He sets up a null-hypothesis that the results are not significant and then seeks to disprove it, thereby establishing the opposite. Under these circumstances the range of tolerance for sampling errors should be liberal, since it is then more difficult to discredit the hypothesis. Convention has established these limits so that the play of chance might yield equally conclusive results only once in a hundred trials.

The table of areas to which reference has already been made (see p. 160 and footnote) and the standard errors of the various statistical measures provide the means by which the one-out-of-a-hundred rule is applied. This table shows that a range equal to 2.576 standard errors laid off in both the positive and the negative directions from the center of the normal curve of error includes 99 percent of the total area. Consequently, there is just one chance in a hundred of random sampling resulting in a difference equal to, or in excess of, the 2.576 standard errors. This becomes, as it were, the breaking point between the probable and the improbable in testing the significance of any particular difference.

Some writers have employed three standard errors in setting up the zone within which errors of sampling may be presumed to account for the results secured. Although this is a convenient round figure, it is unnecessarily conservative as judged on the basis of the one-in-a-hundred rule of thumb. Even the figure 2.576 is more conservative than the rule requires, if one is seeking to determine what allowance to make for errors of sampling that take place in one direction only. A deviation of 2.33 standard errors is sufficient for testing the significance of differences having like signs.

The application of the one-percent level of significance may be illustrated by the results obtained in one of a series of blindfold tests conducted by a cigarette manufacturer. This particular test was made on the campus of a large eastern university. Each of 148 students were blindfolded and asked to smoke and rate four leading brands of cigarettes. Their ratings are shown in the table below.

TABLE 15

PREFERENCE VOTE IN A CIGARETTE POPULARITY TEST

Brand	*First Choice*	*Percent First Choice*
X	43	29
Manufacturer's brand	40	27
Y	35	24
Z	30	20
	148	100

To test the significance of this experiment, we set up a null-hypothesis that there is no distinctive difference in the four brands.

The most probable percentage of first choices for any one brand is then 25. Either of two questions may now be asked. First, how much more or less than 25 percent must any brand receive in order to discredit the hypothesis? Expressed in this way, the sign of the difference is unspecified, so we shall use 2.576 standard errors as setting the maximum for chance variation. Secondly, we may ask how much more than 25 percent must any given brand receive in order to establish a significant superiority? In this second phrasing the difference is specified as positive, so that 2.33 standard errors provide the breaking-point or level of significance. By substituting the appropriate values ($p = 25\%$, $q = 75\%$, and $N = 148$) in the formula $\sqrt{\frac{pq}{N}}$, we obtain 3.56 percent as the standard error. Hence, a positive difference equal to 2.33 x 3.56 or 8.3 percent is ample allowance for sampling errors. The addition of this amount to the hypothetical percentage of 25 gives the value 33.3 as the minimum percentage of first choices required in a sample of 148 to establish a clear-cut preference for any one of the four brands. Since the leading brand received only 29 percent of the vote, the test was obviously without significance.

Whereas the one-percent level was taken to indicate significance in the preceding discussion, there is need for emphasizing that such a division is quite arbitrary, since there are many possible levels of significance—indeed, the number is infinite. The problem of the statistician in testing the significance of differences is to set the level high enough (at a point sufficiently removed from the assumed population value) so that no true hypothesis will be rejected as false because of

TABLE 16

PROBABILITIES OF OBTAINING SAMPLE VALUES BEYOND VARIOUS LIMITS THAT HAVE BEEN SPECIFIED IN UNITS OF THE STANDARD ERROR

Deviation from Population Value in Terms of the Standard Error	*Probabilities Assuming Direction of Difference Is Unspecified*	*Probabilities Assuming Direction of Difference Is Specified*
.6745	.50	.25
1.00	.32	.16
2.00	.05	.025
2.33	.02	.01
2.567	.01	.005
3.00	.003	.0015

certain purely random errors of sampling and yet low enough so that no false hypothesis will be crowded into the acceptable range. The probabilities shown in Table 16 are a few of the many possible levels of significance that may be read from a table of areas.

STATISTICAL TECHNIQUES APPLICABLE AS TESTS OF SINGLE DIFFERENCES

A convenient basis upon which to discuss the various statistical techniques used to determine the significance of differences is that afforded by the inclusiveness of the test. In the first category we shall consider tools that are applicable in testing single differences, such as the deviation of a sample value from some population value and the difference between two values both of which relate to samples and are consequently subject to sampling errors. The following outline will serve to give systematic arrangement to the techniques generally applicable to marketing research problems in which the interpretation of single differences is involved.

Outline of Statistical Techniques Applicable to the Testing of Single Differences

I. Techniques applicable to testing differences in frequencies
  A. Frequencies expressed in absolute terms
    1. Standard error of a sample frequency
    2. Standard error of the difference between two sample frequencies
  B. Frequencies expressed in relative terms
    1. Standard error of a percentage or relative frequency
    2. Standard error of the difference between two sample percentages
II. Techniques applicable to testing differences in magnitudes
  A. Magnitudes expressed in terms of the arithmetic mean
    1. Standard error of the arithmetic mean
    2. Standard error of the difference between two sample arithmetic means
  B. Magnitudes expressed in terms of averages other than the arithmetic mean [1]

EXAMPLES OF TECHNIQUES APPLICABLE TO TESTING SINGLE DIFFERENCES IN FREQUENCIES

The market analyst is one of a great company of persons seeking the application of statistical tools to social and economic problems.

[1] Subtopics similar to those under II-A might be listed for each of the various types of average.

The common denominator to which their varied problems may be reduced is the form of data themselves. Counting and measuring are twin processes by which masses of statistical material are produced. When things are counted, the resulting frequencies may be tested directly in their absolute form or converted into relatives and then tested. The first of the illustrations that follow deals with a sample frequency in absolute terms.

As an advertising feature, a large New York department store selected samples of five brands of golf balls and subjected them to a testing machine which recorded the number of hits each brand made upon a target as the balls were automatically released and allowed to roll down a milled chute. Taking the average number of hits for all brands as the best estimate of the population frequency, it is possible to test the significance of the apparent superiority (or inferiority) of any particular brand. The leading brand in this experiment scored 5,395 hits in 6,000 trials whereas the average number of hits for all brands was only 4,862. Since the standard error of an absolute frequency (usually called the standard error of sampling and indicated by the symbol σ_s) is given by the formula $\sqrt{\frac{f\,(N-f)}{N}}$ we may test the superiority of the leader by substituting the appropriate values and solving as follows: [2]

$$\sigma_s = \sqrt{\frac{4{,}862\ (6{,}000 - 4{,}862)}{6{,}000}}$$
$$= 30.4.$$

The difference between the average frequency and the score of the leading brand is 533, which is 17.5 times the standard error of sampling—a difference decidedly significant.

By expressing the absolute frequencies as relatives we may apply the standard error of a percentage and obtain identical results. For instance, the average percentage of hits for all brands was 81 as compared to 89.75 percent for the leader, resulting in a difference of 8.75 percent. The standard error of the percentage is computed below and applied as a test of significance. The results will be seen to

[2] Since the formula for the standard error of sampling may be readily converted into that for the standard error of a percentage by dividing through by N, the two are always interchangeable. It should be noted that the symbols f and p are assumed to represent population parameters, either true or hypothetical. Sample values, however, can be used without serious error provided the sample itself is fairly large.

check exactly with those obtained above. Substituting in the relation $\sigma_p = \sqrt{\frac{pq}{N}}$, we have

$$\sigma_p = \sqrt{\frac{81\%(19\%)}{6{,}000}} = 5\%.$$

Converting the difference, 8.75 percent, into units of the standard error, we obtain $\frac{8.75}{.5}$ or 17.5 standard errors.

If the population value is known (or can be reliably estimated), the two formulas illustrated above provide sharp and specific tools by which the difference between such population frequency and the frequency in some specific section of the population may be tested. The population frequency may be established by census, by registration, or possibly by extensive surveys. For example, if the analyst knows what proportion of the families in the United States own automobiles, subscribe to certain magazines, have incomes within certain brackets, and so forth, he may test the proportion of families of similar characteristic within any specific market area for the significance of variation from the country's average. The importance of such tests as a means of determining the homogeneity of the population can scarcely be exaggerated.

Often the population frequency is not known, but the analyst may have two sample frequencies that he desires to test for the significance of their difference. If the samples are equal in size, the frequencies may be handled in their absolute form and their difference tested by a combination of the two standard errors of sampling. In the illustration that follows the samples were unequal, so that it became necessary to compute relative frequencies and test by the standard error of the difference of two percentages.

In a market survey of the Ross Federal Service, Inc., published in *Sales Management,* the relative popularity of brands of toilet soap was studied. A gross sample of 1,055 persons was taken and returns were divided on the basis of sex. Certain interesting and significant differences were revealed between the preferences of men and women. For instance, Lifebuoy soap received 103 votes from the sample of 581 men, whereas only 55 women out of a total of 474 voted a similar preference. Reducing the vote to relative terms, Lifebuoy received 17.7 percent of the men's vote, but only 11.6 percent of the women's.

Can such a difference in relative popularity be accounted for by random sampling? This is the type of question that is continually confronting the market analyst and one for which the standard error of the difference of two percentages provides an answer. The formula $\sqrt{\frac{p_1 q_1}{N_1} + \frac{p_2 q_2}{N_2}}$ affords a measure of the sampling errors about the true difference when the two population percentages p_1 and p_2 are given. Since these are usually not known, the sample percentages may be substituted as estimates, provided the samples are fairly large. A more logical procedure, however, is to combine the sample percentages into a weighted average (represented by the symbol p_0) which is then used as the relative frequency for a hypothetical population from which both samples are assumed to have been taken. Hence, zero becomes the hypothetical true difference, with a standard error [3] (represented by the symbol σ_{D_p}) equal to $\sqrt{p_0 q_0 \left(\frac{1}{N_1} + \frac{1}{N_2}\right)}$. The weighted average percentage is easily obtained directly from the absolute frequencies by substituting in the formula $p_0 = \frac{f_1 + f_2}{N_1 + N_2}$. Substituting and solving, we have

$$p_0 = \frac{103 + 55}{581 + 474}$$
$$= 15\%.$$

Assuming 15 percent to be a fair estimate of the true proportion of all consumers preferring Lifebuoy, we substitute and solve to determine the standard error of the difference between sample percentages as follows:

$$\sigma_{D_p} = \sqrt{15\%(85\%)\left(\frac{1}{581} + \frac{1}{474}\right)}$$
$$= .22\%.$$

The actual difference between the two percentages is 17.7 — 11.6, or 6.1 percent. Applying the test of significance (6.1 ÷ .22), we obtain 28 standard-error units, a number so much greater than the level of significance (2.576) that we may readily accept the value 6.1 percent as indicative of a very real difference between men and women as

[3] See Hornell Hart, "The Reliability of a Percentage," *Journal of the American Statistical Association*, Vol. XXI (March, 1926).

regards their degree of preference for this particular brand of toilet soap.

In the problem just illustrated the two sets of frequencies were assumed to be independent. In some instances the relative frequencies may be correlated and the assumption of independence is untenable. For example, when relative choices are divided between two brands, the total must equal 100 percent. Consequently, any increase in the relative vote for one brand will automatically reduce the relative vote for the other. If the vote is distributed among a considerable number of brands, the inverse correlation between any two is so slight that no correction is needed. When choice is limited, however, the formula for the standard error of the difference of two percentages takes the expanded form $\sqrt{\frac{p_1q_1 + p_2q_2 + 2p_1p_2}{N}}$ in which N is the number in the sample from which both percentages are derived.[4]

EXAMPLES OF TECHNIQUES APPLICABLE TO TESTING SINGLE DIFFERENCES IN MAGNITUDES

Tests of sample magnitudes and differences of magnitudes are somewhat less useful to the market analyst than are tests of sample frequencies. This is due partly to the fact that he measures less frequently than he counts. More important perhaps is the greater tendency to keep away from statistical inference when analyzing market variables. The more frequently used data are those relating to incomes, rentals, amounts consumed, ages of equipment, distances from market, and so forth, and since the results are often confined to the cases actually studied, no theory of sampling is involved.

Probably the most important reason for the market analyst's failure to apply tests of significance to magnitudes more often is the difficulty of obtaining a measure (or at least an estimate) of the variation in the population. An average is fairly easy to compute. The market analyst uses per capita data constantly and this, of course, is an arithmetic mean. The average, however, may mean much or little, depending upon the amount of variation in the population, and seldom does the market analyst know this. Without it (or some reasonable estimate of it) no test of the significance of an average magnitude can be made.

[4] For proof of formula see T. H. Brown, *The Use of Statistical Techniques in Certain Problems of Market Research,* "Harvard University Business Research Studies," No. 12.

For example, the formula $\frac{\sigma}{\sqrt{N}}$ used in estimating the sampling errors of the arithmetic mean assumes that σ, the standard deviation of the population, is known. Since this can rarely be obtained, the market analyst can only estimate the variation in the population, substituting the standard deviation of the sample. For fairly large samples, such as those with which the market analyst usually deals, this hostage to expediency results in no substantial loss of accuracy.

The following data represent partial results of a garret-to-garage inventory taken by the Market Research Corporation [5] of some 2,000 homes during the months of March and April, 1934. The sample was distributed by income classes, size of city, and geographical location. The two makes of washing machine that are here compared as to length of service were selected because of their apparently distinctive age characteristics. A conclusion as to the difference in age characteristics cannot be reached, however, until averages are computed and tests of significance are applied.

TABLE 17

WASHING MACHINES CLASSIFIED BY YEAR OF PURCHASE

Year of Purchase	*Easy*	*Kenmore*	*All Makes*
1930 and earlier	17	21	168
1931	11	14	115
1932	13	6	84
1932–34	132	9	808
	173	50	1,175

By converting the years of purchase into years of service and arbitrarily using 5 years as the age for all those purchased in 1930 or prior thereto, we may compute averages and standard deviations for the two makes and for all makes as of the year 1934.

TABLE 18

MEASURES OF AGE CHARACTERISTICS OF WASHING MACHINES

	Easy	*Kenmore*	*All Makes*
Arithmetic mean	4.27 years	2.24 years	4 years
Standard deviation	1.38 years	1.45 years	1.56 years
Number in sample	173	50	1175

[5] Pauline Arnold, "The Washing Machine Market: What and Where It Is," *Advertising and Selling,* XXIII (September 27, 1934), 25.

In applying tests of significance we may approach the problem from several angles, only two of which will here be illustrated. First, we shall test whether the average age of each is distinctly different from that of all makes. The standard deviation of the gross sample will be used as a reasonable estimate of the age variation in the population of washing machines. The standard error of the mean for the first make is $\frac{1.56}{\sqrt{173}}$ or .12, whereas that for the second is $\frac{1.56}{\sqrt{50}}$ or .22 years. The difference between the average of each make and that of all makes is easily tested by converting each deviation into units of the respective standard errors.

TABLE 19

APPLICATION OF TEST OF SIGNIFICANCE

Make of Machine	*Arithmetic Mean*	*Deviation from Mean of All Makes*	*Standard Error of the Mean*	*Deviation in Standard Error Units*
Easy	4.27 years	+ .27 years	.12	+ 2.25
Kenmore	2.24 years	− 1.76 years	.22	− 8.00

From the entries in the last column it may be seen that errors of sampling might possibly account for the margin by which the average age of Easy washing machines exceeds that of all makes since the chances are just slightly more than one out of a hundred that the excess in the sample average would have occurred if the population averages had been identical. It is a practical certainty, however, that the average age of Kenmore washing machines is less than that of all washing machines.

The second approach to testing the significance of a variation similar to that shown above is through the standard error of the difference of two sample means. We shall assume that our data are limited to the 223 observations contained in the two ownership groups. The difference between the two sample means is 2.03 years. The significance of this difference may be tested by substituting in the appropriate formula [6] and solving as indicated below:

[6] Whereas the formula for the standard error of the difference of two means assumes that the standard deviations of the respective populations are known, sample values must usually be employed as estimates of these parameters. In cases similar to the one illustrated, in which an assumed true difference of zero is being tested, consistency and logic suggest the use of a weighted composite standard deviation of the two samples as the best estimate of the variation in the hypothetical universe.

$$\sigma_{D_m} = \sqrt{\frac{\sigma_1^2}{N_1} + \frac{\sigma_2^2}{N_2}}$$
$$= \sqrt{\frac{(1.38)^2}{173} + \frac{(1.45)^2}{50}}$$
$$= .23 \text{ years.}$$

Converting the difference between the two means into units of the standard error, we have

$$\frac{M_1 - M_2}{\sigma_{D_m}} = \frac{2.03}{.23} = 8.8.$$

A difference equal to 8.8 standard errors is so much greater than the level of significance (2.576) that we may easily accept it as indicating a very real difference in the length of service of the two makes of washing machine. The interpretation that the sales managers of the respective companies might place upon this situation constitutes an important step of the analytical process, but one that extends beyond the limits of this discussion.

STATISTICAL TECHNIQUES APPLICABLE AS TESTS OF MULTIPLE DIFFERENCES

The same tests of significance that were illustrated above might be applied successively to testing multiple differences. The process of successive pairing, however, would be laborious, and the conclusions would necessarily apply to specific differences. The techniques discussed in this section are designed to provide a simultaneous test of a whole series of differences. The twofold division that was used in discussing tests of single difference will be retained as the basis for our treatment of multiple differences.

Outline of Statistical Techniques Applicable to the Testing of Multiple Differences

I. Techniques applicable to testing differences in frequencies
  A. Frequencies expressed in absolute terms
    1. Chi-square test
    2. Analysis of variance
  B. Frequencies expressed in relative terms
    1. Lexis ratio
    2. Analysis of variance
II. Techniques applicable to testing differences in magnitudes

A. Magnitudes expressed in terms of arithmetic means and standard deviations
   1. Analysis of variance
   2. Correlation analysis

It may be observed from the outline that several approaches are usually available for the solution of a single problem. Usually the various approaches will provide consistent answers. When different conclusions seem to be indicated, the source of the apparent inconsistency may usually be found within the assumptions upon which the respective techniques are based.

CHI-SQUARE AS A TEST OF SIGNIFICANCE APPLICABLE TO MULTIPLE DIFFERENCES OF FREQUENCIES

The most useful statistical tool for testing a series of hypothetical frequencies is the Chi-square test. Designed by Karl Pearson, the test was originally used as a criterion for testing hypotheses about frequency distributions. Its present use extends to the testing of practically any hypothesis that may be set up into a series of frequencies. The following data are typical of those to which the market analyst may profitably apply the Chi-square test. The information was collected and published by *Major College Publications* from a gross sample of 1,130 college students, users of various makes of typewriters.

TABLE 20

USERS OF TYPEWRITERS CLASSIFIED BY SEX AND BY MAKE OF MACHINE

Make of Typewriter	*Men*	*Women*	*Total*
Underwood	269	137	406
Remington	187	108	295
Royal	128	87	215
Corona	106	34	140
L. C. Smith	40	17	57
Miscellaneous [a]	10	7	17
	740	390	1,130

[a] Category includes Woodstock, Monarch, and Oliver.

The great variation in frequencies leaves little doubt about the significance of preference as among different makes of typewriter. A more interesting question raised by the classification is whether or not sex is really as significant as the twofold division of the data assumes it to be. In other words, has the market analyst overclassified the information and made a division here that the data themselves do not support?

In order to answer the question as stated we set up a series of theoretical frequencies based on the null hypothesis that sex has nothing to do with the make of typewriter used. The value of Chi-square is then determined by applying the formula $\Sigma \frac{(f_o - f)^2}{f}$ in which f_o relates to each of the observed frequencies and f to the corresponding theoretical. If the actual frequencies and the theoretical were identical, the value of χ^2 would obviously be zero. The essence of the test, therefore, is to determine whether the discrepancies between theory and observation are no greater than one might expect from random sampling. The hypothesis is generally rejected when the discrepancies are so great (and χ^2 so large) that random sampling could account for them (and the large value of χ^2) in only 5 trials out of 100.[7]

The theoretical frequencies for men users and women users that appear in Table 21 were computed by multiplying the total number of users for each make of typewriter by the ratios $\frac{740}{1{,}130}$ and $\frac{390}{1{,}130}$, respectively. The same theoretical frequencies could, of course, be secured by multiplying the total number of users of each sex by the series of ratios representing the frequency of each make to the total. Hence, the hypothesis that is here set up to be tested can be expressed in either of two forms. It may be stated, for instance, that the proportion of the sexes among the users of each make of typewriter is assumed to be identical with that for all makes or that the proportion of the various makes of typewriters found within each sex is the same as that for both sexes in combination.

[7] This particular level of significance for χ^2 has been suggested by R. A. Fisher. In discussing the value of P which is the symbol indicating the probability that random sampling would result in a value of χ^2 equal to, or greater than, that obtained, he states, "If P is between .1 and .9 there is certainly no reason to suspect the hypothesis tested. If it is below .02 it is strongly indicated that the hypothesis fails to account for the whole of the facts. We shall not often be astray if we draw a conventional line at .05, and consider that higher values of χ^2 indicate a real discrepancy." *Statistical Methods for Research Workers.*

TABLE 21

COMPUTATION OF CHI-SQUARE FROM SAMPLE OF TYPEWRITER USERS CLASSIFIED BY SEX AND BY MAKE OF MACHINE

Make of Typewriter Used by Men	*Observed Frequencies* f_o		*Theoretical Frequencies* f		$f_o - f$	$\frac{(f_o - f)^2}{f}$
Underwood	269		266		+ 3	.03
Remington	187		193		− 6	.19
Royal	128		141		− 13	1.20
Corona	106		92		+ 14	2.13
L. C. Smith	40		37		+ 3	.24
Miscellaneous	10		11		− 1	.09
Total men users		740		740		
Make of Typewriter Used by Women						
Underwood	137		140		− 3	.06
Remington	108		102		+ 6	.35
Royal	87		74		+ 13	2.28
Corona	34		48		− 14	4.08
L. C. Smith	17		20		− 3	.45
Miscellaneous	7		6		+ 1	.17
Total women users		390		390		11.27
Total of both sexes		1,130		1,130		

Before we can interpret the value of 11.27 for χ^2 we must determine the number of degrees of freedom used in its computation. These are equal to the number of entries that may be made in the table of theoretical frequencies before the others have been predetermined by those already entered.[8] In the table shown above, for example, the entry 266 as the first in the series predetermines the number 140 as the seventh in the series, since the sum of the two is assumed by the hypothesis to equal 406, the total number of both sexes using Underwood typewriters. The same reasoning applies to each of the other four makes of typewriter. The miscellaneous group within each sex is predetermined, since the totals are assumed to check to 740 and 390, respectively. Hence, there are only five degrees of freedom in the computation of this value of χ^2.

[8] In general the number of degrees of freedom in a twofold classification of frequencies is equal to $(n - 1)\ (k - 1)$ in which n is the number of captions and k the number of stubs. In this example n is 2 and k is 6 so that the number of degrees of freedom is 5.

To obtain the probability that errors of sampling would produce a value of χ^2 equal to or greater than 11.27, we consult the table of χ^2 [9] values. Entering the table with 5 degrees of freedom, we find a χ^2 value of 11.07 associated with a probability of .05, indicating that random sampling will result in a value as large as or larger than the one obtained slightly less than 5 out of 100 trials. Hence, if we accept the conventional dividing line of .05, we shall reject our hypothesis as having failed to account for the real underlying distribution.

A more decisive answer is obtained when the distribution of men users is tested against hypothetical frequencies determined from the sample of women users. The percentage frequencies [10] of the latter applied to 740, the total number of men users, produced the theoretical frequencies shown in the following table.

TABLE 22

COMPUTATION OF CHI-SQUARE FROM THE DISTRIBUTION OF MEN USERS

Make of Typewriter	*Observed Frequencies* f_o	*Theoretical Frequencies* f	$f_o - f$	$\frac{(f_o - f)^2}{f}$
Underwood	269	269	+ 9	.31
Remington	187	205	− 18	1.58
Royal	128	165	− 37	8.30
Corona	106	64	+ 42	27.56
L. C. Smith	40	33	+ 7	1.49
Miscellaneous	10	13	− 3	.70
	740	740		39.94

Five is again the number of degrees of freedom, since the last entry in the column of theoretical frequencies is predetermined by the first five. If we enter the table of χ^2 with this number, we see that the value 39.94 is so improbable that it lies beyond the range of values covered in the table. Thus, our hypothesis must be rejected as definitely untenable, that is, men users of typewriters (assuming our sample of men users to be a random drawing) exhibit preferences definitely different

[9] The reader may consult a table of χ^2 in any of the more inclusive texts dealing with the general body of statistical methods. For an unusually comprehensive discussion of the nature of χ^2 and its distribution the text *Statistical Methods Applied to Economics and Business*, by F. C. Mills, is particularly recommended.

[10] The percentage frequencies computed from the sample of 390 women users are as follows: Underwood 35.1; Remington 27.7; Royal 22.3; Corona 8.7; L. C. Smith 4.4; and miscellaneous group 1.8.

from women users (assuming the universe of women users is distributed in the same relative manner as the sample).

Still a third hypothesis may be tested by comparing the actual frequencies in the sample of women users with theoretical frequencies distributed in the same relative fashion as we found in the sample of men users. The computation of χ^2 yielded a value of 17.17 which also indicates a definite discrepancy between the theoretical and the observed frequencies.

Although slightly different hypotheses were advanced in the three tests, the results point to the same general conclusion. Certainly the classification by sex has produced a series of results distinctly different from what one might expect if the criterion were unimportant. Therefore, if sex is not itself a significant factor in determining the choice of typewriter, possibly some characteristic associated with sex, as well as with the sale and use of typewriters, has resulted in the significant differences observed.

The theoretical frequencies in the examples given above were estimated from a knowledge of the sample. In the following illustration the hypothesis is determined *a priori*. The data are those previously used in illustrating the concept of significance.

TABLE 23

APPLICATION OF CHI-SQUARE TO THE DISTRIBUTION OF CIGARETTE PREFERENCES

	Brands of Cigarettes				
	X	*Own Brand*	*Y*	*Z*	*Total*
Observed first choices	43	40	35	30	148
Theoretical first choices	37	37	37	37	148
$\frac{(f_o - f)^2}{f}$	.97	.24	.11	1.44	2.76

By setting up the null hypothesis that there is no distinctive difference in the various brands tested we can make a theoretical distribution of choices on purely rational grounds, giving each of the four brands one quarter of the total vote. The value 2.76 for χ^2 (with three degrees of freedom) is definitely not significant. Hence, the *a priori* distribution of first choices is a tenable hypothesis, and the data fail to support the presumptive preference.

Several general observations are appropriate relative to the use and the interpretation of this effective statistical tool. First, every application requires the setting up of some kind of hypothesis (either estimated empirically or set up *a priori*) regarding the distribution of frequencies in a universe from which the sample with its observed frequencies is presumed to have been drawn. Secondly, the observed frequencies are assumed to relate to a random sample so that if purposive selection or any sort of force prejudicial to the play of chance were operative, the Chi-square test (as well as other statistical tests based on the theory of probabilities) would be inappropriate. A third condition is that the expected frequencies in each category must be relatively large if the reliability of the test is not to be impaired. Snedecor [11] suggests that no expected frequency should be less than 5 and when possible all should be 10 or more.

A fourth stipulation relates to the nature of the conclusion to which Chi-square points. Since the results are expressed in terms of probabilities, a rejected hypothesis is not necessarily false; neither is a tenable hypothesis necessarily true. A rejection simply means that if the theoretical frequencies accurately account for the underlying distribution, the observed frequencies of the sample would have been very improbable, but nevertheless possible. Tenability, on the other hand, means that the assumed distribution in the population could quite easily be true—an assertion decidedly different from the flat statement that it *is* true. In a given problem several equally rational hypotheses may be shown by χ^2 to be tenable, but obviously they could not all be true.

Finally, the significance of any variable that may be the criterion for a classification is not to be determined solely from the evidence provided by the χ^2 test or other statistical devices. There may be involved what G. C. Whipple has called "the fallacy of concealed classification." [12] This arises when the factor really responsible for the significant differences in categories is correlated with the one that is being tested. As a consequence, the tested criterion becomes the carrier of, and is erroneously given the credit for, influences that the unnamed and frequently unsuspected factor has produced. Market studies in particular are subject to this type of error, since usually there are a considerable number of factors influencing the purchase and consumption of goods and most of these variables are rather

[11] See Snedecor, *Statistical Methods*, p. 160.
[12] See *Vital Statistics*, John Wiley & Sons, Inc., New York, 1923, p. 290.

closely interrelated. In the presence of such multiple relationships one can easily mistake causes and attribute an influence to factor A that may really be due to B, to C, and so forth, or to a combination of all of them.

LEXIS RATIO AS A TEST OF SIGNIFICANCE APPLICABLE TO MULTIPLE DIFFERENCES AMONG RELATIVE FREQUENCIES

As a test of significance involving a series of differences among relative frequencies, no statistical tool is more effective than the ratio that bears the name of its originator, William Lexis. The argument is technical, but not involved. When the incidence of some event (such as the show of a head in the throw of a coin) is controlled by a constant probability, repeated samples of uniform size will yield occurrences of that event with relative distribution approximating the successive terms in the binomial expansion $(q+p)^n$ in which p is a constant probability, q its complement or $1-p$, and n the number in each sample; the product of the number of drawings and each term yields the absolute frequencies expected in each of the $n+1$ categories. In this binomial distribution the arithmetic mean (which is the average number of occurrences in each sample) is given by pn with a standard deviation of $\sqrt{pqn}$. By dividing each of these expressions by n we obtain corresponding measures in relative terms, so that the formulas become: arithmetic mean $=p$, standard deviation $=\sqrt{\frac{pq}{n}}$.

From these formulas it is evident that the expected mean of a series of relative frequencies is simply the underlying probability that is assumed to control the occurrence of the event. The expected standard deviation is given by the same formula that has been previously explained as the standard error of a relative frequency. Hence, if the analyst is in a position to know p (or to estimate it from repeated samples), he can set up *a priori* the variation in relative occurrences that should prevail under the assumed conditions of uniform samples drawn from a population characterized by a constant probability of the event occurring. Then if the actual variation closely approximates this ideal, the universe from which the samples were drawn may be regarded as homogeneous and influenced by the same constant probability. Lexis expressed the relationship as a ratio $\frac{\sigma_A}{\sigma_B}$ in which numerator and denominator relate, respectively, to standard deviation actual and standard deviation binomial.[13] The value of this ratio obviously approaches unity as the conditions in the sampled population approach those assumed in the binomial expansion. The departures from unity, especially if their significance is in doubt, should be appraised in terms of the standard error [14] of Lexis ratio (σ_L) given by the formula $\frac{.707L}{\sqrt{N}}$.

Portions of the following data have been used in a previous section to illustrate specific tests of single differences in frequencies. The complete table is here provided in order to illustrate the use of Lexis ratio in testing the significance of variation of relative frequencies about their average.

TABLE 24

APPLICATION OF LEXIS RATIO IN CONSISTENCY TEST INVOLVING FIVE BRANDS OF GOLF BALLS

Brand of Golf Ball	*Number of Shots*	*Number of Hits*	*Percentage of Hits*	*Deviations from Mean* d	*Deviations Squared* d^2
Brand A	6,000	5,395	89.9	+ 8.8	77.44
Brand B	6,000	5,103	85.0	+ 4.0	16.00
Brand C	6,000	4,948	82.5	+ 1.5	2.25
Brand D	6,000	4,660	77.7	− 3.3	10.89
Brand E	6,000	4,205	70.1	− 10.9	118.81
			405.1		225.39

Arithmetic mean = 405.1 ÷ 5 = 81.0%

$$\text{Standard deviation (actual)} = \sqrt{\frac{225.39}{5}} = 6.7\%$$

$$\text{Standard deviation (Bernoulli)} = \sqrt{\frac{(81)(19)}{6{,}000}} = .5\%$$

$$\text{Lexis ratio} = \frac{\sigma_A}{\sigma_B} = \frac{6.7}{.5} = 13.4$$

Since the actual standard deviation is somewhat more than 13 times the theoretical, there seems to be no room for doubting the significance

[13] Also known as a Bernoulli distribution after James Bernoulli, who formulated the theorem by which probabilities are calculated from the binomial expansion.

[14] See Rietz, *A Handbook of Mathematical Statistics*.

of the variation. As a check upon our judgment, however, we shall apply the standard error of the Lexis ratio and test as follows: [15]

$$\sigma_L = \frac{.707L}{\sqrt{N}} = \frac{.707}{\sqrt{5}} = .31$$

$$\frac{L-1}{\sigma_L} = \frac{13.4-1}{.31} = 40.$$

Since Lexis ratio shows a departure of 40 standard errors from unity, the test amply confirms our previous judgment. Whatever the true probability may be for obtaining a hit with each of the five brands of golf balls, we can be reasonably certain that it is not the same for the different brands. Heterogeneity or the significance of differences among relative frequencies has been demonstrated.

The general field of marketing research offers numerous opportunities for the application of tests similar to that just illustrated. Usually the conditions required for the application of Lexis ratio either are present or may be arranged. Subdivisions of a gross sample may, of course, be treated in the same manner as samples that are individually drawn, provided the subsamples are relatively large, since otherwise the standard error of Lexis is so large that only the most extreme cases will be revealed as significant. The number within each sample or subsample is also important, since it conditions the size of the standard deviation Bernoulli and of the Lexis ratio itself. With very large samples, such as were used above, the value of σ_B becomes so small that it serves as a sensitive seismograph, revealing slight yet significant tendencies for the probability of an event to change from one sample to another.

A final condition for the application of Lexis ratio is that the events to which the relative frequencies relate must be clearly defined and independent. The fact that the frequencies are in relative terms is likely to create the erroneous impression that any series of relatives, such as those based on equal magnitudes, can be subjected to the test. Not only must the relatives be derived from frequencies or things counted but also each unit of frequency must be regarded as an in-

[15] Since the hypothesis that is here being tested is that the true Lexis ratio is unity, we assume unity for the value of L in the standard error formula. In other circumstances, as for example in setting up the fiducial limits within which the true value of L is likely to fall, we should employ the sample value of L in our formula as our best approximation. It should be noted that N in the formula relates to the number of samples rather than to the number in each sample.

dependent event similar to the tossing of a coin or the rolling of a die, where a success is clearly defined. The relative frequencies that are often compiled to show the respective popularity of each of a number of brands of merchandise within a given sample are not independent and consequently cannot be properly analyzed by the Lexis ratio. Every increase in the relative vote of one brand automatically decreases the relative vote for each of the others. If, however, we were to divide the gross sample into a considerable number of equal subsamples and compute the relative frequency of a particular brand within each, we should then have a problem with a series of relatives, each of which would be quite independent and to which the Lexis ratio could be appropriately applied.

ANALYSIS OF VARIANCE AS A GENERAL TEST OF SIGNIFICANCE

Whereas the Chi-square test [16] and the Lexis ratio have found most general application in testing differences in frequencies (the former in tests involving absolute frequencies and the latter requiring frequencies in relative terms), the analysis of variance has been used most extensively for gauging the significance of differences in a series of magnitudes. The general technique was developed by R. A. Fisher,[17] and it has become one of the most widely used tools of research in agriculture and genetics, fields in which the name Fisher has been written large. Its use in the field of marketing research, however, has made little progress, partly because the method itself is a bit more technical than market analysts are in the habit of using and partly because the problems with which the market analyst deals are concerned largely with human reactions and consequently are not so amenable to controlled experimentation as those found in agriculture.

The following hypothetical data pertaining to the amounts of a product consumed within a given period by each of twenty-five families will serve to illustrate the general argument of the technique as well as the procedure in testing the significance of a single criterion of classification.

[16] The original derivation of Chi-square assumed a distribution of sampling errors in frequencies. At present Chi-square is understood as a more general test applicable to any series of normally distributed sample values (either frequencies or magnitudes) where the standard errors are known.

[17] Fisher, *Statistical Methods for Research Workers,* chap. viii.

TABLE 25

UNITS OF PRODUCT CONSUMED BY EACH OF TWENTY-FIVE FAMILIES CLASSIFIED BY INCOME GROUPS

	Income Classes				
	A	*B*	*C*	*D*	*E*
	8	6	4	3	3
	7	7	5	4	2
	5	4	6	5	3
	6	5	6	3	4
	9	8	4	5	3
Class Means	7	6	5	4	3

Mean number of units consumed per family for all income groups = 5.

We may begin the analysis by setting up the null hypothesis that we have drawn a random sample of consumers from a homogeneous population (that is, homogeneous as regards the consumption of this particular product). From what has been said previously of homogeneity we know that if the hypothesis be true we shall be unable to choose any basis of classification, such as income, age, nationality, place of residence, and so forth, that will provide us with subdivisions of families having any greater similarity than we already possess in the unclassified data. Since the variability within any sample series of observations is definitely limited, we may regard classification (assuming a single criterion) as an attempt to break the total into two parts, one representing variability within classes and the other variability among classes. Our purpose is to increase the latter at the expense of the former, and only when the differences that we have introduced among classes are of an order of magnitude significantly greater than those found within classes has the principle of our classification been successful.

In the sample of data shown above, income has been employed as the single criterion for subdividing the data. The number of items within each class has been made uniform, but this is not a necessary condition. To test the significance of this classification we shall measure first the total variability within the unclassified sample of 25 observations. This equals $\Sigma(m - \overline{M})^2$, in which m is each observation and $\overline{M}$ is the arithmetic mean of the series. Next we shall measure the variability among classes by computing $\Sigma f(M_c - \overline{M})^2$, in which M_c relates to each class mean and f to the number of observations upon which each class mean is based. The variability within classes may be secured either by subtracting the variability among classes from the total or by substituting in the expression $\Sigma(m - M_c)^2$ and computing it independently as a check.

The actual computation is usually facilitated by considering all deviations as measured from the assumed mean of zero and making the necessary corrections. In this way the computation begins by squaring all the original observations together with the class means and the grand mean. The following table contains the necessary work-sheet values.

TABLE 26

SQUARED VALUES REQUIRED FOR THE COMPUTATION OF VARIANCES

	Income Classes				
	A	*B*	*C*	*D*	*E*
	64	36	16	9	9
	49	49	25	16	4
	25	16	36	25	9
	36	25	36	9	16
	81	64	16	25	9
Squares of Class Means	49	36	25	16	9

Square of the grand mean of all income groups = $\overline{M}^2 = 25$.

The formulas for computing the sums of the squares of the deviations (corrected for the assumed origin at zero) and the substitutions are as follows:

Total variability (sum of squared deviations of observations about grand mean):

$$\Sigma m^2 - N\overline{M}^2 = 705 - 625 = 80$$

Variability among classes (sum of squared deviations of class means about grand mean weighted by class frequencies):

$$\Sigma f M_c^2 - N\overline{M}^2 = 675 - 625 = 50$$

Variability within classes (sum of squared deviations of observations about respective class means):

$$\Sigma m^2 - \Sigma f M_c^2 = 705 - 675 = 30$$

Comparison of the component variabilities requires that account be taken of the respective degrees of freedom. For the total variability these are equal to $N-1$, or 24 divided between the components as follows: among classes, $n-1$ or 4 degrees of freedom; within classes, $N-n$ or 20 degrees of freedom. The variance (as distinct from variability) is secured by dividing the appropriate degrees of freedom into each sum of squared deviations. The computation is shown in the following table.

TABLE 27

COMPUTATION OF VARIANCES

Source of Variance	*Sum of Squares of Deviations*	*Degrees of Freedom*	*Variance*
Among income groups	50	4	12.5
Within income groups	30	20	1.5
Total	80	24	3.3

If the sample were drawn at random from a homogeneous normal population, the three variances shown in the last column would be of the same general order of magnitude and each would provide a fair estimate of the variance in the population. If it can be shown, therefore, that their order of magnitude is distinctly different, the null hypothesis of homogeneity will have been discredited and our criterion of classification will have been established as significant.

Two approaches are open for determining whether the variance among classes is distinctly greater than that within. The first was developed by R. A. Fisher and is based on the difference of the logarithms of the variances, a difference that Fisher designated by the letter z from whence comes the name of the test.[18] The F-test that was developed later by G. W. Snedecor employs the concept of the ratio with the larger of the two variances in the numerator. Since Snedecor's test provides the same conclusion with less arithmetical computation it has been the one employed. Using the variances found in Table 27, we have

$$F = \frac{\text{larger variance}}{\text{smaller variance}} = \frac{12.5}{1.5} = 8.33.$$

[18] For a complete discussion of the function of z and its various applications see Fisher, *Statistical Methods for Research Workers*, 6th ed., 1936.

If the two variances were identical, *F* would have a value of unity. Our result appears so much greater than unity that there can be little doubt about its significance. Consultation of the Table of *F* constructed by Snedecor [19] provides an explicit answer. Entering the table with 4 and 20 degrees of freedom for numerator and denominator, respectively, we find that random selection would yield an *F* as large as 4.43 only once in a hundred trials, if the underlying population were homogeneous. Having obtained an *F* much in excess of this one-percent value, we can safely conclude that the population of consumers from which the sample was drawn was nonhomogeneous. If income as the criterion of our classification was not the source of these distinctive class differences, then some factor correlated with income was responsible.

It frequently happens that two criteria are used in classifying data, and both require testing for significance. The following data [20] will serve to illustrate the extension of the analysis of variance technique to a twofold classification.

TABLE 28

STOCK TURNOVER RATES IN DRUG STORES

Drug Store	*Compacts*	*Creams*	*Dentifrices*	*Perfumes*	*Lotions*	*Face Powder*	*Shaving Creams*	*Soaps*	*Toilet Brushes*	*Razor Blades*	*Means of Rows*
A	.9	1.3	3.7	1.2	1.6	1.4	2.5	2.6	1.7	5.9	2.28
B	.6	.9	2.3	.8	1.1	1.0	2.9	1.6	1.1	1.6	1.39
C	.5	.9	3.5	.5	1.3	.5	2.0	1.4	1.9	3.7	1.62
D	.6	1.1	5.0	.8	1.3	1.1	2.7	2.6	1.3	5.3	2.18
E	.9	1.2	2.4	.9	1.1	.5	3.0	1.1	1.6	2.8	1.55
F	.7	1.3	2.9	.6	1.3	2.4	3.7	2.0	1.0	4.8	2.07
Means of columns	.7	1.12	3.3	.8	1.28	1.15	2.8	1.88	1.43	4.02	$\overline{M} = 1.848$

When data have been classified in a two-way table as shown above, their total variability may be divided into three components: variability among columns, among rows, and residual (sometimes called interaction). The sums of the squared deviations representing the first two are obtained as in the preceding problem. Ordinarily the residual is not calculated directly, but is obtained by subtracting the sum of the other two components from the total.

[19] See Snedecor, *Statistical Methods*, for a table of values of F and a discussion of its various applications.

[20] Data are contained in Wroe Alderson and Nelson A. Miller, *Costs, Sales and Profits in the Retail Drug Store*, United States Department of Commerce.

As in the preceding problem, computation is facilitated by starting from an assumed mean of zero in each case and squaring all the values tabled above, including the marginal entries of means of rows, of columns, and of all observations combined. The following table of squared values provides all the material needed for the subsequent computation.

TABLE 29

SQUARED VALUES REQUIRED FOR COMPUTATION OF VARIANCES

Drug Store	*Squared Values of Stock Turnover Rates*										*Squares of Means*
A	.81	1.69	13.69	1.44	2.56	1.96	6.25	6.76	2.89	34.81	5.1984
B	.36	.81	5.29	.64	1.21	1.00	8.41	2.56	1.21	2.56	1.9321
C	.25	.81	12.25	.25	1.69	.25	4.00	1.96	3.61	13.69	2.6244
D	.36	1.21	25.00	.64	1.69	1.21	7.29	6.76	1.69	28.09	4.7524
E	.81	1.44	5.76	.81	1.21	.25	9.00	1.21	2.56	7.84	2.4025
F	.49	1.69	8.41	.36	1.69	5.76	13.69	4.00	1.00	23.04	4.2849
Squares of Means	.49	1.2544	10.89	.64	1.6384	1.3225	7.84	3.5344	2.0449	16.1604	

Square of grand mean of all turnover rates $= \overline{M}^2 = 3.4151$.

A simple extension of the formulas used in a single criterion classification serves to provide the several sums of squared deviations in a twofold classification. The formulas and the degrees of freedom applicable to each component of variation are shown below.

TABLE 30

FORMULAS AND DEGREES OF FREEDOM FOR TWOFOLD CLASSIFICATION

Source of Variability	*Sum of Squares of Deviations*	*Degrees of Freedom*
Among columns	$\Sigma f M_c^2 - N\overline{M}^2$	$n-1$
Among rows	$\Sigma f M_r^2 - N\overline{M}^2$	$k-1$
Residual	$\Sigma m^2 - \Sigma f M_c^2 - \Sigma f M_r^2 + N\overline{M}^2$	$(n-1)\ (k-1)$
Total	$\Sigma m^2 - N\overline{M}^2$	$N-1$

The various sums required in the formulas are readily obtained from the table of squared values. Substitution provides the following total and component variabilities:

Variability among columns: $274.89 - 60(1.848)^2 = 69.984$
Variability among rows: $211.947 - 60(1.848)^2 = 7.041$
Residual variability: $300.63 - 274.89 - 211.947 + 204.906 = 18.699$
Total variability: $300.63 - 60(1.848)^2 = 95.724$

Account must now be taken of the degrees of freedom upon which each component of variability is based. The following table contains the various mean-squares resulting from the division.

TABLE 31

COMPUTATION OF VARIANCES

Source of Variance	*Sum of Squares of Deviations*	*Degrees of Freedom*	*Variance*
Among types of merchandise	69.984	9	7.776
Among drug stores	7.041	5	1.408
Residual	18.699	45	.4155
Total	95.724	59	

If the classification of rates of turnover either by type of merchandise or by drugstore has been significant, we assume that the respective variances arising from such classification will be found significantly greater than the residual variance. This unassigned portion of variance is assumed to measure the influence of all the factors of which no account has been taken and which are not correlated with either store or type of merchandise. For this reason it may be used as a yardstick of what has been called "experimental error." The F tests and the values for the one-percent and five-percent levels of significance as provided by Snedecor's tables appear below.

	One-Percent Level	*Five-Percent Level*
$F = \frac{7.776}{.4155} = 18.72$	2.83	2.09
$F = \frac{1.408}{.4155} = 3.39$	3.45	2.42

The first value of F exceeds both levels of significance by such a large margin that there can be no reasonable doubt that there is a real difference in the rates of turnover as among various classes of merchandise. Since the second value of F lies between the two levels of significance, we may conclude that the differences in rates of turnover among stores is probably significant, but not definitely so.

A few words of caution seem here to be appropriate. In using the residual variance as a yardstick to measure the influence exerted by random forces one must assume that the two criteria of classification are independent. When they are correlated, the influence properly attributable to classification tends to be dispersed between the two bases, and the residual variance becomes diluted with a spurious element, non-random in character.

A second condition pertinent to the applications illustrated above is that the observations themselves must be independent and equal in importance. Since ratios and percentages are ordinarily weighted by their respective denominators before they are averaged, it is necessary to assume that the divisors were approximately of the same size in order to apply a simple or unweighted average. Whereas this assumption is reasonably valid in the illustration used above, there are many situations involving ratios and percentages in which it would not be true.

The technique of variance analysis is also applicable when frequencies of attributes are the subject of investigation. Here again, however, the observations are comparable only if we assume that they have been derived from equal random samples representing each subdivision of the major universe. For example, if it were desired to test the geographical homogeneity in consumer preference for a particular brand of cigarette, a series of random samples taken within each geographical region would produce a series of frequencies whose variance might be employed as the yardstick to test the region-to-region differences. If the comparison of interregional and intraregional variances revealed the former as being significantly greater, one could conclude that geography was exerting a decided influence upon the market of the particular brand.

A twofold classification of frequencies might be tested in a manner similar to the twofold classification of magnitudes, but once again it is essential that sampling be conducted in such a manner that the differences in frequencies be independent of the sampling procedure. For instance, if the frequency of use of each of k brands of cigarettes were to be tested simultaneously with the frequency of use of all brands in each of n geographical areas, we should require a two-way table of nk entries derived from nk independently drawn samples of equal size. If this sort of two-way frequency table were used, it would be a matter of indifference in the application of the analysis of variance whether the absolute or the relative frequencies were employed, since the validity of the test is no way impaired by addition, subtraction, multiplication, or division, so long as any such operation is applied in a uniform manner to every entry in the table. This feature of the technique is especially convenient when dealing with decimal fractions or with large numbers. Moving the decimal to the right in the case of decimals and subtracting a uniform amount from all entries when the numbers are large substantially lessens the labor of computation.

CHAPTER XII

Statistical Methods of Testing the Adequacy Of Market Samples

IN THE PRECEDING CHAPTER some of the more important statistical techniques for detecting significant differences in market data were discussed. These methods serve as sensitive divining rods by which the market analyst detects the really important factors that underlie and condition a specific market. Some of the factors he may identify as important without recourse to statistical analysis. The unknown and doubtful elements provide the opportunity for applying the various definitive tests. Thus, through a combination of general knowledge, *a priori* reasoning, and statistical analysis the analyst defines the conditions for a reliable sample.

TESTS OF ADEQUACY AS RELATED TO TESTS OF SIGNIFICANCE

The question of the size of sample becomes a part of the order of business only after the market analyst has disposed of all the previous steps dealing with the planning of the sample. If either the major or the minor universes have been vaguely defined or if the proportions of each of the latter have been inaccurately determined, no amount of data gathering will serve to overcome such deficiencies. An experienced photographer, for example, does not expect numerous exposures to provide clear and vivid pictures of his subject, unless he has first set his camera to take proper account of distance, light, and position of subject. The market analyst must also "set his camera" if clear pictures of the market are to be obtained, but the significant variables in market photography are factors such as income, occupation, sex, nationality, and geographical location. When the market photographer has taken cognizance of these, he may properly concern himself with the number of exposures—that is, with the size of his sample.

DIFFERENCES OF OPINION AS REGARDS PROPER SIZE OF SAMPLE

In 1934 the editors of *Sales Management* conducted a questionnaire survey in which the following question was placed before 250 sales executives distributed over the United States: "What is the smallest number of homes in any community which may be safely considered a typical cross section?" The statistical results of the survey are presented in the following table.[1]

TABLE 32

DISTRIBUTION OF ANSWERS TO QUESTION REGARDING SIZE OF SAMPLE

Percent of Persons Who Answered Specifically	*Percent of Homes Given as Adequate Sample*
28.6	2
20.3	1
16.2	4
13.5	10
9.5	.5
6.8	3
4.1	5
1.0	1.5

The variety of answers in the table serves to illustrate the folly of attempting a specific statement as to the proper size of sample. The most appropriate answer to the question does not appear in the tabulation. Approximately a third of the executives whose opinions were solicited stated that no definite percentage could be given. This would seem to be the proper answer. In general, the size of sample depends on the product, the size and nature of the community, and the degree of accuracy required in the results. A brief review of the various factors affecting the adequacy of a sample seems appropriate before specific tests of adequacy are discussed.

FACTORS AFFECTING THE ADEQUACY OF A SAMPLE

Factor of uniformity.—From the formula previously given for determining the standard error of the arithmetic average $\left(\sigma_m = \frac{\sigma}{\sqrt{N}}\right)$

[1] *Sales Management*, XXXV (1934), 218.

it may be seen that the sampling errors of the mean vary in direct proportion to the standard deviation of the population and inversely to the square root of the number in the sample. Hence, in order to offset greater variation within the population, the number in the sample must be made greater. For instance, if universe B exhibits twice the variation that is found in universe A, a sample drawn from B would need to be four times the size of that drawn from A in order to possess equal reliability.

As a practical matter the analyst seldom has any statistical measurement of the variability within the market area which he is sampling. He does, however, have a pretty accurate impression of the degree of uniformity of the homes in any community. He knows, for instance, that the greater the diversity of income, race, religion, nationality, occupation, and so forth, the larger his sample in that community must be in order to provide reliability. Rural communities and small towns are much more homogeneous as a rule than the "melting-pot" cities. Samples in the latter must be large in order to secure anything approaching a cross-section of the various racial, social, and economic groups.

The proportion of people in any community who are acquainted with the product.—In the preceding chapter it was pointed out that the sampling errors of a relative frequency may be estimated from the formula $\sqrt{\frac{pq}{N}}$ in which p is the percentage, q the complement or $100\% - p$, and N the number of observations in the sample. By assuming a sample of 100 observations and varying the size of the percentage whose sampling errors are being tested, we arrive at the results shown in Table 33.

The last column of the table illustrates the point that is here being discussed. As the percentage increases from 10 to 90, the standard error becomes proportionately less. Hence, the larger the percentage of people in any community who are familiar with a product, the smaller the sample may be and still provide a reliable estimate. For some specialty product used by only a small fraction of the consumers, one might find it necessary to extend the survey to every person in the community.

Definiteness of a product's characteristics.—Some products are purchased on the basis of rather precise specifications. Such charac-

TABLE 33

EFFECT OF SIZE OF PERCENTAGE ON SAMPLING ERRORS

Assumed Percentage (%)	*Standard Error When N = 100* (%)	*Standard Error as a Percent of Assumed Figures* (%)
10	3.0	30
20	4.0	20
30	4.6	$15\frac{1}{3}$
40	4.9	$12\frac{1}{4}$
50	5.0	10
60	4.9	$8\frac{1}{6}$
70	4.6	$6\frac{4}{7}$
80	4.0	5
90	3.0	$3\frac{1}{3}$

teristics as the tensile strength of wire, the life of electric bulbs, and the heat generated in the combustion of fuel represent commensurable qualities that may be rigorously defined. Other characteristics of products may relate to certain vague differences of taste, smell, color, texture, and style—characteristics that can be gauged only subjectively. When personal impressions rather than precise information are the subject of inquiry, there is need for a larger number of observations. In order, however, that increasing the size of sample may compensate for the less definite character of the information, one must assume that the sampling errors (as distinct from the erroneous impressions that consumers may hold) are of a nature that tend to cancel. In other words, the opinions being gathered may frequently be biased but the method of their gathering must be unbiased. If the questions asked tend to elicit incomplete or inaccurate answers, increasing the size of the sample only confirms the distortion.

The quality of the informant.—Sometimes a superior grade of information is obtained from certain groups of persons, and the sample need not be so large. Other things being equal, a sample of interviews with purchasing agents might be smaller than one composed of interviews with housewives. Purchasing agents are assumed to be specialists in their field. Their opinions usually rest on a solid foundation of fact. Housewives are more likely to guess, but in order that increasing the sample may compensate for this tendency, we must assume that the errors of guessing and of inaccurate observation are of the compensating type.

The method of gathering the information.—Information obtained by a mail questionnaire is usually somewhat less reliable than that obtained by personal interview. Similarly, the information secured through unskilled interviewers is usually less precise than that obtained by persons experienced in the field. This lack of precision in the method of collecting data may be offset by increasing the sample, provided, as before, the errors are of the compensating type.

Knowledge of the total population.—A final important factor in conditioning the size of sample is the amount of information available as regards the total population. The three following situations may be identified. First, one may know, or have reason to believe, that the population is reasonably uniform with respect to the measured characteristic. Secondly, the population may be subject to heterogeneous influences, but a knowledge of these forces and the part they play in the major universe enables the analyst to assign definite proportions for each subdivision of the sample. Finally, one may be sampling a heterogeneous population, but there is lacking the information by which to estimate the proper proportions within each subdivision of the sample.

When the first condition outlined above is present, an adequate sample is secured by drawing from the population at random until a stability in the characteristic measured is observed. When the second condition applies, the analyst resorts to stratified random selection with the proportions in the sample fixed by the proportions in the major universe. The sources of heterogeneity are thus held constant, and the errors of sampling are concentrated within each homogeneous subdivision of the population so that the sample need contain no greater number of observations than would be needed in sampling a homogeneous universe. This control of the heterogeneous forces is reflected in the standard errors of measures computed from stratified random samples. For instance, the standard error of the mean derived from a stratified sample is equal to $\sqrt{\frac{\sigma^2 - \sigma_s^2}{N}}$, in which the variation of the major universe (σ^2) has been reduced by the variation among strata (σ_s^2).

The third possible condition is that of a population whose heterogeneous elements are known only qualitatively. The first task of the analyst is then to estimate the relative importance of each minor universe so that proper proportions shall be obtained within each subdivision of the sample. Let us assume, for instance, that age is a dominant factor affecting attitudes toward products of the cinema. Suppose, however, that an investigator who sought to obtain a cross-section of a certain community's opinions could find no statistical data upon the number of persons of different ages. The sample would then have to be both large enough and varied enough to provide stable estimates of the number of persons falling within the various age groups. Not until such estimates were obtained could the analyst devote attention to the stability of the responses received. Thus, when heterogeneity of the population is not controlled, the errors of sampling between groups must be brought within acceptable limits before any attention can be given to the errors of sampling within groups.

The financial advantage that comes from being able to control the heterogeneity of the population is an important consideration in the making of any nation-wide investigation. The greater economy as well as the increased accuracy of stratified selection (as opposed to undifferentiated sampling) is well illustrated by some of the recent efforts made to determine the trend of public opinion. Here it has been demonstrated that a few thousand voters selected with proper regard for the significant elements in the voting population will provide reliable estimates of what would be obtained in a general election. The results of the various election polls conducted prior to the 1936 presidential election did much to shake the confidence of people in the efficiency of large numbers and to increase the opportunities for applying precise scientific methods to sampling.

METHODS OF TESTING THE ADEQUACY OF A SAMPLE

Several devices are available for testing the adequacy of one's sample. The reader should remember, however, that statistical tests of adequacy are never to be interpreted as demonstrating the representativeness of the sample. One could find any number of biased samples that would meet every test of adequacy that has been devised. As a matter of fact, the more one-sided and biased the sampling procedure, the greater is the likelihood that the sample will conform to the various tests of adequacy. The general principle underlying such tests is that as soon as the measures derived from samples attain a certain stability or consistency, adequacy of sample has been attained. Consequently, the effect produced by biased sampling is not unlike that which obtains in a game of chance when a player is accorded the privilege of "stacking the cards." In both instances consistency of results is made easy.

The application of a test for adequacy of sample assumes that the conditions necessary for the collection of unbiased data have been fulfilled. The precise meaning of adequacy will then depend upon the degree of accuracy required by the problem. The most important factor conditioning the latter is the purpose of the study. Sometimes the decisions of management turn upon very rough and approximate answers. For instance, if the problem of selecting the better of two package designs were to be placed before a jury of consumers, the poll could be terminated as soon as a clear-cut majority were indicated. If a number of package designs were entered and the competition were close, the poll might have to be made quite extensive in order to secure a definite plurality. Occasionally the conditions of the problem may require that the sampling error be reduced to no more than one percent of the sample value. The result is then said to have a precision index of one percent. Each reduction, however, in the margin of sampling errors requires a more than proportionate increase in the number of observations. Hence, a point is soon reached beyond which increased precision is not worth the effort made to secure it.

The methods used in testing adequacy of sample may be divided into three categories. The first is represented by graphic devices known as "stabilization charts." The second is comprised of the various statistical formulas that indicate the reliability of statistical measures. Certain features of the methods in these two categories are combined to form the third procedure of group rotation and testing for significant differences.

STABILIZATION CHARTS IN TESTING ADEQUACY OF SAMPLE

The test of adequacy most often applied by persons engaged in the making of market surveys is that of increasing the size of the sample by equal increments until a consistency of results is obtained. To assist in determining the approximate point of stabilization, the results are plotted upon a simple coördinate sheet of graph paper with increments of the sample indicated upon the horizontal scale and units in which the results are recorded along the vertical axis. The point of adequacy is assumed to have been reached when the curve of successive results ceases to oscillate and approaches a horizontal static position, the ordinate of which is assumed to be a reliable estimate of the population value.

A major criticism of this type of stabilization test is that one can never tell from the mere fact of stabilization whether or not the individual accretions or subdivisions of the sample are similar or not. The additions themselves might be exceedingly diverse, with no central tendency in evidence, and yet, because each increment receives less and less weight as it is merged with the average of all the preceding increments, the effect of the diversity is largely dissipated. Hence, the uniformity of results that is approached in a gradually expanding sample is in the nature of a forced stability about some value which, if the population be highly heterogeneous, fails to be indicative of a true central tendency. The effect is analogous to the results obtained by a chemist who combines the small portions of each of a series of distinctly different elements and then proceeds to increase the mixture by equal dosages from first one and then another of the constituent elements. Obviously, the composition of the mixture would be less altered by each additional dosage even though the dosages themselves remained consistently different throughout the experiment.

As a means of overcoming this possible disadvantage, a modified form of the stabilization test can be applied. If we start with a relatively large body of data, the first step consists in dividing the returns into a certain number of random groups of equal size. If an analysis by groups shows a close parallelism in results, the sample is deemed adequate. If discrepancies of considerable magnitude appear, another sample is taken. By using the same random method of grouping as before, additions are made to each previous subdivision, and the results are again tested for similarity. This threefold process of sampling, grouping, and analysis continues until the results by groups tend to parallel and approach a common figure that is the best estimate of the population value.

Whereas this method of applying the stabilization test is more laborious than the one above, it is free from the criticism that a stabilization is being in any way forced. Chance presumably rules the grouping, and the essence of the test consists not alone in the fact that successive results from each subgroup shall exhibit a tendency toward stability but also that in the process of stabilization these several cumulative groups shall approach a common population average.

TESTS OF ADEQUACY INVOLVING STATISTICAL FORMULAS

This second general category of tests for the adequacy of a sample assumes familiarity with the various standard error and probable error formulas. Since N is one of the variables upon which the sampling errors of any measure depend, the analyst can estimate the other variables and solve for N to obtain any desired degree of accuracy. The procedure will be illustrated with respect to the arithmetic mean. Other applications can be made by adjusting the standard error or probable error formula to fit the particular measure desired.

We shall assume that a manufacturer with a national sales organization desires to determine the average number of hours per week which the salesmen of his organization spend in the actual selling process. If the data from which a sample is to be drawn are represented by weekly reports from the men in the field, how many weekly reports should the analyst draw to obtain an adequate sample?

The first step in answering the above question is to define the degree of precision required in the answer. Must the average time be correct to the minute or to the hour? The errors of observation plus a certain possible "loaded" error in the figures themselves would seem to make accuracy to the hour quite sufficient. In other words, sufficient reliability will have been achieved when we can say with practical certainty that the true average selling time per week for the entire sales organization does not vary more than a half hour either way from our sample estimate.

The definition of accuracy in this case, as in all cases, is a relative matter. To attempt to reduce the sampling errors much below the errors of observation in the data themselves is to seek false accuracy. Moreover, the range of tolerance given to sampling errors must be related to the order of magnitude expected in the answer. If, for example, the terms of the above problem were to be altered so that annual selling times were made the subject of analysis, we should have to increase the range of tolerance. By the same token, we should have to decrease it if our analysis were to be made of data representing daily selling time.

The precision index, to which reference has previously been made, may be readily combined with the appropriate standard error formula to provide an estimate of the number of observations. For example, the desired precision for a mean estimated to be 20 hours and a range of tolerance for sampling errors of ½ hour either way would be $\frac{.5}{20}$ or .025. The general formula combining the precision index with the standard error of the mean is then

$$\text{Precision of Mean} = P_M = \frac{2.576\sigma}{M\sqrt{N-1}}$$

in which the constant factor 2.576 is the number of standard errors required to give the probability of 99 chances out of 100 that the true value will fall within the limits. The right-hand term $\frac{\sigma}{\sqrt{N-1}}$ is the formula for the standard error of the mean when the standard deviation of the universe is not known and must be approximated. Solving the formula for the value of N in terms of the other variables, we have

$$N = \left(\frac{2.576\sigma}{P_M \times M}\right)^2 + 1.$$

By estimating the values of the mean and of the standard deviation to be 20 hours and 2 hours, respectively, we substitute and solve for N

$$N = \left(\frac{2.576(2)}{.025 \times 20}\right)^2 + 1$$
$$= 107.$$

Thus, under the assumed conditions the sample should contain in the neighborhood of 100 observations. The value of N obtained in this manner must be interpreted as approximate since it is secured from estimates of the mean and of the standard deviation.

To save the trouble of solving for N, special tables and charts have been prepared from which one may read directly the number of observations necessary to meet a specified standard of accuracy.[2] The use of such tables for predetermining the size of sample assumes that

[2] See George R. Davies and Dale Yoder, *Business Statistics*, New York, Wiley, 1937, p. 402; also Brown, *The Use of Statistical Technique in Certain Problems of Market Research*, pp. 10–13.

the analyst is able to estimate the terms that provide the argument for entering the table. Unless this can be done with a fair degree of assurance, the safer procedure is to set up the standard of accuracy required, but to await the actual accumulation of data before deciding what size of sample is going to be required. As soon as the number of observations is sufficiently large to reduce the coefficient of precision to a magnitude equal to or less than the standard, it may be assumed that an adequate sample has been gathered.

TESTS OF DIFFERENCES BETWEEN ROTATED GROUPS OF OBSERVATIONS

The principle of group rotation and testing for significant differences was first suggested by William J. Reilly.[3] The specific procedure, as he has outlined it in *Marketing Investigations,* is one that is capable of modification and elaboration. The following exposition is, therefore, intentionally more general and should point to a wider application of the technique.

The sample being tested for adequacy is divided at random into a series of consecutively numbered groups—the precise number of groups is immaterial so long as it is even and not too great to be handled conveniently. With k, any even number of random subdivisions, the analyst can make $k/2$ pairings of results. The series of differences may then be tested for significance by applying the appropriate statistical formula.

To illustrate the principle of rotation, we shall assume 10 groups or subdivisions of the sample and draw up the following list of paired groupings:

Groups		*Groups*
1, 2, 3, 4, 5	paired with	6, 7, 8, 9, 10
2, 3, 4, 5, 6	paired with	7, 8, 9, 10, 1
3, 4, 5, 6, 7	paired with	8, 9, 10, 1, 2
4, 5, 6, 7, 8	paired with	9, 10, 1, 2, 3
5, 6, 7, 8, 9	paired with	10, 1, 2, 3, 4

In order to illustrate the principle of testing for significant differences, we shall assume that the observations relate to the answers given in response to a specific question chosen from among those used in a personal interview survey. Taking 1,000 replies as a convenient

[3] Reilly, *Marketing Investigations,* p. 154.

sample to be allocated at random into 10 groups of 100 observations each, the analyst records the affirmative answers contained within each of the groupings shown above. In the first set of paired groupings we shall assume the percentage of affirmative answers to be 55 and 58, respectively. The difference of 3 percent may now be tested for significance by applying the formula for the standard error of the difference between two uncorrelated percentages $\sqrt{p_o q_o \left(\frac{1}{N_1} + \frac{1}{N_2}\right)}$. (See section of preceding chapter dealing with tests of single differences in frequencies.) By substituting the appropriate values and solving, we have

$$\sigma_{D_p} = \sqrt{(56.5)(43.5)\left(\frac{1}{500}+\frac{1}{500}\right)}$$
$$= 3.15 \text{ percent.}$$

Since the standard error is as large as the difference itself, it is obvious that this particular difference is not large enough to be significant. This identical procedure may be employed in testing each of the other differences obtained from the paired groupings. If any of the differences exceed the limit of 2.576 standard errors (the deviation previously set as allowable to chance), the sample is regarded as inadequate, and additional data must be collected and tested.

Tables of maximum chance differences between samples may be easily compiled by substituting each of a series of average percentages (p_o) in the appropriate formula. For example, if we assume samples of some specific size we can solve the expression

$$\sqrt{(6.64)\ p_o q_o\left(\frac{1}{N_1}+\frac{1}{N_2}\right)}$$

to obtain the maximum sampling difference of two percentages.

The formula as given is simply the standard error of the difference of two sample percentages multiplied by 2.576 (6.64 under the radical), which is the number of standard errors required to indicate a significant difference. In the problem illustrated above the maximum allowable difference is

$$\sqrt{(6.64)\ (56.5)\ (43.5)\left(\frac{1}{500}+\frac{1}{500}\right)}, \text{ or 8 per cent.}$$

To convert this result into terms of absolute frequencies, we need only to multiply by N (in this case 500). Hence, 40 is the maximum difference in the number of affirmative answers that random selection should give between two groups of 500 returns each when the average percentage of affirmative answers is 56.5.[4] As the average of the two percentages approaches either extreme of the percentage scale extending from zero to one hundred, the maximum allowable difference becomes less.

By replacing the formula for the standard error of the difference between two uncorrelated percentages by other formulas appropriate for testing sampling differences in other measures, the procedure here illustrated may be extended for use with the measurement of magnitudes. The assumption underlying the procedure is that if randomness characterizes the division of the sample, the difference between successive groupings should be of an order of magnitude consistent with chance. Consequently, when the maximum allowable difference is exceeded, the analyst has reason to believe that his sample was not large enough to provide statistical stability.

RELATIVE ADVANTAGES OF METHODS OF TESTING ADEQUACY

Simplicity is a distinctive advantage of the stabilization chart. It may be used by persons unfamiliar with the various statistical formulas for testing the reliability of measures. Its limitations were discussed in a previous section.

The principal advantage of the more technical approach involving the use of statistical formulas is the opportunity it affords for adjusting the size of the sample to the particular purpose of the study. Hence, it is generally more economical than the stabilization chart, since the latter method occasionally leads to the collection of a needlessly large sample. A most salutary feature of the statistical approach is the simple fact that it forces the analyst to take thought as to the degree of accuracy required in his results before he begins the collection of data.

[4] In the table prepared by Reilly, showing maximum allowable differences in frequencies applicable to the group rotation method, a maximum of 33 is shown when the smallest of the two percentages is somewhere between 56 and 65 and $N = 500$. Since this table was prepared from the standard error of a percentage rather than the standard error of the difference of two percentages, the readings from the table are consistently below those that would be obtained by use of the formula given above. The discrepancy is reduced somewhat by the fact that the range of tolerance used in the preparation of the table was 3 standard errors rather than the more precise number 2.576. See *Market Investigations*, p. 154.

A second advantage of the more precise and technical approach is that it provides the analyst with a means of calculating in advance of experience the probable cost of a proposed survey. By appraising the expected benefits in terms of the probable cost, many unprofitable ventures into the field of research might be avoided.

Finally, the procedure provides for an independent check upon the adequacy of any sample. Only a person who has access to the original body of data could duplicate the stabilization chart or the group rotation method. An independent investigator, however, can estimate by means of the various standard-error formulas whether or not the sample has been adequate to support the conclusions drawn. We must assume, of course, that the independent analyst has been given certain summary measures and the size of sample from which to make the test. The progress of scientific effort in any field may well be gauged by the possibility and the prevalence of such independent checks.

A word of warning seems appropriate to the application of any test of adequacy. Previous knowledge as to the minor universes is essential if errors are to be avoided. The gross sample may satisfy the most rigorous test of adequacy, but if the analyst proceeds to compute measures and to draw conclusions from various small subdivisions of the sample, he may find that the number of observations within these subsamples is entirely inadequate. In general, the tests should be applied to the smallest subdivision of the universe about which conclusions are to be drawn. If the smallest subdivision of the sample is adequate, the sample is probably large enough to satisfy the tests in all larger parts. One company engaged in market research follows the rule of thumb that the smallest of the various minor universes must be represented by at least 25 observations or interviews. From this it is able to estimate the gross sample. The results obtained by applying an arbitrary method of this kind will be generally superior to those obtained by using more technical methods, unless the latter are applied with discrimination.

CHAPTER XIII

Methods of Analyzing Market Data

THE ANALYSIS of market data is not a process wholly distinct from that of the collection of market data. A certain amount of analysis has been shown to be necessary in the collection procedure itself. Moreover, the degree of precision employed in the analysis cannot well be decided apart from the methods and conditions surrounding the collection of the data. Analysis and collection are best regarded as mutually interdependent. The analyst of market data must look continuously to the person who collects them if he is to be conversant with the distortions and inadequacies of his basic material. On the other hand, in order to provide the significant facts, the collector must keep constantly in mind the type of analysis to be performed upon the data.

TYPES OF ANALYSIS AS RELATED TO THE PROBLEM

The two general types of analysis discussed in Chapters III to VII which dealt with the analysis of sales may be duplicated in analyzing the market. A cross-section study made as of a given time period results in a static picture. Like the static type of sales analysis, it is concerned with problems whose solutions rest upon current data. The evaluation of sales territories for the purpose of allocating a current sales budget to various salesmen or to various district managers represents a problem of the static type. When the analyst is engaged upon this type of problem he has little interest in either the past or the future, but desires rather to know the present sales opportunities in territory A, for example, relative to territory B. Upon such information, he distributes his quotas.

In the dynamic analysis of markets cognizance is taken of the influence of the time factor. Trends are the important consideration, and the technique of analysis must be adapted to the showing of these changes through time. Whereas any single static analysis is used principally as a basis for comparing the relative positions of territories, products, brands, companies, and so forth, at some particular point in time, the dynamic analysis compares these variables over a period of time. Consequently, the dynamic analysis is of greater significance in dealing with problems that cast their shadows before them for some considerable period into the future. Long-term market planning and the determination of sales policies are likely to rest principally on analyses of the dynamic type.

THE AMOUNT OF ANALYSIS AS RELATED TO THE PROBLEM

A great many market studies have not involved an analysis more complicated than a simple classification and tabulation of data. Numerous surveys deal with the brand preferences of consumers. Some are made directly with the consumer, whereas others deal with the problem indirectly through dealer inventories and dealer questionnaires. Once tabulation has been made showing the numbers of people using or preferring each of a series of brands of articles, there is little more that one can do. At most, the actual numbers using each brand can be converted into percentages of the total. The conversion into percentage terms, however, is of doubtful value unless the actual figures accompany the percentages.

Insofar as the purpose of any study can be served by resorting to the relatively simple analytical processes, it would be folly to employ any of the more technical methods of statistical analysis. In general, one's aim should be to keep the analysis as simple as possible without losing the possible effectiveness of the data. Simplicity of analysis, however, ceases to be a virtue as soon as it fails to bring forth the essential significance of the data. Respecting the thoroughness of analysis, one research authority has stated that

> the thoroughness with which research data have been analyzed and interpreted can easily be judged by the skill employed in the technique of manipulating or recasting data in those forms which make them most meaningful. One could establish, indeed, an arbitrary measure of skill in the degree of completeness with which meanings, inferences or evidence have been derived from manipulated data. Many published pieces of research indicate to a

trained analyst that often no more than 10 to 20 percent of the inherent evidence in the data used has been discovered. . . . Much research effort is often wasted, because the research worker does not know what to do with the data he has collected.[1]

Market analysts have failed to extract much of the real metal of significance contained in the raw statistical ore they have gathered. The greater portion of this failure can be traced to the analyst's reluctance to employ methods so technical that they will not be intelligible to business executives. Unlike the chemist or the engineer, the market analyst deals with problems that fall within the range of the business manager's knowledge and experience. Yet some of the more effective tools for handling these problems are so technical that the analyst feels constrained to explain the tools before using them. Eventually a knowledge of statistical methods may become sufficiently widespread to enable those engaged in marketing research to drop the exposition and concentrate on application and interpretation. In the meantime anyone who ventures to use anything more complicated than a percentage or an average feels a certain compunction unless he makes his exposition twofold—one dealing with methods, the other dealing with their application.

METHODS OF ANALYSIS

A detailed explanation and description of all the various statistical methods used in the analysis of data would extend much beyond the scope of this study. The purpose of the present chapter will have been achieved by a brief enumeration of the various categories of methodology, and some reference to the general type of problem in the handling of which a knowledge of the methods is desirable.

The following classification of analytical methods has been found serviceable in giving instructions in this field: (1) methods of classification and tabulation of data; (2) graphic methods of presentation and analysis; (3) averages and measures of dispersion; (4) index numbers as a special form of average; (5) time-series analysis; and (6) correlation analysis.

Each of the above categories will be briefly discussed as a means of indicating the bearing which each has upon the general problem of analyzing market data.

[1] Schluter, *How to Do Research Work.*

THEORY OF CLASSIFICATION

"There can be no doubt that improper classification of questionnaire returns is responsible for much error in marketing research." [2] Such is the opinion of Dr. Paul Felix Lazarsfeld, who has made significant contributions to the literature dealing with psychological aspects of marketing research. Dr. Lazarsfeld gives the following four requirements of a psychologically satisfactory classification. The grouping must be (1) articulate, (2) psychologically adequate, (3) logically correct, and (4) psychologically pertinent.

The whole purpose of the classification process is to put into groups those elements which are similar, so that a greater degree of homogeneity is found within groups than between groups. In the pursuit of this purpose, however, the number of groups frequently multiplies to such extent that the interpretation of the results becomes difficult. To overcome this handicap without losing any of the advantages of classification, the grouping should be made "articulate" through the use of major and minor categories. The major categories are usually few in number and correspond to the major headings of an outline. The minor categories represent a series of subgroupings within the major classes, so that almost any degree of fineness in grouping may be pursued without loss of significant relationships.

To be psychologically adequate, the basis of classification must recognize the obvious and the conventional categories when these are suggested by the nature of the problem. When the nature of the data is such that no readily perceptible or well-established basis of classification is suggested, the analyst should seek the psychologically adequate basis in the actual situation or process with which the problem deals. For example, if the problem were one in which data relative to the characteristics of a product were to be classified, the analyst might endeavor to place himself in the position of the consumer about to purchase or to use the product and might inquire what mental processes would be involved.

A classification is logically correct when it recognizes levels of generality within any given subdivision and prevents the grouping of different aspects of a subject into coördinate categories. For example,

[2] For a full discussion of the psychological problems involved in the classification of marketing data see *The Technique of Marketing Research*, chap. xi.

if a person were to make a statistical table of the agate lines of advertising found in various New York newspapers and were to use such major headings as "Evening Newspapers," "Morning Newspapers," and "Sunday Newspapers," he would be guilty of mixing two levels of generality. To overcome the difficulty, the third category should be dropped and the second should be shown with two subclasses designated as "Week-days" and "Sundays." Again, if one were to make a study of magazine reading preferences of people and were to list as coördinate categories groups such as bankers, sales managers, railroad executives, best customers of best stores, airline passengers, social registerites, and so forth, he would be confusing different aspects of the respondents within the same level of generality.

The final requirement of a satisfactory classification is that it shall be psychologically pertinent in that it shall have taken into account differences in interpretation of questions, as well as differences in the aspects of responses. To fulfill this requirement, it is necessary that each question be critically examined in order to determine the various possible aspects which a respondent might have in mind when answering. The responses must then be classified in accordance with the particular aspect to which each response belongs. For instance, in answering a general question such as "Why did you purchase Brand X?" the respondent might reply under any one of three general categories.[3] The first relates to an individual's own purpose, attitudes, and predilections, which are referred to as tendencies. The second relates to all outside influences, such as advertising, window display, recommendation by a friend, and so forth. The third category includes all attributes of the product itself, such as taste, color, package design, price, and so forth.

MECHANICS OF CLASSIFICATION AND TABULATION

Both hand and machine methods are available for the tabulation of statistical data. Which of these the analyst employs depends upon the quantity and the nature of the information that is being handled. Decision as to the more economical method must rest upon intimate knowledge of all the conditions surrounding each survey. The principal variables influencing the decision are: the number of schedules or

[3] Categories are those given by Paul Felix Lazarsfeld in an article "Art of Asking Why in Marketing Research," *National Marketing Review*, Summer, 1935.

questionnaire returns, the number of questions per questionnaire, the number of cross classifications desired, the costs of obtaining competent tabulators, the rental charge for use of mechanical equipment, and, finally, the type of information. All of these have a connection that is obvious, save perhaps the type of information, and this is important because it affects the ease with which the information may be coded for mechanical tabulation.[4]

The great advantage of the machine method of classification consists in its almost limitless possibilities for classifying and combining the data. By the process of repeated classifications significant differences can frequently be revealed. It then becomes the task of the investigator to find, if possible, the reason or reasons for these differences. Not infrequently the factor or factors responsible for the significant variation can be uncovered by continuing the classification process. For instance, if a company discovered significant differences in its per capita sales among territories, a further classification of sales should be undertaken on the basis of other criteria such as income, race, size of town, occupation, style of product, and so forth. Then, if two or more series are found which exhibit significant differences, a correlation may be sought between the variables in the hope of identifying the causal factor. Proof of causality, however, must be established by processes other than those of a purely statistical nature.

GRAPHIC METHODS OF PRESENTATION AND ANALYSIS

Usually one of three purposes is dominant in the construction of a chart or a graph. The first purpose a graph or a chart may serve is that of a storehouse for reference material. For example, a statistical map showing by one of a variety of means factors such as population, number of income-tax returns, number of retail outlets, and number of users of the product constitutes a reference type of chart. Like a general statistical table, it is a storehouse of data pertaining to significant market factors.

The second general purpose for which a graphic device may be used is to clarify or make more vivid some certain piece of specific

[4] For a discussion of the development and principles of mechanical tabulation see George Walter Baehne, ed., *Practical Applications of the Punched Card Method in Colleges and Universities,* New York, Columbia University Press, 1935, pp. 1–20.

information. The Gantt progress chart and the clock chart (two types of graphic presentation that have been used to show the relative accomplishment of salesmen with respect to their individual quotas) are examples of this second type.

The third category of graphs is represented by those that are analytical in purpose. The break-even diagram which was discussed in Chapter V is typical of diagrams in this class. An examination of the diagram provides an estimate of net profit or net loss at each of a series of sales volumes. An analysis of a slightly different sort is provided by ratio charts, as when the analyst plots total sales against sales by territories for the purpose of comparing percentage changes and relationships. Correlation diagrams are in part explanatory and in part analytical. Sales-trend lines projected to obtain estimates of future sales serve a similar dual purpose.

The brief treatment that has been accorded to each of the three major purposes served by graphic methods must not be taken as an index to the importance of this subject. There is little, however, that is unique in the application of graphic methods of sales control. Time and space must here be conserved by referring the reader to any one of a number of textbooks that deal exclusively with graphic methods of presenting and analyzing facts.[5]

AVERAGES AS TOOLS OF MARKET ANALYSIS

Markets are aggregates of a great many units, such as persons, families, retail outlets, factories, mines, homes, and so forth. The essence of market measurement is the collection, organization, analysis, and interpretation of numerical observations relative to these market units. The two most commonly used methods of summarizing a mass of statistical data are simple summation and averaging. Whereas simple summation is most effective for certain types of problems, the human mind can usually grasp with greater ease the significance of some form of average, such as the arithmetic mean, the

[5] The following general texts are cited as typical of the publications in this field: H. Arkin and R. R. Colton, *Graphs: How to Make and Use Them*, New York, Harper, 1936; W. C. Brinton, *Graphic Methods for Presenting Facts*, New York, The Engineering Magazine Company, 1914; A. C. Haskell, *How to Make and Use Graphic Charts*, New York [now Norwood, Mass.], Codex Book Company, 1922; Karl G. Karsten, *Charts and Graphs*, New York, Prentice Hall, 1923; and Bruce D. Mudgett, *Statistical Tables and Graphs*, Boston, Houghton Mifflin, 1930.

median, or the mode. Since the mean is derived simply by dividing the sum of a series of observations by the number of items, knowledge of the individual magnitudes is not essential. This simplicity of computation makes it the most widely used, as well as the most frequently abused, of the various kinds of average.

Any elementary statistical textbook is replete with explanations and illustrations for the computation of all types of averages. The emphasis of the present section is upon the deceptive nature of an average and the danger of placing too great confidence in its use as a summary measure of a market's characteristics. Large and very significant differences often lurk within the shadow of an average. Not infrequently these differences are sufficiently large to vitiate the whole concept of a representative value. For instance, if one were to compute the per capita income for a community containing a few very wealthy persons, but a great number of the very poor, he might easily find the average income well above that for the country as a whole, but the market for goods (especially convenience goods used by middle-income classes) would be much less than in some more homogeneous community in which neither the excessively rich nor the extremely poor were to be found.

One of the hardiest perennials of loose statistical inference is that which concerns the use of per capita sales data—a hybrid form of the arithmetic mean. One will frequently see the per capita retail sales of a given city compared with those of another city or with those of the United States as a whole. The latter is a pure statistical average, since numerator and denominator relate to the same body of persons. Total retail sales within the country are divided by the country's total population, and we can assume a certain identity between dividend and divisor as regards the units represented.[6] In computing per capita sales data for cities and towns, however, the numerator (sales) is augmented by the purchases of non-residents and diminished by the outside buying of residents. Only if we assume the highly improbable condition that the sales to non-residents of a town or city equal the outside purchases of residents (both as regards volume and number of persons involved) would a simple division of sales by population pro-

[6] Even in the country as a unit there is a certain small element of spuriousness in the average due to purchases at retail across the borders. The per capita sales are augmented by internal purchases of foreigners and diminished by foreign purchases of nationals.

vide a true per capita average. The spurious element introduced into the average when this hypothetical condition is absent need not in itself destroy comparability, provided all per capita data are in error in the same direction and to the same relative degree—a condition that would be true if the percentages of business lost and gained remained constant from city to city. But this condition is as unreal as the former.

Probably the nearest approach to pure statistical averages representing per capita sales for limited geographical units are those prepared by trading areas. New difficulties, however, are then encountered in defining the trading areas. Different estimates of per capita sales may be obtained for a city's trading area, depending upon what boundaries one accepts as truly defining the area from which the city draws its trade. Conditions of this sort constitute the breeding ground for statistical charlatanry since reliable data may so easily be prostituted to show what the analyst desires.

Where spuriousness of one form or another is likely to creep into an average, great care must be exercised to provide supplementary information. For instance, if total sales by cities or towns were given, these might prove more illuminating for some purposes than the per capita figures. Only by providing every possible opportunity for other investigators to check methods of analysis and processes of reasoning can market analysts hope to improve the general quality of research that is being done in this new and fast developing field.

Frequently the measures computed are legitimate and free from bias, but the conclusions drawn are either erroneous or open to serious question. An illustrative case is afforded by the interpretation which a national research organization placed upon the results of a consumer survey made to determine the relative popularity and amounts consumed of various brands of coffee. Since the low-priced coffees showed the highest average number of pounds used per month, the research organization drew the conclusion "that there is not much real saving in the use of a cheap grade of coffee, that the less one pays for coffee, the more one has to use of it." [7] Since no account was taken either of the size of family or of the coffee-drinking habits in the various income groups, the conclusion was quite unwarranted.

An illustration used by William J. Reilly in his stimulating book

[7] *Advertising and Selling*, XXIII (August 2, 1934), 19.

Straight Thinking indicates the great care needed in interpreting market averages and per capita sales in particular. One company found that in seven of its sixty-two sales territories the per capita sales of the product had declined about the same amount within the two preceding years. These seven territories were grouped together on the assumption that they represented the same situation and required the same kind of treatment. Actually, however, there are no less than five possible combinations of circumstances that might have yielded the same results. They are as follows: (1) a decline in sales total, the number of customers remaining constant; (2) the sales total constant, but an increase in the number of customers; (3) a decline in both the volume of sales and the number of customers, but a smaller proportional decline in the latter; (4) an increase in both the volume of sales and the number of customers, but a very much greater increase in the latter; and (5) a decline in sales volume, with an increase in the number of customers.

The listing of these possible combinations should serve to emphasize the importance of supplementary information in interpreting summary measures, especially an average in which both dividend and divisor are subject to change.

MEASURES OF DISPERSION OR VARIATION

Measures of dispersion afford perhaps the best safeguard against the too-ready acceptance of an average. Unfortunately the market analyst often has no knowledge of the variation in the data with which he deals. Frequently he uses secondary data, for which only the total and the number of observations may be given. This is true, for example, with much of the census data respecting sales, rentals, wages, values produced, and so forth. Whereas averages may be computed, there is no way of knowing how much variation there may be among the observations. Yet it is upon such information that the significance of an average depends.

Classification in terms of magnitudes partially overcomes the difficulty mentioned above. The frequent use, however, of large and varying class intervals and the lumping of extreme cases into open-end classes combine to make the computation of any except the cruder measures of variation impossible.

Possibly the most irritating aspect for those who seek to test the significance of market measurements is the frequent publication of averages obviously computed from samples, yet unaccompanied by any measure of variation. Frequently the size of the sample will be given, but such information by itself is of little practical value. In order to estimate sampling errors and to appraise the significance of differences between averages, one must know (or at least have some estimate of) the variation in the population.

INDEX NUMBERS

Most index numbers are a form of average. Whereas a single series of values may be converted into relatives and called an index, the usual procedure consists in combining into a composite a number of series by some method of summarization. Market indexes represent one member in a family of four. The other three are: index numbers of prices, indexes of physical volume (including business activity, production, and trade), and index numbers of seasonal variation. Although the market analyst should be familiar with all four members of the index family, the present purpose will be served by confining the discussion to those employed in the measurement of markets. The types of market index, the methods of construction, and some of the more significant contributions in this field are considered in the following chapter.

TIME-SERIES ANALYSIS

Any series of values ordered in time is referred to as a time series. The dynamic analysis of sales and of markets presupposes a knowledge of the statistical technique appropriate for studying variation exhibited over a period of months or years. Since the application of these techniques was discussed earlier in connection with the dynamic analysis of sales records, no additional treatment of these analytical devices is here required.

CORRELATION ANALYSIS

The methods used in measuring the relationship between two or more sets of data have been extensively treated in standard statistical textbooks.[8] The purpose of the present section is to summarize the

[8] For a most comprehensive treatment of correlation methods the student is referred to Mordecai Ezekial, *Methods of Correlation Analyses*, John Wiley, New York, 1930.

specific applications that market analysts have made of this important branch of statistical methodology.

Sales, costs, and markets are the three areas of study into which correlation methods have brought a new and higher degree of precision. The use of correlation technique in the control of sales and costs was discussed in Chapters V and VII. Market analysis presents three major problems in the solution of which a knowledge of correlation can prove most helpful. These are: (1) the selection of factors that influence the sales either of a specific product or of goods in general; (2) the weighting of different factors for the purpose of compiling a composite market index; and (3) the setting of territorial sales quotas.

The selection of significant market factors and the assignment of weights in the construction of a composite market index are problems more appropriately discussed in connection with the general subject of market indexes. Some of the advantages, as well as a few of the dangers, that accompany the use of correlation analysis will receive attention during the course of that discussion.

CHAPTER XIV

Types of Market Indexes and Methods Of Construction

A MARKET INDEX is any quantitative measure that serves to indicate the opportunity for the sale of goods. There are at least three bases upon which such quantitative measures may be classified.

TYPES OF MARKET INDEXES

A market index may represent a single statistical series or a composite of a number of statistical series. The amount of analysis required for an index of the simple or single-series type is very limited, whereas that for one of the composite type can lead into paths as devious as any that the methods of statistics have to offer.

As to use or purpose, we may distinguish two broad categories of market indexes. The first embraces indexes designed to measure the potential sales of a specific product or group of products. The second is composed of those used to measure the sales opportunities for products in general. The former are called specific market indexes; the latter are usually referred to as general market indexes or indexes of general purchasing power. A specific market index should never be used to serve the purpose of a general, but under certain conditions and circumstances the general index may quite properly be used either in place of or as a part of a specific market index.

The time factor provides a third basis for classifying market indexes. Into one class we may place the static indexes used to indicate relative sales opportunities by territories. In the second class are the dynamic indexes which emphasize the changes taking place in sales opportunities over a period of time. If the static type of index is computed at frequent intervals of time and continued over a considerable time period, it serves to reflect not only the current position but also previous and prospective future positions. A dynamic view of the market is thereby secured. Hence, static market indexes, when computed frequently and continued over a period long enough to reveal trends, become indexes of the dynamic type.

MARKET INDEXES OF THE SIMPLE TYPE

In the following discussion of indexes of the simple type the reader should keep in mind the distinction between the method of constructing an index and the use to which it is put. A simple market index (one based upon a single statistical series) may, for instance, be designed to measure the sales opportunities for a specific product or to indicate the purchasing power of the market in general. The same thing may be said of a composite market index (one compiled from a number of statistical series).

The most common simple type of index is that which measures the market for a specific product. When either the purchase or the previous possession of one product is a necessary condition for the present or future purchase of some other, the purchase or ownership of the former may be used as a simple specific market index for the latter. It may often measure the potential sales with a greater degree of accuracy than can a composite index made up of many variables.

In the category of the simple general market index (a single statistical series used to measure general purchasing power) the outstanding example is that of the total Retail Sales Index compiled by the United States Bureau of Foreign and Domestic Commerce.[1] This general market index is one of the best guides on the general consumer market that we have. It measures not only what people are buying but also where and how much they are buying.

The fact that a great many companies find the Retail Sales Index a helpful guide in spotting the weak places in the distribution of their

[1] The retail sales index has been compiled from data contained in the Census of Distribution. It represents a conversion of total retail sales by counties and by cities into a series of percentages with both the state's total and that of the United States as a base. The index may be found in a series of special bulletins the first of which carries the title "An Aid for Analyzing Markets in Connecticut." Others in the series bear this identical title save for the necessary substitution of the name of the appropriate state or geographical area. The states and areas now covered include Ohio, Illinois, Michigan, Pennsylvania, Missouri, New York, New Jersey, New England, and the Pacific South-

product does not alter the general character of the index. It means simply that a general market index has found usefulness in a specific capacity.

SOME LIMITATIONS OF SIMPLE MARKET INDEXES AS USED TO MEASURE SPECIFIC MARKETS

Most of the limitations of simple market indexes apply particularly to those used to measure a specific market. Usually the simple specific index is lacking in the proper degree of selectivity. Automobile registrations, for example, might serve reasonably well as an index to the potential sales of motor oil in various sections of the United States but be quite inadequate as an index to the possible sales of anti-freeze solutions. The number of houses wired for electricity might be used to indicate the relative importance of territories as markets for popular-priced electric toasters, but the same index would be inadequate to measure the sales potentials for electric ranges. Temperature data would most certainly need to be a factor in any index of demand for anti-freeze solutions and such variables as electrical rates, competition of other fuels, and income would require inclusion if proper selectivity were to be achieved in an index of demand for electric ranges.

At the other extreme we may find a simple index that is too restrictive in character in the sense that it rules out of possible consideration important segments of the real market for a particular product. The number of doctors and medical students might serve reasonably well to indicate the relative importance of territories as markets for stethoscopes, but it would be decidedly too restrictive to indicate the potential demand for clinical thermometers. To keep the market index free from elements that bear little or no relationship to the sale of the product and at the same time make it inclusive enough so that no considerable body of consumers will be omitted is the consummation for which market analysts strive.

Perhaps the most serious objection that might be raised against indexes of the simple specific type relates to the circuity of reasoning frequently involved in their selection. For example, the manufacturer of a well-known make of typewriter once employed the circulation figures of the *Saturday Evening Post* to set sales quotas, since the circulation data followed the company's sales within two percent in each major sales division. Presumably the perfect standard would be one that followed the company's sales without a single deviation. But this is placing "the cart before the horse." Any legitimate test of agreement should come after the selection of the index series, not before it. The standard, if it is to be a standard, must be selected on the basis of *a priori* reasoning and common sense. Then, if subsequent analysis reveals significant variations in the sales of certain areas, it is probable that the distribution is at fault, not the index that serves as the standard.

THE PURPOSE OF THE INDEX AS A FACTOR IN SELECTION

A practice that is inappropriate as applied to the selection of a specific market index may be quite satisfactory as a means of finding a barometer for the general market. The circle of reasoning is broken in the second case because the purpose of a general market index is, not to indicate what sales in general ought to be in each of a series of market areas, but rather to reflect the *status quo*. Hence, the concept of a standard in the sense of a goal to be attained is without any real significance except as it is applied to some specific product or group of products. It can scarcely have meaning as applied to the purchasing power for all products at any given time and place, since this is rather definitely fixed—fixed by the economic resources of the community and its ability to produce. From this it follows that the selection of a statistical series to measure the general market is primarily a problem of estimating the relative extent of wealth-creating activities within various geographical units. For this purpose the total sales of all products affords one of the best possible guides.

Long before the Federal Government took its first census of distribution, pioneers in the field of marketing research used retail sales by counties in Pennsylvania [2] as a sort of statistical divining rod by which they could determine what series could profitably be used to measure the general market. Now that data regarding sales, both retail and wholesale, are available for the country as a whole, there is less need for a divining rod to search out indexes to the general buying power. Whatever merit, for the purpose of a general market index, the market analyst might find in a combination of significant factors, he would very likely find in even greater measure in the simple

[2] Retail sales data were available in Pennsylvania when they could not be found for other states. The early use of the retail sales tax in that state resulted in this very useful statistical by-product.

index of retail sales. As a consequence, some of the better-known composite indexes of general purchasing power have fallen into disuse. Those who created them at considerable expense can now purchase for a few cents the Retail Sales Index. As a measure of general consumer ability to buy goods, the latter is a better tool than many of the indexes that market analysts have hitherto been able to fashion for themselves out of the more limited statistical facilities at their command.

LIMITATIONS OF THE RETAIL SALES INDEX

The Retail Sales Index is not without its limitations. These must be appreciated if it is to be used properly. The first limitation would apply with even greater force to some of the earlier composite indexes of the general market. Most of these were never revised or brought up to date. The retail sales index is as current as the census data from which it is compiled, but changes taking place in the intercensal periods have to be accounted for, if at all, by various supplementary yardsticks.

A second limitation of the Retail Sales Index arises out of the manner in which statistical data in general are reported. Data are given by political subdivisions, with the city, county, or state as the geographical unit. Sales, however, are made in trading areas that frequently ignore political boundaries; and trading areas differ with products, as well as with merchants. Therefore, in order that the Retail Sales Index may be applied to a specific situation, it must usually be modified to correspond to the trading area of the individual enterprise. By adding the indexes of a number of counties, it is frequently possible to build up an index appropriate to the specific needs of the merchant. When the boundaries of the trading area cut across county lines, the index of retail sales may be approximated either by estimating the portion of the county or by adding the indexes of only those towns and cities from which the merchant draws his business. For those who shun the trouble of tailoring their trading areas to fit their specific needs there are a number of custom-made trading areas available.[3]

[3] The various trading area maps included in the *Market Data Handbook of the United States*, published by the United States Bureau of Foreign and Domestic Commerce, deserve specific mention.

A third limitation of the Retail Sales Index is similar to the second in that it also relates to the necessity of modifying the index to fit a specific purpose. The index indicates by sections the relative amounts of money spent on all commodities, but specific commodities might present an entirely different picture. The factors influencing the purchase of commodities are so varied that as one moves from the small town to the large city, from a wealthy community to a poverty-stricken one, from a cold climate to a warm one, or from a community composed primarily of people belonging to a particular nationality, occupation, or religious belief, to a community presenting decidedly different aspects of each of these characteristics, the proportion of the income that goes to purchase any particular product is bound to show considerable variation. The use of the Retail Sales Index as a standard for judging the distribution of a specific product would seem justified only if purchase of the product were primarily a function of ability to buy. In other circumstances the index should either be modified or included simply as one factor in a composite index tailored to fit the specific needs.

Those who compiled the Retail Sales Index fully recognize its limitations and have been careful to point out the need for more specific barometers. For example, Charles B. Elliot, author of *An Aid for Analyzing Markets in Connecticut*, states:

> The ideal index would show for every commodity, or at least every related group of commodities, the actual percentage sold in each political subdivision of the United States. If we knew the actual sales of all commodities by states, counties, and cities, a series of such indexes could easily be calculated each of which would then be a specific index for a particular commodity. The census was not able, however, to show actual commodity sales—the data simply were not obtainable. But it does show total sales by kinds of outlets, and we believe that this information will eventually enable marketing men to work out indexes which will supersede the estimated general indexes hitherto used as well as the total retail sales index developed in this report.

The author of the report then illustrates how the sales data by types of retail outlets may be utilized to give a more nearly accurate estimate of certain specific markets than could be obtained from the total Retail Sales Index. The necessary statistical data, gathered originally from the *Census of Distribution*, have here been consolidated into convenient tabular form. The percentages shown as indexes relate in each instance to the county of New Haven in Connecticut, which has been taken as the base, or 100 percent, in making the comparison.

TABLE 34

COMPARISON OF GENERAL AND SPECIFIC RETAIL SALES INDEXES

City	*Population*	*Retail Sales Index*	*Index of Retail Food Sales*	*Index of Retail Shoe Sales*
New Haven	162,655	48.96	38.03	56.39
West Haven	25,808	2.84	4.65	00.56

The Retail Sales Index is here shown to be an inaccurate indicator of the sales potentials for distribution of both food and shoes. West Haven is undervalued as a market in which to sell food and overvalued as a market for shoes. If one were to enlarge the geographical unit of comparison to include entire trading areas, those differences arising from metropolitan versus suburban shopping habits would tend to cancel. Other differences, however, that arise from racial, climatic, and occupational characteristics would remain, regardless of the geographical unit chosen.

MARKET INDEXES OF THE COMPOSITE TYPE

The chief purpose for which indexes of the composite type are now constructed is that of evaluating the market for a specific commodity or service. The limitations of the simple market barometers make necessary the construction of indexes of this more complicated variety. The two principal steps to be taken in the construction of a composite market index are: (1) an enumeration and evaluation of the various factors that determine the market either for a specific commodity or for products in general; and (2) the combination of the more important factors into a market index.

In the process of selecting and appraising the factors that are to be combined into a composite index one should keep in mind the three conditions without which no market can exist. First, there must be people. Secondly, the people must possess the funds to enable them to buy. Finally, those with power to buy must be inclined to use that power in a specific direction. Willingness to buy is the necessary complement of ability to buy, if demand is to become effective.

FACTORS USED IN THE APPRAISAL OF MARKETS

Population.—At the time of the 1930 census there were more than 122,000,000 persons in this country scattered over 3,073 counties in varying degrees of density with 75 percent of the population concentrated in 28 percent of the counties.[4] In an earlier stage of our economic development, when the vast majority of the population were engaged in agricultural pursuits, the number of people provided a fairly reliable index to the market in a given area.

> With increasing competition for the consumer's dollar, not only among producers of similar commodities but also among producers of utterly unlike kinds of things such as furniture and automobiles, the market analysts discovered that population alone did not furnish a usable basis for estimating the consuming power of different sections of the country.[5]

The population factor quite obviously fulfills the first section of the threefold condition set forth above. It tells where the people are, but nothing as to their ability to buy or their desire to buy. To make the population factor more selective, some companies have eliminated certain groups as being of little or no significance as far as the sale of their particular product is concerned. This amounts to the introduction of additional factors. For example, if a company employs native white population as the basis of market estimates, it has actually used the three factors: population, nativity, and color.

There is a real danger in the elimination of any segment of the population purely on *a priori* grounds. In some instances company officials have been reluctant to admit the importance of certain types of customers, but this attitude does not become the market analyst. In cases of doubt empirical tests should be made before any important population group is eliminated.

Number of income tax returns.—This factor is a rather exclusive measure of people's ability to buy. It has been called the qualitative factor, as contrasted with the quantitative factor of population. Its efficacy, however, on this score is subject to the fiat of the United States Congress, which controls the regulations under which returns

[4] Based on the U. S., Bureau of the Census, *Census of Population,* 1930.

[5] Charles B. Elliot, *An Aid for Analyzing Markets in Connecticut,* U. S. Bureau of Foreign and Domestic Commerce, 1932.

of the taxpayer are made. Moreover, income data underemphasize the importance of the rural and small-town communities, where much of the income is received in kind.

For a commodity or service whose purchase is confined very definitely to persons of considerable wealth, income-tax data provide the means of securing the necessary exclusiveness. The tardiness that characterizes the publication of income data, the changes that Congress writes into the income tax law, and the fluctuations in the general price level are factors tending to decrease the effectiveness of incomes as an exclusive measure of the ability to buy.

Number of retail outlets.—The number of retail stores provides a very rough measure of the number of consumers and of their willingness to buy. In order that it might serve as an accurate measure, we should have to assume that both the average number of people per store and the average sales per store remained constant from one market area to another. Since neither of these assumptions is true, the margin of error involved in using the number of retail outlets as a market indicator may be considerable.

The logical application for any variable that is so directly connected with retail selling is for estimating sales to retailers rather than to consumers. Various types of store equipment might be cited as an example. In any case, the index is quantitative rather than qualitative. The qualitative element might, however, be introduced if the stores are subdivided into classes according to the volume of business done. Occasionally a classification by type of outlet will provide the analyst with a more selective group for his specific product.

Value of retail sales.—The advantages and the limitations of total retail sales as an index of the simple type have already received extended treatment. The present discussion is concerned with the use of retail sales as the purchasing-power factor in the construction of a specific composite index. The form in which the series should be expressed for this purpose will also be considered.

There is considerable argument and no little misunderstanding among those engaged in market research concerning whether total retail sales or per capita retail sales furnish the better basis for comparing sales territories. For some purposes, as in a correlation study between retail sales and some other market factor, one can remove the influence of population on each variable by placing each of the series on a per capita basis. In the absence of this correction, spuriously high correlation would usually be obtained between two market series. The quantitative influence exerted by population would tend to produce agreement even where none existed on the per capita basis.

For purposes other than the specific one mentioned there would seem to be a real advantage in leaving retail sales in total form. The aggregate is an unadulterated concept that shows quite accurately what volume of business is available and where it is to be found, whereas any per capita retail sales figure is likely to be a statistical hybrid. The source of this hybridism comes from the fact that cities, counties, trading areas, and so forth, are not self-contained economic units. City limits, county lines, and even the boundaries of trading areas are crossed and recrossed in daily business transactions. For example, the total retail sales of New York City include sales made to visitors from all parts of the world, yet the divisor is limited to the number of persons residing within the city limits. The result is a hybrid that is misleadingly high for New York (or for any other metropolitan community) and misleadingly low for the small towns and the country regions.

Automobile registrations.—Automobile registration data are an obvious ingredient for the construction of an index to measure sales potentials of automobile equipment. For various complementary goods, such as camp stoves, cameras, tents, and so forth, the registration series would provide a desirable, though less obvious, component.

Among the more important advantages possessed by the series are: the ease with which the data are obtainable, the timeliness of these data, and the opportunities offered the analyst through break-downs of the series by makes and types of cars to adapt the series to his specific need and make his index more selective. The unclassified registration data are usually too inclusive as an index to purchasing power, especially in rural communities where persons of the lowest income level may own an ancient automobile as their only piece of property. On the other hand, the difficulties and the expense of car ownership in metropolitan areas of our large cities make the registration series too exclusive as a test of purchasing power. At best, we may consider the index as setting the upper limit of the market for commodities and services that are directly related to the use of the motor car. In this sense it indicates demand or willingness to buy, rather than general purchasing power.

Registration figures have been analyzed into percentage form by the Bureau of Foreign and Domestic Commerce and set forth as the automobile appliance index for various cities and counties of the United States. The index appears in the same series of bulletins that contain the retail sales index.

Houses wired for electricity.—The number of houses wired for electricity sets the upper limit of the market for all kinds of electrical appliances used in the home. The increased development of water power and the wider distribution of transmission lines have brought electrical service into homes of many low-income receivers. Consequently, a list of wired homes is no longer the "bluebook" of purchasing power that it once was. Other factors, such as the wide variation in electrical rates, the local competition offered by gas for cooking and heating purposes, and the proximity to transmission lines, decrease the usefulness of the series both as a measure of general purchasing power and as an index to the potential sales of electrical equipment. The series resembles automobile registrations in that its real effectiveness is obtained in combination with some other factor or factors to indicate the market for certain specific products requiring the consumption of electrical current.

Houses equipped for gas.—Most of what has been said in the preceding section concerning data on number of houses wired for electricity might be appropriately repeated with respect to houses equipped for gas. Marketing men consider both these indexes of sufficient importance to warrant their inclusion along with the automotive appliance index in the series of bulletins published by the Department of Commerce under the general title "Aids for Analyzing Markets."

Climatic conditions.—Persons engaged in agricultural research and that phase of general economic research that deals with the forecasting of prices have given weather conditions a position of first importance. Those engaged in the measurement of markets, however, have not appreciated sufficiently the importance of weather as a factor in determining the sales for a very considerable group of products. The quality and type of fuel consumed, the quantity and type of clothing worn,

me of the foods, and many of the articles of common use are in-
ienced by weather conditions.

Occasionally *a priori* reasoning is sufficient to indicate the desir-
ility of including rainfall and temperature data in estimating the
tential sales of a particular product. Correlation analysis provides
empirical test of association that is particularly appropriate in
termining the effect of weather on sales. The hazard of circular
asoning is not present, since weather is so obviously independent
at there can be little question of its being the causal factor if a high
gree of association can be established. The fact that data pertain-
g to weather conditions are usually complete and up to date is an
ditional boon to anyone desiring to use this factor as one of the
riables in a correlation analysis.

Value of product series.—For measuring the potential market of
ecific geographical areas in which certain industries are dominant,
e value-of-products series offer a logical component for a market
dex. The value series are most effective when used as barometers for
e sale of industrial products. The demand for consumers' goods
pends less on value of products than on the number of wage earners
d the total wages paid. The degree to which the value of products
associated with the number of wage earners and the total wages paid
pends primarily upon the extent to which machinery is used in the
oductive process.

The assumption of an association between the value of products
d the potential sales of goods is obviously weak unless one includes
ther large geographical areas. It is only necessary to compare the
iying power of a factory town or of a fishing village with that of a
gh-class residential community in which industrial activities are
her excluded or restricted to appreciate the danger of using the
lue series to appraise small communities. If the index is to be applied
a consumers' good, the areas of comparison must be large enough
r both industrial and residential communities to be included. The
lue of goods produced and the value of those consumed might then
ow reasonably high correlation.

Some of the specific value series that one might use, granting the
nitations and safeguards mentioned above, are: value of manu-
ctured products, value added by manufacture, value of farm crops,
lue of mineral products, and value of fishery products.

Banking and financial series.—Banking and financial series may be conveniently grouped into three categories. The first includes the purely quantitative series pertaining to the numbers of financial institutions. An enumeration of the banks, investment houses, trust companies, insurance companies, brokerage houses, and so forth, within each of a series of territories serves fairly well as an index for certain types of producers' goods, such as tabulating and calculating equipment and office supplies of various kinds. As an index, however, for consumers' goods there is little one can say in favor of this category of financial series. At best these data show where money is kept, which may be quite different from where it is spent.

The second category emphasizes persons rather than institutions. The number of bank depositors, of stockholders, of policy holders, and so forth belong here. These are fairly good indexes of purchasing power, but they are hardly safe guides to follow in estimating effective demand for consumers' goods. They show where the legal claims to funds reside, but this is not the equivalent of showing where the money is spent. The latter is the important thing from the point of view of the market for goods.

Into the third category go the various value series such as volume of bank deposits, debits to individual accounts, bank clearings, value of life insurance in force, and new-paid-for life insurance. Since the value series are quite sensitive to change, they are used primarily as dynamic barometers of general business conditions rather than as components of indexes to the sale of any specific product.

Building series.—Most of the series under this heading have their greatest usefulness to companies whose products are used in the building industry. The series most frequently used are: number of building permits, volume of building contracts, number of vacancies, number of leases, and volume of real estate sales. The first two series are rather sensitive barometers to the sale of all kinds of building materials, supplies, and equipment. The sale of these products is a logical sequel to the issuance of building permits and the letting of contracts to build. The second two series (vacancies and leases) stand in a reciprocal relationship to each other. Declining vacancies and increasing number of leases indicate a growing demand for space which sooner or later will express itself in new buildings. Real estate sales are included, since preparations for buildings usually go hand-in-hand with the purchase of real estate. Even though the property is already improved, alterations and additions are frequently made at the time of purchase. This is likewise true in the signing of new leases.

Miscellaneous series.—The preceding catalogue of market factors would be deficient without the inclusion of such series as department store sales, mail order sales, chain store sales, home telephones, and magazine circulation. The data for each of these series can be easily obtained and are always current.

The three sales series in combination provide a fair basis of estimating the relative strength of territories during the intercensal period. The tendency for department stores to be concentrated in the large cities results in an undue emphasis upon urban buying. Since mail order sales, however, emphasize the rural areas the two series tend to complement each other. Whereas chain stores are fairly well distributed between urban and rural sections, they are rather overweighted with low-cost and small-item merchandise.

The home telephone series has frequently been used to indicate the presence of persons with better-than-average purchasing ability. The general reliability of the series as an index is materially diminished by the unequal importance attached to home telephones in rural and in urban areas. The nearness of one's neighbors, the use of apartment house central switchboards, and the convenience of public telephones tend to place the home phone for a city dweller in the comfort or even luxury class, whereas to the rural inhabitant living miles from town a home telephone is almost a necessity. Moreover, the density of telephone homes, even in cities of equal purchasing power, tends to vary considerably. The most serious limitation, however, is the logical difficulty of establishing any *a priori* connection between the possession of a home telephone and the purchase of any particular commodity or service. Only under the special circumstance in which a seller makes exclusive use of the telephone for establishing sales contacts would there exist a direct and causal relationship.

Magazine-circulation data, especially those of magazines having national circulation, have often been used as market indexes. Special merit has frequently been claimed for composites of circulation data representing magazines ranging from the high-priced periodicals to the low-priced popular publications. An obvious weakness of any index that assumes an ability to read the English language is its tendency to underestimate demand in non-English speaking communities and in those containing a large percentage of illiteracy. Other less obvious limitations of a circulation index are: the tendency of some publishers to force circulation for advertising reasons, the padding of reported circulation, and the differences in reading habits of people in different sections of the country. Circulation data have been used as a basis both in distributing advertising costs to market areas and in establishing sales quotas. The first use finds a logical justification, provided the data used pertain to those magazines in which the company does its advertising. The second use is less easily justified. To establish quotas on the basis of magazine circulation is to ignore the effect of newspaper and outdoor advertising and to overlook several other very important variables, such as the relative opportunity in different areas for the sale of the product and the relative capacities of members of the sales organization to make sales.

SPECIFIC GUIDES FOR SELECTING MARKET INDEX SERIES

In the selection of market index series it is well to keep in mind the three conditions previously mentioned as necessary for the existence of a market, namely, people, purchasing power, and a desire to purchase. The market index should so far as possible include factors that give weight to each of these major conditions. Aside from this general injunction there are a number of specific points that might be set down as worthy of attention. As regards the data themselves the following constitute a check list of desirable characteristics: (1) accuracy, (2) recency, (3) completeness, (4) comparability, (5) continuity, (6) relevancy, and (7) inclusiveness.

The first of the above-mentioned characteristics is not likely to cause trouble for those who have had first-hand experience in the collection of statistical data. Such persons are likely to be much more critical than those lacking this experience. Recency of the data is obviously important in a dynamic society where market areas are continually changing their relative importance. Completeness requires investigation, since some series are not reported for all sections of the country. Comparability may be lacking in the series, either because the number of reporting firms has changed from time to time or because the definition of the unit has not been the same in different sections of the reporting area. Continuity is obviously important in keeping the market index itself comparable over a period of time. If any series has been discontinued or is likely to be discontinued, much of the effectiveness of the comparison is lost. Relevancy of the data pertains particularly to the purpose of the index. If the index is to measure the market for some specific company or commodity, each series should bear some direct relationship to the company's sales or to the sales of the specific product. Inclusiveness as the last-mentioned characteristic is one of degree. Some market series are too inclusive in that they embrace persons who are neither present nor potential users of a product. Others are too exclusive and rule out many actual and potential buyers. The aim of the analyst in selecting the component series of the index is to balance exclusiveness against inclusiveness so that non-users will be eliminated without ruling out any substantial section of either the present or the potential market.

As a safeguard against omitting or overlooking any important statistical series a check list of all those that either have been or may be used as market indicators can easily be prepared. The factors discussed in the preceding sections might well provide the starting point, and the list could be classified and extended to accommodate other series which have not been mentioned or discussed.

A final consideration of considerable importance is the estimate of cost. If the market analyst is to avoid the painful experience of committing himself beyond his resources, he will carefully estimate in advance the expense of collecting the data and of compiling and keeping the market index up to date.

CORRELATION ANALYSIS AS AN AID IN THE SELECTION OF MARKET FACTORS

Correlation analysis is one of the most useful, as well as the most abused, of statistical techniques. In the words of Bowley, it is an instrument of "elegance and power if delicately handled and warily interpreted." Its use for the selection of market indexes is legitimate, provided the following conditions have been observed. First, no two series should be correlated without first removing, as far as possible, the spurious effect which a common third factor may exert upon the results. Secondly, no series should be selected solely on the basis of a high correlation coefficient. Finally, no series should be used as a test for the selection of market indexes, unless its use can be defended on *a priori* grounds. Each of these conditions deserves elaboration.

The first condition springs from the oft-repeated error of overlooking the possible spurious effect of a common third factor in correlating sales data. The common influence of population, for example, would tend to produce fairly high positive correlation between the sales of such diverse products as bread and diamonds. If both series were first placed on a per capita basis, there is no reason to suppose that any significant relationship would appear. If anything the relationship might be inverse, since the wealthy people who can afford diamonds would tend to substitute luxury foods for the staff of life.

The second condition for the legitimate appiication of correlation is perfectly general and would apply to any field of inquiry. Correlation technique is simply a tool to lend precision to the analyst's processes of reasoning, and unless some logical explanation can be found for a high correlation coefficient there is probably something spurious about the association, and one should be most chary in using the results.

The third condition is important, because the existence of a test series is essential in selecting market factors. The test series in every case is made the dependent variable and paired either successively or simultaneously with a number of other variables. Those showing the highest degree of association are then chosen as the significant factors for the construction of a composite market index. As previously pointed out, the sales of any individual company are subject to forces peculiar to that company's sales organization and are therefore lacking those characteristics required of a true test series. This deficiency tends to be overcome as we consolidate the sales experiences of a number of companies competing with one another within each market area. For example, the per capita data derived from total retail sales would be the net resultant of the experiences of a number of companies, so that the weak spots in the sales organizations of some companies would tend to cancel the particularly strong sections of others, leaving their combined performance representing approximately what is desired of a test series.[6]

[6] That all companies selling a particular product and competing with one another might have weak spots within the same market area is a condition much less likely to occur than any theoretical probability ratio would indicate, simply because the stron sections of a given sales distribution are more likely to occur where competition is weal

METHODS OF COMBINING MARKET FACTORS

As soon as the market factors have been chosen, the task of combining them into some sort of composite index begins. For this step of the analysis each factor must first be expressed in a form appropriate for the taking of an average or for the computation of a total. Secondly, the weights must be assigned to the various component series so that each will exercise an influence on the composite index in proportion to its importance. Finally, the weights are applied, and through either an averaging or a summation process the composite index is derived.

Two principal methods are available for putting the component series into appropriate form. The first method requires that the data for the various geographical units of the market be expressed as percentages to some form of average, which is usually either the arithmetic mean or the median. Each percentage thus computed will be either greater or less than 100 percent, depending upon whether or not the particular unit of the market is above or below the average of all the units.

The second method also makes use of percentages, but substitutes the total of all market units as the common divisor in place of the average. Consequently, each market area is shown as a certain percentage of the total, and when all the percentages relating to the market units have been added, their sum is equal to 100 percent.

Although each method of reducing the data to comparable terms has its proponents, there would seem to be little to choose between them. The reduction of all observations to percentages of the total is probably easier to understand and interpret, but if the geographical unit of comparison is small, such as the city or the county, the computation of the component percentages may have to be carried to a half dozen places beyond the decimal in order to obtain the necessary number of significant figures.

The second step in constructing the composite is the assignment of weights. Here we find three methods in current use. First, the weights may be guessed. One may assume, however, that the guessing is intelligent, that is, based on wide experience and broad general knowledge of the way in which each series tends to reflect sales opportunities.

The second method is trial-and-error. It consists in trying several different combinations of weights, until the weighted composite gives the best approximation of the variable that was employed as the test series.

The third method is provided by partial correlation, a statistical technique that apportions the weights empirically. The first person to employ this more technical approach was L. D. H. Weld, research director of McCann-Erickson Company. Whereas the mathematical basis of the technique is somewhat involved, the concept itself is relatively simple. We shall assume that the sales of a particular product are conditioned by three principal factors. It is the purpose of partial correlation analysis to provide estimates of the degree of relationship between sales as the dependent variable (usually on a per capita basis) and each of the three independent variables when the influences exerted by the other two are held constant. The abstract numerical values that express these degrees of relationship are the coefficients of partial correlation. Each coefficient is assumed to express a pure relationship in the sense that it indicates the importance of a given factor after the disturbing influences exerted by the others have been removed. Hence, they provide logical weights to be applied to their respective variables in deriving the composite index.

MISCELLANEOUS EXAMPLES OF COMPOSITE MARKET INDEXES

The limitations of space do not permit an extended and detailed treatment of each of the various indexes that have been selected as examples of the composite type. The references given in the footnotes, however, will enable those having a special interest to obtain whatever details they desire.

H. G. Weaver's Index of Purchasing Power.—One of the first composite market indexes to receive wide publicity was developed by H. G. Weaver, director of customer research for General Motors.[7] Mr. Weaver's original purpose was to compile an index that could be used in distributing advertising and other sales effort in the marketing of automobiles. The inquiry, however, became sufficiently extensive to produce a general index which, in the words of its author, was "so basic in its nature that it may be used as a foundation upon which to

[7] See *Harvard Business Review,* Vol. IV (No. 2, April, 1926).

build sales quotas for practically all kinds of consumer merchandise."

Four statistical series were employed, in which the data by states were converted into percentages of the total for the entire country. The four component series were: value of products, number of retail outlets, population, and the number of income tax returns. The method of trial-and-error was used to develop formulas appropriate for each of the four homogeneous groups into which the forty-eight states were divided. The test of appropriateness in each instance was the income by states over the twelve years preceding. Weights were applied to the component series, and by a process of juggling, a combination of weights was finally discovered that resulted in an index approximating the test series. After the most effective formula was found for a given state, it was applied to the counties within the state. The composite index was published as a series of relatives showing not only what proportion each state bore to the total national market but also what proportion each county bore to the state in which it was located.

The author of the index set it forth disclaiming all pretense of having compiled a perfect indicator of purchasing power. After naming a number of its limitations, chief of which was its failure to reflect current conditions, he somewhat apologetically said,

> A limited knowledge of mathematical processes has made it necessary for the writer to avoid the more complicated statistical processes, and while it is felt that the development of the basic method could not have been accomplished through the purely scientific approach, the value of mathematical procedure is fully recognized, and it is hoped that these studies may be pursued by others who are more fortunately equipped with the tools of the statistician.[8]

Nelson H. Seubert's Indexes of Demand by Commodity Classes.— Two years after H. G. Weaver's Index of Purchasing Power appeared, Nelson H. Seubert [9] published his six series of indexes purporting to show the relative demand for commodities under each of six major categories. Population and the number of income tax returns were the only factors used in constructing each of the six indexes. Population was called the "quantity factor," and the number of income tax returns the "quality factor." A "luxury factor," consisting of incomes in excess of $10,000, was introduced and combined with population to provide the index for the very exclusive luxury class of goods.

[8] *Ibid.* [9] Nelson H. Seubert, *Editor and Publisher,* Vol. LXI (August, 18), 1928.

The data for each geographical unit were first expressed as percentages of the United States total. The percentages were then weighted and combined, the weights being quite arbitrarily chosen according to the particular commodity class that was being considered. The six classes and the weights assigned to each factor were as follows:

Class 1. Cheap necessities and bulk staples. Quantity factor, 90 percent; quality factor, 10 percent.

Class 2. Moderate-priced necessities and packaged staples. Quantity factor, 70 percent; quality factor, 30 percent.

Class 3. Quality-priced necessities and staples together with cheap luxuries and low-priced nonstaples. Quantity factor, 50 percent; quality factor, 50 percent.

Class 4. Fancy-priced necessities and staples together with moderate-priced luxuries and nonstaples. Quantity factor, 30 percent; quality factor, 70 percent.

Class 5. Quality-priced luxuries and nonstaples. Quantity factor, 10 percent, quality factor, 90 percent.

Class 6. Fancy-priced exclusive luxuries of high unit value. Quantity factor, 10 percent; exclusive luxury factor, 90 percent.

If *a priori* reasoning should prove inadequate for deciding into which of the six classes a given product should be placed, the author recommended the use of an empirical test. This consisted in making a comparison of the percentage distribution of the particular company's sales with each of the six sets of indexes and selecting as appropriate the class index in which the differences were found to be least.

Any of the six indexes could be readily adapted to the market areas of a given company, since each index was available by cities, counties, states, and even retail shopping areas, the last-named unit being defined in accordance with the data set forth by J. Walter Thompson Company in *Retail Shopping Areas*. Unless a company had national distribution, however, the indexes would not be appropriate. To adjust the indexes so as to make them applicable to a smaller market area would involve the recomputation of the whole index series.

Edmond E. Lincoln's Index of Reasonable Sales Expectation.—In the same year that Nelson H. Seubert's indexes appeared, Edmond E. Lincoln who was then economist for the International Telephone and Telegraph Corporation published an index designed to measure the current wholesale market for electrical supplies. For this purpose he divided such economic factors as he considered important into two categories: (1) basic factors and (2) variable factors.

The first group consisted of nine factors that were considered fundamental and were relatively stable over a period of time. The second group consisted of three factors, all of which were quite sensitive to change. Since current data were available on the second group, a combination of the two groups resulted in keeping the composite index up to date. Through the interplay of personal judgment and trial-and-error testing, the following system of weights was developed for each group. In the final composite the group of basic factors was given twice the weight allowed to the variable group.

TABLE 35

FACTORS COMPRISING THE INDEX OF REASONABLE SALES EXPECTATION

Basic Factors

	Weight
Urban white population	20
Population in territories served by central stations	20
Value of production added by manufacture	10
Central station capacity	15
Residence meters	5
Total horsepower of industrial plants	10
Capitalization of industrial plants manufacturing electrical material or products incorporating electrical material	10
Number of telephone stations now owned by Bell System	5
Railroad mileage and passenger cars	5
	100

Variable Factors

Building permits as compiled by Bradstreet's	50
Production of electrical energy	25
Bank debits outside New York	25
	100

From the final composite index showing reasonable sales expectation for each of its 18 sales districts the management of the International Telephone and Telegraph Company was able to make a number of illuminating comparisons. To facilitate the drawing of conclusions, it placed in adjacent columns the following information: reasonable expectation based on the composite index, distribution estimates based solely on population, distribution estimates of competitors' business, actual distribution of the company's sales over the two preceding years, and finally, the actual distribution of profits, both gross and net, over the two preceding years.

District C will serve to illustrate the form of the information as well as the use which management was able to make of it. The composite index indicated that 10 percent of the total national sales was quite within reason for this district, yet the company was getting only 6.8 percent of its business there. The district's population was such that it should have had 9.1 percent of the total sales. Competitors, it was estimated, were getting 7.7 percent of their business out of the district. Apparently something was wrong with the company as far as District C was concerned.

An investigation showed that the territory had just what the market index had indicated—a market that was only partially developed. Competitors had already seized the opportunity and were rapidly developing the territory. It was decided that the company should open new branches in that district and aggressively go after the business that was there.

Fuller Brush Company's Index of Buying Habits.—Messrs. Everett R. and Philip W. Smith, of the Fuller Brush Company, anticipated the index of retail sales by half a decade in the construction of an index based upon sales experiences of a small group of ten companies. Whereas previously constructed indexes were based on the assumption that a heterogeneous group of factors combined into a composite provided the best estimate of what people might reasonably be expected to buy, the Smiths cut the Gordian knot by setting out to determine the actual spending habits. To this end they secured the cooperation of nine other companies, all of which were leaders in their respective fields. The ten companies agreed to pool their sales information and to break down their total sales by territories, using percentages rather than actual values for this purpose. From these percentages the clearing house prepared national and local averages so that each of the collaborating companies was able to appraise its own percentage of sales in a given territory with that secured by the group. The requirements for membership in the group were as follows: (1) the product had to be universally in use in every home, as far as possible; (2) the product had to be universally desirable on the part of the consumer; (3) the product had to have national distribution and finally, (4) it had to fall within a low and fairly steady price range. The maximum price was set at five dollars.

Since the information on sales distribution was gathered quarterly, the index reflected currently the actual buying habits of people in various parts of the country. Shifts in the relative positions of sales areas and trends could be detected quickly enough to enable management to plan more effectively. Concerning this particular virtue of the index Everett Smith, one of its coauthors, says,

> We have found in our experience and with our group of companies that a period of two years makes such a radical change that if a company really has thorough distribution, they may be led badly astray on their sales quota. The watching of trends in our sales figures and in the quotas of the group has been particularly instructive. Of course, unless the figures are quite current, the trend cannot be watched except over a long period of years and in that case they are not particularly useful today.[10]

The McCann Index.—The General Market Index[11] prepared by the director of research of McCann-Erickson, Inc., represents a departure from the beaten trail more in the methods of analysis than in the general character of the index. Dr. L. D. H. Weld, with the aid of his assistant, Miss Margaret Booss, employed correlation technique both for the selection of the factors and for weighting them in compiling the composite. The steps they took can be only briefly outlined here.

First, a number of factors which they considered important were correlated individually with estimated incomes by states, and the most important of these (those showing the highest correlation) were selected for the variables in a multiple correlation analysis. This enabled the investigators to assign weights to the various series in proportion to the part that each variable played when all were considered simultaneously. The weights were applied and a composite index found.

The second step consisted of constructing the composite index on a county basis for Pennsylvania. It was assumed that if the combination of factors found to reflect differences in state incomes also accurately reflected differences in retail sales in Pennsylvania (the only state for which retail sales data were then available), the

[10] Percival White, *Sales Quotas,* p. 32.

[11] L. D. H. Weld, *The McCann Index of General Buying Power,* Bulletin of the H. K. McCann Company, New York, 1930.

reverse situation would be equally valid, and Pennsylvania retail data could be used as a sort of proving ground for series that would measure national purchasing power. The close agreement revealed by the high coefficient of correlation demonstrated the essential validity of the assumption.

The third step represented a new start, with Pennsylvania retail sales as a measuring stick for testing the adequacy of statistical market barometers. Twenty-five additional series were selected, and the individual correlations indicated the selection of five or six for more intensive study and greater refinement of analysis. The application of partial correlation technique enabled the investigators to measure the net influence of each variable in this small select group. The partial coefficients of correlation indicated the degree of association existing between each of the selected factors and the test series when the other variables in the group were held constant. The four factors exhibiting the highest net relationship were selected for constructing the composite General Market Index. The factors selected were: number of income tax returns, number of domestic lighting customers, bank deposits, and the combined circulation of four leading magazines. Weights in proportion to the partial coefficients of correlation were assigned in the taking of the weighted average for the composite.

As tests of the composite index, two additional correlations were made, one with Pennsylvania retail sales by counties, the other with the sales of a group of nationally advertised articles by states. Since the former correlation coefficient was .85 and the latter .92, it appeared that the composite index was quite satisfactory and even better on the national scale than on the limited experimental basis.

The final step consisted in constructing the index for each of 3,073 counties in the United States. The information, kept on a card index, one card for each county, is used by the McCann Company for a number of purposes, such as the sorting of advertising media to determine which are essentially quality as opposed to quantity media, to aid in selecting the factors for determining the market for a specific product, and to aid in allocating sales pressure.

The B. B. D. O. Buying Power Index.—The advertising agency of Batten, Barton, Durstine and Osborn Company [12] also applied the correlation technique, with the retail sales data of Pennsylvania as

[12] C. F. Haring, "The B. B. D. O. Buying Power Index," *Advertising and Selling*, XXII (November 9, 1933), 16–17.

the test series. Starting with the assumption that a five-year average of retail sales by counties would eliminate irregularities due to local booms and depressions, the company reduced the average sales by counties to percentages of the state's total and ran correlations with each of twenty market factors selected for the test. An unweighted average of the following three factors was finally chosen as that combination resulting in the closest correlation (correlation coefficient was .997): population, number of income tax returns, and number of retail outlets. These three factors became the B. B. D. O. formula for sales opportunity—"people with money—with places to spend it."

The remarkably close correlation between the unweighted average of the three market factors and the Pennsylvania retail sales gave the company confidence in the applicability of the formula to the counties of other states in which no retail sales data were at that time available. The application of the formula resulted in a B. B. D. O. index for each of the 3,073 counties in the United States. Since the total sales opportunity for the country at large was the base, or 100 percent, each county index showed what proportion of the country's total sales a company having national distribution could reasonably expect that particular county to give. For example, the B. B. D. O. index of .145 for Cumberland County in Maine indicated that .145 percent of the sales made nationally could be expected from that county.

Regional Trade Barometers.—Persons charged with the responsibility of directing sales and advertising efforts have long recognized the need of a dynamic type of buying power index—one that will reflect changes in the current business situation as shown by people's overt acts of buying and at the same time be sufficiently specific as to geographical regions to enable management to allocate selling effort. The *Regional Trade Barometers* [13] prepared by Dr. L. D. H. Weld and published currently in ***Dun and Bradstreet Monthly Review*** represent a distinctive contribution in this direction. These new barometers combine the virtue of currency that characterizes various indexes of general business activity with that of market relevancy.

The problem that Weld and his staff solved in order to obtain the new series of sensitive trade barometers fall under three headings: (1) problems associated with the delineation of the districts or regions; (2) problems associated with the selection of the factors; and

[13] L. D. H. Weld, *Regional Trade Barometers*, reprinted from *Dun and Bradstreet Monthly Review*, Sept., 1936.

(3) problems concerned with the combination of factors into an index.

In defining the 29 geographical regions into which the United States was divided, the authors of the index sought to give effect to such factors as the sales districts and trading areas used by many large companies, the availability of the data, and the homogeneity of economic conditions within each geographical region. For practical purposes the state lines were followed as much as possible, and the boundaries of the Federal Reserve districts were respected, with very few exceptions.

The task of selecting the factors to be combined was made more difficult because of the limited number of series meeting the requirements. The data of any series used had to be not only reliable but also quickly available, since timeliness was regarded as a most desirable quality in the index. Moreover, the series had to be sensitive to business changes and representative of the flow of trade as opposed to industrial production. After much experimentation, the following four series were selected: bank debits, department store sales, new car sales, and life insurance sales.

The four series listed above were weighted and combined into a single index for each geographical region and for the country as a whole. The seasonal variation was left in each of the component series, but it was removed later in a single operation by applying the twelve-month moving average method to the composite. No attempt was made to correct for trend, since the geographical differences in trend were considered to be a significant feature of the indexes. Each of the 29 indexes begins with January, 1928, and is published currently in *Dun and Bradstreet Monthly Review,* with the monthly average for the five-year period 1928–32 as base.

Indexes of this dynamic type help to fill one of the long-standing gaps in the marketing executive's statistical equipment. The adjustment of current selling activities to current sales quotas, the allocation of advertising, and the making of sales forecasts by territories are among the more important uses to which the *Regional Trade Barometers* may be put.

APPRAISAL OF MARKET INDEXES

The inauguration of a regular United States census of business has resulted in less need for private agencies to undertake the construction of market indexes. This is particularly true of indexes of the general market type, since the Retail Sales Index of the Bureau of Foreign and Domestic Commerce probably measures the relative strength of markets for goods in general with a greater degree of accuracy than that secured in indexes that private agencies have constructed.

In the field of specific-market indexes there is as great need as ever for the compilation and combination of statistical series that will give effect to the circumstances peculiar to the marketing of particular products. The naïve acceptance and unsupported use of any general market index to allocate sales effort for a specific product is gradually becoming less common. Critics have rather effectively demonstrated the danger of accepting the sanguine claims of publishers regarding the general applicability of certain indexes. Unfortunately the tests that have been made to disprove these rather exaggerated claims have included other indexes whose authors never intended that they should be used for specific purposes unless supplemented by other series.

Lyndon O. Brown [14] has made a rather comprehensive statistical appraisal of the various methods of constructing market indexes. His tests of accuracy were applied to ten methods with the actual sales distribution of twelve products ranging from shoes to automobiles serving as the basis of appraisal. The results of the tests indicated that most of the general market indexes were inaccurate when applied to specific products. The multiple correlation technique, as a method of distributing sales by territories, was found to be distinctly superior to any of the other methods tested.

[14] Lyndon O. Brown, "Quantitative Market Analysis Methods," *Harvard Business Review*, Autumn Number, 1937.

CHAPTER XV

Combination and Application of Analyses

ANALYSIS, planning, and checking constitute the three major steps in controlling the operations of the business enterprise. The preceding chapters have dealt primarily with the analytical processes as these apply to the control of sales. The present chapter deals with planning and checking as these activities are related to analysis.

INTERRELATION OF PLANNING AND ANALYSIS

Sales plans are to the sales manager what blueprints and specifications are to the engineer. They give point to all the previous analytical soundings, testings, and borings made upon sales, costs, and markets in that they combine and coördinate the results into a systematic program against which subsequent performance may be checked. Any serious discrepancy that may occur between plans and performance calls for further analysis to reveal causes and further planning to correct the deficiency. Hence, the process of control is something of a spiral that begins with the analysis of a body of data and extends upward through planning and checking only to return at a more advanced point to the analytical stage for additional material to be used in the revision of plans and the correction of defects.

SPECIFIC ASPECTS OF SALES PLANNING

One of the greatest benefits to be derived from the formulation of sales plans and the general budgetary procedure is the need for taking thought, and the management becomes acutely aware of this as soon as it attempts to establish standards of operation. The conflicts of personal interests and of impersonal statistics cannot be left to the healing influence of time. They must be settled in an orderly manner in advance of experience, and it may be safely assumed that the difficulty of planning is more than compensated for by the quality of the decisions that grow out of the orderly consideration of many points of view.

As applied to the sales department, planning serves the following four major functions: (1) it provides for the combination of analyses into an estimate of sales high enough to challenge the best efforts of all those connected with the selling of goods and yet low enough to be achieved; (2) estimated sales are apportioned by time periods (usually the month) so that performance can be checked at frequent intervals; (3) responsibility is allocated within the sales department so that each member from the salesmanager down to the salesman in the field has his appointed task to do; and (4) adjustment of conflicts is made easier if and when the sales department and some other major functional division fail to synchronize their activities.

COMBINING SALES ESTIMATES

Chapters III–VII of this study dealt specifically with the analysis of sales records, and the term "probable sales" was coined in order to designate any estimate based solely on the company's previous experience as revealed through the sales journal. Largely to check experience against opportunity and to reveal sources of income not previously explored, the market was made the subject of analysis in Chapters VIII–XIV. Here the term "potential sales" was used to designate the estimate of what could be sold in any given market area within any allotted period of time. Any considerable discrepancy between probable sales and potential sales constitutes a problem in planning. Qualitative rather than quantitative considerations usually dominate in bringing the two estimates of sales into some reasonable and workable relationship. The final estimate that is incorporated into the general budget will usually represent a compromise between the two.

Comparison and compromise assume that the two estimates of sales are in identical terms. Probable sales, however, are usually in concrete terms (dollar values or number of units of the product), whereas potential sales often take the form of a distributive market index. The latter shows what proportion of the total business each of a series of territories can be expected to provide. These proportions can be readily converted into concrete terms, provided an estimate is available of the total potential sales. When this information is not at hand, a fairly accurate estimate of the company's ideal sales volume may be developed from a detailed study of some specific section of its market. The first step consists in selecting that market area which fulfills all reasonable expectations for efficient distribution. The actual sales within such area may then be taken as a standard from which an estimate of potential sales for each of the other territories and for the market as a whole may be made. The following proportion is the general form of the series of proportions that may be set up: index of model sales area is to the index of sales area X as the actual sales of model area are to estimated sales of area X.

In using the market index in the first part of the proportion one must place great confidence in its accuracy and general fairness. Moreover, if the actual sales in any territory are to be used as a standard to gauge potential sales in the less efficient areas one must assume a direct positive relationship between current selling efficiency and the opportunity for future sales—a condition that would be true only of merchandise subject to repeat orders. If the product is of such durable nature that its sale puts the purchaser out of the market for an indefinitely long period, a detailed analysis might be made of some specific section of the distribution area, and from the single sales potential thus developed others could be estimated by applying a series of proportions similar to that illustrated above. The proportion as modified would be as follows: index of analyzed sales area is to the index of sales area X as the potential sales of analyzed area are to the potential sales of area X.

PLANNING THE SALES BY TIME PERIODS

The information upon which a distribution of expected sales by time periods can be made is to be found in the results of the dynamic analysis of sales records. Chapters VI and VII dealt with the definition, measurement, and combination of the four categories of force that influence series ordered in time. Month-by-month estimates of sales are obtained by projecting the results of the dynamic analysis From such estimates a series of percentages may be easily computed, showing what proportion of the yearly sales may safely be scheduled for each month.

The accuracy of sales estimates derived solely from a statistical analysis of sales data may be immediately challenged. The estimates may range either too high or too low, depending upon such factors as the effectiveness of previous distribution, the amount of sales effort planned, the strength of competition, the degree of saturation of the market, and the precision of the measurements themselves. Fortunately, the monthly percentages are not seriously affected by such sources of error in the estimates. In the first place, the discrepancies are likely to be in the same direction, so that the monthly proportions will tend to remain stable even when the concrete values are out of line. For example, a dynamic analysis of previous sales may provide estimates of sales that supplementary analyses of the market and a consideration of sales policies may either increase or decrease considerably without affecting the percentages that can be sold each month. Secondly, errors made in estimating the percentages of total sales that can be sold each month are much less disturbing than errors in predicting the total sales figure. So long as the latter is estimated closely, the month-to-month errors tend to cancel, and on a cumulative scale they will iron themselves out completely at the end of the year.

PLANNING FOR THE DISTRIBUTION OF RESPONSIBILITY

The sales budget represents a coöperative task for which each member of the sales department must assume some definite responsibility. The assigning of this responsibility is known as sales-quota making. The quota procedure may be definitely integrated with the sales budget, or it may represent a subsidiary activity performed by the sales department quite independently from the budget system *per se*. In some instances quotas may be assigned even though no budget system is used. Logically, however, sales-quota making is an activity subsidiary to that of formulating and directing the budget. The principal function of both budgets and quotas is to make each person's responsibility definite and to coördinate the activities of everyone within the business enterprise toward the common goal of net profits.

Sometimes the members of the sales department are asked to estimate their own future sales performance, management acting in an advisory capacity to check the overzealous and to spur the indolent and the cautious. More often management is the active agent and assigns the quotas to the various selling units, subject always to the individual's acceptance and approval. Whether the general approach to quota making is "from the bottom up" or "from the top down," certain conditions or requirements may be enumerated as representing the characteristics of a good quota system. Among the more important requirements are:

1. The quota system should provide each selling unit with a goal that is equally difficult to obtain. On no other basis can the comparison of persons in terms of percentage of quota attained be justified.

2. The system should encourage balanced selling effort by breaking down each salesman's quota into a series of subdivisions representing, as it were, subquotas by products, by types of outlets, by time periods, by size of city, by customers (such as old and new), and by markets (such as the developed as against the undeveloped).

3. The cost of selling each quota is a debit to be set opposite the credit of expected sales performance. Without this simultaneous consideration of selling costs with sales quotas the setting of selling tasks can easily become enmeshed in an expensive competitive race after unprofitable sales volume.

4. The system itself should be economical to operate. Nothing can be gained from the setting of standards if the cost of their maintenance and operation exceeds any reasonable estimate of their productiveness.

5. Flexibility is needed in the quota system to provide for various unforeseen circumstances. Two territorial quotas may constitute equally difficult tasks, but suddenly they may become unequal because of some shift in local economic conditions. Also, all quotas may occasionally have to be raised or lowered, depending upon some unforeseen factor in the general business situation.

6. The success of any method of sales quota depends upon the cooperation of the members of the sales department. Unless "the knights of the road" are convinced of the essential fairness and reasonableness of the quota procedure, their discontent may lead to sabotage and a failure of the system. Technical methods have their place in the determination of sales quotas only on the assumption that they can be explained in sufficiently non-technical language to enable the salesmen to understand the basis upon which their individual tasks have been determined.

7. The follow-up that is so essential for an effective quota system is the work of the sales promotion department. By various advertising and selling aids they can assist the salesmen to achieve their quotas.

8. The check-up in which performance is matched against quota is provided through a system of reports and charts. These serve the dual purpose of keeping management informed as to the success of their sales plans and of showing each salesman the progress he is making. The salesman should know at least once a month his standing with respect to his quota and in relation to the performances of others in the sales organization. Comparison of the individual's performance with quota should be shown on a cumulative, as well as a specific, time-period basis. Temporary slumps and fortuitous increases cancel out in the cumulative sales record, so that the salesman's real productiveness is revealed.

9. A final requirement of the quota system deals with incentives. In some instances no inducement other than that provided by the administration of the quota system itself is needed. As special incentives for quota achievement some companies offer prizes. Others tie their method of compensation to the quota system. Salesmen, for example, may be paid a combination of salary and bonus, the latter graduated in terms of the percentage of quota attained. In the following schedule illustrating the graduated payments it will be seen that inducements of increasing magnitudes are offered to the salesman

TABLE 36

SCHEDULE OF BONUS PAYMENTS [1]

Percentage of Quota Attained	*Percentage of Salary Given as Bonus*	*Increments in Percentage Bonus*
70	2	
75	5	3
80	9	4
85	14	5
90	20	6
95	27	7
100	35	8
105	37.5	2.5
110	40	2.5
115 [a]	42.5 [a]	2.5 [a]

[a] For higher percentages of quota the increment in percentage bonus remains at 2.5.

---

[1] Schedule given by Carle M. Bigelow in *Economics and Mathematics of Sales*, an address delivered at 15th national convention of the Society of Industrial Engineers, Rochester, New York, Oct. 18, 1928.

until he meets his quota. Thereafter the scale becomes proportionate, and equal increments in bonus are granted for equal increments in the percentage of quota attained. This method of scaling may be modified in a number of ways so that bonus schedules may be drawn for use with each line of product and each type of customer.

METHODS USED IN ESTABLISHING SALES QUOTAS

Numerous methods of setting quotas have been used. To identify distinctly different categories of method is not easy. Evidence of the difficulty is afforded by the varying number of classifications that writers upon this subject have given. Labels such as "guesswork" and "scientific" have appeared repeatedly in the discussions of quota systems. Since there is an element of guessing in every forecast, the use of such contrasting labels is somewhat misleading. The use of the term "scientific" for any method implies that the others are somehow "unscientific." Omission of labels of this sort would seem to be the first condition for an impartial discussion. Hence, they have been expurgated from the following descriptive outline of quota methods.

Fixed-percentage method.—Perhaps the simplest method of setting sales quotas is that which applies a fixed percentage to previous performance. For example, if the sales forecast of a company for the ensuing year is 5 percent above the sales for the current year, each salesman will be expected to exceed his current year's performance by that same percentage. The principal objection to this simple procedure is that its premise is frequently false. It assumes that past performance provides an adequate standard for setting goals and appraising future performance. Under this method the mediocre and lazy salesman working in a territory of great undeveloped market resources might easily make his quota year after year, whereas the efficient and industrious salesman who is approaching the saturatior point in his territory might be actually penalized for his previous industry.

A second objection to the method is its failure to take cognizance of the varying effect of the business cycle in different sections of the market area. Some sections may be suffering severe economic depression, while others may be enjoying a fair degree of prosperity. Other dynamic factors that frequently affect the relative opportunity for selling goods are represented by the weather and the amount of advertising that is done in various sections of the market. Rarely do the dynamic market factors affect every part of the market in the same way, and yet the application of a fixed percentage assumes this uniformity.

If the reader is looking for the advantage of the method, he may find it in the simple dogmatic way in which the quota is set. No salesman can fail to understand the method, and if he is unaware of differences in sales opportunities, he may accept the procedure as an equitable one.

Quotas determined by salesmen.—A second method of quota setting places the responsibility for making the estimates upon members of the sales organization. The salesmen, in conference with the general sales manager, discuss the opportunities for the sale of goods in their respective territories. The method has very distinct advantages, especially if the informal conferences are supported by adequate statistical data from the home office showing previous performance and market possibilities. It is extremely flexible in that the quota can be tailored to suit the temperament of the individual salesman. Some salesmen are inclined toward optimism and exaggerate what they think they can do, whereas others may be unduly conservative. Some may work better if their quotas are placed beyond their reach, whereas others may get discouraged unless they can equal or exceed their quotas. Of all such personal differences cognizance may be taken in the informal conferences out of which the quotas develop.

Possibly the most distinctive advantage of the method is the opportunity it affords to impress each salesman with his own importance. The latitude he is given to make his own plans and to be responsible for them serves to secure his coöperation and best efforts toward achieving whatever quota he and his immediate superior may decide upon. Some have called it the "psychological quota" because of this feature.

There are several disadvantages, however, connected with this procedure. Anybody connected with the sales organization is likely to be an optimist. His general temperament is one that is given to the use of superlatives and an exaggerated enthusiasm. Quotas set by persons of this frame of mind are not likely to afford a reliable basis for either the planning of sales or the measurement of subsequent performance.

The above objection is partially overcome if the informal conferences are adequately supported by analyses of statistical data dealing with sales and markets. Some companies have attempted to preserve the advantages of individual quota setting by combining estimates made by men in the field with those of a technically trained staff of the home office. The former emphasize the individual and personal elements, whereas the latter place stress upon the cold and impersonal data that have been analyzed to show what can be done.

Method of pooled sales experience.—The third method of setting sales quotas makes use of what may be called "pooled sales experience." An outstanding example of this procedure is afforded by the Fuller Brush Company's Index of Buying Habits.[2] The method is based upon the reasonable hypothesis that a single company may have weak spots in its sales organization, but a combination of non-competing companies selling products of the same general price class are very unlikely to have the same combination of weaknesses. Consequently, an index formed from their pooled sales experience reveals the current potentialities in each of the various territories that are common to the coöperating companies.

The chief advantage of this method is its currency. Too often census data and market indexes are out of date by the time they are published. In this method an opportunity is afforded to obtain a current body of data respecting the relative spending proclivities of people residing in various sections of the country and possessing incomes adequate for the purchase of commodities in a particular price class.

The principal objection to the method is that it fails to take cognizance of peculiarities in the buying habits of people as respects different products. The method assumes that anyone who has expended a certain average sum for nine products (ten companies collaborated) should also be interested in the purchase of the tenth. Since buying habits with respect to different products are not likely to exhibit the same pattern of variation from territory to territory, it would be a matter of coincidence if the sales of any specific product should conform to the average of the group.

A modification of this "pooled sales" plan has been used by companies selling directly competing products of the same price class. In this modified procedure we may assume that the same buying habits condition the sales of all competitors, and the objection raised against

[2] See chap. xiv.

the plan described above is overcome. There is, however, a new objection in that we must assume that the total market area has been uniformly exploited by the various competitors. If one percent of the sales of all shoes, for example, were made in city A, we could hardly expect a particular shoe manufacturer to have the same percentage of his sales in that city unless his sales organization extended over the entire market area from which the statistical data were drawn. If the pooled sales index of non-competing products was deficient in not taking cognizance of differences in buying habits for different products this method is deficient in that it does not recognize differences in public favor and intensity of distribution for the different brands of the same product.

Quotas determined by simple market indexes.—A fourth procedure for estimating quotas is represented by the use of some simple market-index series, such as the number of automobile registrations (excellent for certain accessories), magazine circulation, the number of houses wired for electricity, the number of home telephones, the value of building contracts, the number of retail outlets, and the number of income tax returns. The uses and limitations of these and other series have been discussed in the preceding chapter. Writers upon the subject of market indexes have emphasized repeatedly that no single series will serve satisfactorily as an index to the potential sales of every commodity. The claims made by publishers of many popular magazines would lead one to believe, however, that their circulation figures were a made-to-order answer for any problem of sales allocation. Unless some direct connection between the sales of the particular product and the proposed index series is discernible, the allocation can hardly be other than arbitrary.

Quotas determined on basis of composite market indexes.—A fifth possible basis for the distribution of sales quotas is to be found in some combination of a number of market factors. Occasionally one of the published indexes of the composite type may be suitable. Some of the more widely known indexes of this category were discussed in the preceding chapter. In most instances, however, the better practice is to construct an index to meet the specific needs. The problems incident to the selection and the combination of market series have been previously reviewed.

Quotas determined by application of correlation analysis.—The use of correlation analysis in the establishment of sales quotas represents a sixth possible means for allocating responsibility for the accomplishment of the total sales budget.[3] If a single market factor provides an adequate barometer, simple correlation technique is sufficient. Usually, however, several factors must be taken into account as significant determinants of the potential sales. The problem then becomes one requiring the application of multiple correlation technique. By substituting into the multiple regression equation the known values of the independent variables, estimates of the dependent variable (potential sales by territories) can be readily computed.

In the experimental work of Lyndon O. Brown, to whose study reference has already been made,[4] correlation analysis was shown to be distinctly superior to nine other bases that he employed in making the tests. Using the sales statistics of twelve commodities, he found the mean error of all methods to be 21.5 percent, whereas the mean error of the best method (multiple correlation) was only 12.1 percent.

The importance of multiple correlation technique as applied to the problem of quota determination should not be judged by the number of companies using the procedure. Its significance springs rather from the future possibilities that quota setting affords for use of the technique. Those who are equipped to employ this precise but somewhat technical approach are certain to find opportunity for service.

PREDICTION OF DISTRIBUTION COSTS

The ultimate purpose of quota making has not been achieved unless either a larger or a more stable net profit is secured. Hence, expenses (primarily the costs of distribution) must be brought under control along with sales. The necessity of considering the two sides of the income statement simultaneously has been emphasized repeatedly. The present section deals briefly with the classification of distribution costs and with certain general methods of estimating their amount.

The costs of distribution are generally assumed to begin at the shipping door of the factory and to include all outlays incurred to convert the product into cash. With time sequence as our criterion of

[3] For an interesting application of correlation technique in quota setting see Cowan, *Sales Analysis from the Management Standpoint.*

[4] Lyndon O. Brown, "Quantitative Market Analysis Methods," *Harvard Business Review,* Autumn Number, 1937.

classification, we may group such outlays into two major categories: (1) outlays incurred for obtaining the order; (2) outlays incurred for filling the order and collecting the money. Each of these two major categories may be subdivided as shown in the explanatory outline below.

I. Outlays incurred for obtaining the order.
   1. Advertising and sales promotion costs. These may be regarded as preparatory costs incurred to obtain and maintain customer good will.
   2. Direct selling costs. This subdivision includes salesmen's salaries, bonuses, commissions, traveling expenses, and whatever costs are incurred in maintaining the sales office.

II. Outlays incurred for filling the order and collecting the money.
   1. Warehousing and storage costs represent expenditures made in anticipation of orders.
   2. Packing, transportation, and delivery costs are the order-filling expenditures.
   3. Credit, collection, and financial management costs provide for the *quid pro quod* of the transaction, namely, the delivery of cash to the seller on terms convenient to the buyer.

A combination of several techniques may be used in predicting distribution costs. If data are available for any considerable time period, estimates can be made independently of the sales record by applying the technique of time-series analysis to each item of expense and projecting the analysis forward. A more logical procedure, however, is to establish various significant relationships of costs to sales, since the last-named variable is the source of funds out of which expenses are paid. For the establishment of these relationships the two types of static analysis discussed in Chapters IV and V are available. Since ratio analysis is the more common type, it will be the first to be discussed.

Any expense can be expressed as a percentage of the corresponding dollar volume of sales, and when so expressed it will tend to fall into one of three categories, namely, (1) expense relatives that remain more or less constant irrespective of the dollar volume of sales, (2) expense relatives that tend to increase with increments in the dollar volume of sales, and (3) expense relatives that tend to decrease as sales increase.

Some selling expenses belong in the first category simply because of executive decree. If salesmen, for example, are paid on a straight commission basis, this item of expense would necessarily show a constant relationship to sales. Advertising is another expense which may bear a constant relationship to sales, because the executives have decreed that a certain part of every sales dollar shall be spent in this manner. No problem of analysis is presented by such expenses, since the forecast of sales definitely establishes the forecast of expense. The real problem of ratio analysis emerges in connection with those expenses that are only approximately proportional to sales. The variation, however, in each expense as a percentage of sales is assumed to be due to a large number of relatively minor factors, so that any considerable number of such relatives will exhibit a central tendency capable of being described by an average. Then the average percentage relationship of each expense to sales becomes the basis for predicting the future outlay in each expense category.

If no clearly defined central tendency can be observed among the expense relatives, or if there is great variation about the average percentage relationship, some form of algebraic function may be needed as an adequate description of the data. For the application of a functional type of analysis the expenses may be either in dollar units or expressed as percentages of sales. When expense relatives are the subject of analysis, however, any relationship of a straight proportional nature between the expense and the sales has already been removed. Consequently, the functional relationships are distinctly different from those obtained when costs in dollars are used. The tabular arrangement on page 275 contains brief descriptive notes upon the more important categories of distribution costs as these are related to the dollar volume of sales.

The selection of an appropriate function is facilitated by the construction of scatter diagrams in which each specific distribution cost item is plotted against sales as the independent variable. In those instances in which the scatter of points about the selected curve type is not great, an estimate of the expense may be made either by reading points from the graph or by substituting the expected dollar volume of sales into the algebraic function that describes the relationship. If any cost item, analyzed in both absolute and relative terms, fails to exhibit a significant and reliable relationship with sales, other variables thought to have a direct and causal connection with costs may be introduced through the use of multiple correlation technique.

TABLE 37

DISTRIBUTION COSTS CLASSIFIED ACCORDING TO THEIR FUNCTIONAL RELATIONSHIP TO THE DOLLAR VOLUME OF SALES

Costs in Dollars	*Means of Description*	*Costs Expressed as Percentages of Sales*	*Means of Description*
Fixed costs	A constant number of dollars	Decreasing	The hyperbola $y = \frac{a}{x}$ that approaches zero as a minimum
Proportional costs	The linear equation $y = bx$	Constant	A constant percentage of sales
Mixed costs partly fixed, partly proportional	The linear equation $y = a + bx$	Decreasing	The modified hyperbola, $y = a + \frac{b}{x}$ that approaches a as a minimum
Progressive costs	Tendency toward the exponential equation, $y = b^x$	Increasing	Tendency toward the linear equation, $y = bx$

DIFFICULTIES IN ALLOCATING DISTRIBUTION COSTS

The costs that are incurred in the production of goods are generally more easily allocated than those incurred in their distribution. There is little to distinguish one unit of the product from another as they pass through the factory and are subjected to highly standardized processes of production. The customers, however, present almost unlimited variety in terms of the possible combinations of variables that influence distribution costs. Such variables as the specific articles ordered, the quantity of each, the method of delivery, the terms of the sale, the frequency of ordering, the promptness of payment, and the amount of service needed in soliciting the patronage operate to make each order a distinct unit and each customer a unique individual. In certain types of business enterprise a million dollars of sales might be recorded without duplicating a single combination of cost variables.

A second obstacle to distribution cost analysis is the intangible nature of the selling function. A plant engineer can prepare a blueprint and submit specifications for a product with reasonable assurance that the completed product will conform and be produced according to schedule. A sales manager in a moment of optimism might prepare the specifications for a sale, but he would have little assurance that a sale would result. This subjective element in selling makes difficult the task of allocating the cost to any specific order or to individual customers.

The decentralized character of much of the selling activity constitutes a third obstacle. The processes of production are usually concentrated within a relatively small area, but a sales organization may be nationwide. Time studies are easily made in the factory, where a single timekeeper can clock a large number of workers. To make distribution time studies, management must either go to considerable expense or let each salesman clock his own activities—an uncontrolled procedure that may occasionally lead to unreliable results.

A fourth difficulty arising in the allocation and standardization of the distribution costs is the great number of possible categories for which costs are desired. The production manager is usually satisfied if he knows costs by products or classes of products, whereas the distribution manager may desire a break-down and allocation of costs by products, by customers, by territories, by methods of delivery, by size of order, or by some combination of these various categories.

A fifth obstreperous element with which the distribution cost accountant must deal is that which concerns the deferment of promotional selling expense. In production-cost accounting each expenditure is assumed to add to the value of the product and enters the balance sheet as inventory until the product is sold. From a theoretical point of view a similar opportunity is available to the cost accountant in deferring promotional selling costs and treating them as assets until the sales for which they were made take place. If the relationship between any specific promotional effort and a future sale were definite and measurable, no serious problem would be involved. Usually, however, the relationship is not easily traced. Until more information is available upon the incidence of general promotional expense, the arguments against deferment seem to outweigh those in its favor.

METHODS OF COST ALLOCATION

The techniques used to allocate distribution costs are conditioned largely by the nature of those outlays. The threefold classification given below provides a convenient basis for the discussion of methods.

1. Direct costs of distribution include all items of expense that can

be recorded as belonging to certain specific territories, departments, types of order, channels of distribution, products, and so forth.

2. Semidirect costs include items that are incurred jointly for the benefit of two or more territories, departments, products, types of order, and so forth. This joint nature of the costs does not preclude their being divided, however, upon some equitable basis.

3. Indirect costs are those expense items that have no apparent connection with any specific territory, department, product, sales channel, or type of order, so that any basis used in their allocation must be an arbitrary one.

A cost that may be direct for one basis of classification may be semidirect or even indirect for some other basis. A salesman's salary, for instance, is usually direct if the classification is by territories, but if the salesman sells a variety of products, his salary would be a semidirect expense to be allocated on some equitable basis in a product classification. Again, promotional advertising is a direct expense for each territory if done locally, but indirect if done nationally. Hence, the first step in any allocation of distribution costs consists in determining what bases of classification are significant for the particular company.

The second step involves the selection of the most economical and equitable means of allocating the costs. The direct costs in any classification present no particular problem, since their distribution is simply a matter of bookkeeping. In a territorial analysis, for example, salesmen's salaries, commissions, traveling expenses, and freight and drayage can be recorded by territories and accumulated to a series of totals. The semidirect and indirect costs constitute the real problems in any cost classification. The bases upon which their allocation is made may be determined either by *a priori* reasoning or by statistical analysis. In some instances a single basis may be adequate, whereas in others a combination of bases may be needed. The data may be easily accessible for some allocations whereas for others the information must be gathered through time and activity studies.

The methods of allocation can be most easily designated in terms of the statistical tools that each tends to emphasize. The average-cost method is by far the most popular of the allocation procedures. It assumes that each cost bears a constant and direct proportion to the magnitude of some variable in terms of which it may be prorated. The variable itself is usually expressed in simple units, for example, the dollar volume of sales, the number of square feet of floor space, the number of shipments, the number of invoices, the hundredweight of goods handled, the number of orders, and so forth. Less frequently it may represent a combination of two variables, and some compound unit such as driver-hours or truck-hours may be needed for the proration. The procedure in either case is to divide the total expense by the number of units and thereby to obtain an average or unit cost. The various unit-cost factors are then applicable as multipliers in obtaining for each product, territory, customers' account, and so forth, its proportionate share of the various total costs.

The ease with which one can apply the average-cost method is its chief advantage. The variable used as a basis of allocation is usually selected by *a priori* reasoning, and the allocation reduces to a problem of simple proportions. The disadvantages of the method are to be found in this assumption of proportionality. If any part of the distributed cost is fixed, the average cost method distributes it in the same proportions as the variable part. Moreover, it assumes that the interclass variations in each cost can be accounted for in terms of a single variable, whereas actually a number of factors may be responsible.

A second possible approach to the problem of cost allocation involves the use of simultaneous equations. The application, however, is limited to those expense items that are, in fact, variable, since at least two sets of observations are required in order to obtain values for the simultaneous solution. If we allow x to represent the variable in terms of which the expense y is assumed to vary, we may select and substitute paired values in the general algebraic form $y = a + bx$ and as a result obtain two simultaneous equations.

To illustrate the procedure, let us assume that 1,000 units can be produced at a total cost of \$1,100 whereas 600 units cost a total of \$500. By substituting for y and x in the general equation $y = a + bx$, we have

$$1{,}100 = a + 1{,}000\,b$$
$$600 = a + 500\,b.$$

A solution of the two equations gives us $a = \$100$ and $b = \$1$. Hence there is a constant element in the expense of \$100 and a variable element amounting to $1 per unit. If the constant part of the expense be distributed equally or upon any other basis than that of a direct proportion to the number of units produced, the results of this method will differ from those secured by the average-cost method. The following tabular comparison assumes a total expense of $1,100 containing a constant element of $100 as shown by the simultaneous solution.

TABLE 38

COMPARISON OF TWO METHODS OF COST ALLOCATION

Territory	*Number of Units*	*Distributed by Average-Cost Method*	*Distribution on Basis of Simultaneous Solution with Fixed Element Shared Equally*		
			Fixed	*Variable*	*Total*
A	100	$110	$25	100	$125
B	200	220	25	200	225
C	300	330	25	300	325
D	400	440	25	400	425
Total	1,000	$1,100			$1,100

A territorial distribution has here been assumed, although other categories would have served the purpose equally well. The comparison reveals that the average-cost method places a somewhat heavier cost upon the territories having the larger number of units. The source of the difference lies in the manner of distributing the fixed element of the cost. The average-cost method lumps the fixed element with the variable element and distributes the total equally to all units, whereas the simultaneous solution segregates the two elements distributing the variable equally to all units and leaving the fixed to be distributed upon some other basis or equally to all territories as in this specific illustration.

A third approach to the problem of cost allocation makes use of correlation analysis. This is the most flexible method, since it provides for the introduction of as many variables as the analyst finds significant in determining costs. For example, the cost of packing may be considered to be affected by variables such as weight, volume, and number of pieces. If data are available (or can be gathered) pertaining to each of these variables, an estimate of the influence of each may be secured through multiple correlation analysis. Whatever constant element may be present in the cost is segregated by the analysis so that it may be allocated separately or lumped with other constant cost elements and treated as a charge against the total sales income without regard to origin.

The technical nature of the correlation approach is the chief obstacle in the way of its being more widely used. If simple correlation is applied, the results are quite similar to those secured by the second method described above. Neither approach is applicable unless the total expense to be allocated is a variable.

SOME LIMITATIONS OF DISTRIBUTION COST ANALYSIS

The limitations that surround the application of distribution cost analysis are of the two general types. First, there are certain technical and financial difficulties in classifying and allocating costs. Secondly, there are definite limitations to the amount of control that management can exercise in applying the results of cost analysis.

The inability to allocate certain expenditures with any degree of precision is probably the greatest obstacle in distribution cost analysis. With large overhead costs and a great variety of products or services, the allocation, in many instances, is likely to be quite arbitrary. Obviously the results one obtains in an allocation can hardly be a safe guide for appraising relative profitableness if certain categories may be made to show either a profit or a loss, depending upon the particular basis used in making the allocation.

A second limiting factor is the cost of making the analysis. There is always the danger that management will become so engrossed in the methods of control that their cost exceeds their benefit. Occasionally the expense of a complete and continuous analysis of costs may be avoided by using the technique of sampling. Periodic studies based upon samples of orders and of customers' accounts have been found to provide substantial accuracy with a considerable saving in the costs of analysis.

Since the ultimate purpose of any sales or cost analysis is either to augment or to stabilize the profits of the business, there is need to emphasize certain conditions that limit the realization of this purpose The first of these is the necessity of considering the long-run point of view in applying the cost principles. Current temporary losses may often be a necessary prelude to future gains. In launching a new product or in opening a new territory the sales may for some time lag behind the expenses properly chargeable to the product or to the territory.

Again, the loss that is sometimes recorded within a given category may be counterbalanced by gains that are real but incapable of being evaluated. Quite frequently a business enterprise may undertake projects and activities primarily for the purpose of creating good will with its customers and with the general public. The statistical and economic services maintained by certain large metropolitan banks fall into this category. The monetary outlay upon these activities is presumed to be counterbalanced by the intangible element of good will that enlarges the whole business income, but whose measurement, if undertaken, would be nothing but a crude sort of guess.

A similar exception to what might be termed the cost-of-service principle is represented by the loss leaders used in retailing. Here also the loss sustained upon certain products or services is assumed to be counterbalanced by additions to income through the sale of other products or services.

Other exceptions that might be taken to the principle of rigorously balancing the costs against income for each category are dictated by necessity. There are certain products and services that must be sold on the principle of charging what the traffic can bear. Sometimes humanitarian motives require that losses be taken on some part of the service or on certain products and that higher charges be made on the balance to offset the losses. Charges for medical aid and other professional services are often made on this basis.

The presence of large overhead costs may operate to produce a similar situation. A particular product, service, territory, account, and so forth may not provide an income sufficient to cover its proportionate share of the overhead expense. Yet its discontinuance would be unwise unless overhead costs could be reduced.

Finally, custom may exercise all the force of necessity as in the case of retailers who stock so-called "accommodation" goods. Sugar, for example, may be sold on such a small margin that it fails to cover handling costs, and yet the merchant can hardly discontinue its sale. He must follow the practice of the trade and serve all his customers with a complete line of merchandise, even though certain customers and certain products tend to decrease his net profits.

SOME CONSEQUENCES OF THE WIDER APPLICATION OF ANALYTICAL METHODS

When analytical methods are applied to a specific body of data, the conclusions presumably relate to the phenomena out of which the basic information grew. The methods themselves are usually of little interest, provided, of course, that their use has become so widespread that they may be taken for granted. In the present study the reverse situation has prevailed in that the methods of analysis and control have occupied the focal point of interest and that the statistical data used were quite incidental, serving primarily as illustrative material. Since no new instruments of sales control have been forged, justification for the emphasis on methodology must come from another quarter. Already accounting and statistics, the two main storehouses from which business managers draw their techniques of control, are bursting with tools, many of which grow rusty because of limited use. This neglect can hardly be assessed to any lack of opportunity for their more general application. The most cogent business facing those who are familiar with these two closely related fields of knowledge would therefore seem to be, not the creation of new methods, but rather the more general and effective use of those already available. The conclusions that may be drawn from a study that emphasizes this objective must relate more to the future than to the past. In the field of distribution the following results might be expected to flow from a wider knowledge and a more general application of the analytical tools discussed in this study.

The first result that might conceivably follow the wider application of sales and cost analyses would be an adjustment of the price lists. If income were found inadequate to cover a product's fair share of the costs, the remedy in some instances might be an increase of prices. Other situations might call for a reduction in prices thereby increasing consumption to the point at which costs could be lowered and profits obtained.

If price adjustments were ineffective in converting losses on certain products into profits, the techniques of production and sale might conceivably be so improved that a satisfactory relationship between income and costs would be secured. Were all remedial efforts to fail, the manufacture and sale of the no-profit products and services would presumably be discontinued, thereby resulting in a realignment of productive energies.

Many changes could be expected in accounts receivable ledgers if each customer were required to provide a sales income sufficient to cover a reasonable portion of the cost of service. Those whose patronage had been solicited at considerable expense would be eliminated from the salesman's calling list, and possibly some less expensive method of solicitation would be substituted, for example, the mail, the telephone, or the telegraph. Pruning the customer list would constitute a drastic measure of last resort, to be taken only after every effort had been made to serve the entire list at a profit.

A fourth consequence that would flow from a more rigorous application of sales and cost analyses would be the wider application of the minimum-order rule. Once a distributor has determined his break-even or no-profit point, he is in a position to establish the minimum size of order for his specific business. The discontinuance of service on the unprofitable small orders might in some instances reduce sales volume, but if profits could thereby be increased one should not be greatly concerned with the volume of goods sold.

Unprofitable prospects and mailing lists represent a fifth area of dead timber in distribution that would gradually come under the axe if costs and income were to be more critically analyzed. Many long mailing lists would be clipped short, and idle curiosity seekers would find it much more difficult to be placed on the prospect list if the characteristics of a prospect were carefully scrutinized and defined. The savings in solicitation costs might then be profitably applied upon those whose interest was *bona fide*. In some instances a classification of the prospects would enable the sales organization to improve its approach and increase the volume of its sales.

Beyond mailing lists and customers' ledgers lies the market, where other possible savings in distribution costs could be effected. Here the rigorous application of sales and cost analyses should result in abandoning many market areas and in substituting less expensive means of selling in certain of the remaining areas. Sections of the market would probably be served with greater intensity, each salesman receiving perhaps a smaller area and a shorter but more select list of prospects, so that the average size of order would tend to increase. Selling by mail and by telephone would be used more often to supplement the very expensive procedure of calling on the prospects in person. More attention would be given to the routing of salesmen in their territories and the relative economy of travel by airplane, railroad, and automobile. There is scarcely a variable that influences marketing costs that could not be studied with profit.

The type of sales personnel would very likely be modified by a wider application of sales and costs analyses. Instead of selling being a sort of free-for-all in which persons of every type may engage, more attention would be given to previous training and experience of applicants with a consequent improvement in the general caliber of the men employed. A classification of salesmen according to type of business or trade served might be more widely employed as a step toward greater efficiency in selling. Other classifications, such as the volume of sales and costs by customers, would be an obvious boon in the more effective supervision and direction of selling activities.

Sales policies would be certain to come in for critical study and modification if sales and cost analyses were to be more generally applied. Ignorance of costs on the part of a few sellers in a competitive field often forces those well informed to go contrary to their better judgment. Price cutting of the sort that undermines legitimate profits would tend to become less prevalent as more distributors became aware of their real costs of selling. Possibly the strongest argument for an extension of cost accounting principles to the distribution of goods is the seller's legal necessity of defending his price structure under such legislation as the Robinson-Patman Act. Since easy terms of sale are frequently the disguise by which price reductions masquerade, they, too, provide an opportunity for substantial revision under searching analysis. The cost of selling on credit, the relative advantages of different terms of credit, and the losses from uncharged interest on overdue accounts are topics upon which there is at present a general paucity of information.

Action by individual companies may not be adequate to achieve many of the economies in distribution toward which analyses point Some wasteful practices have become established as customs of the trade. Others began as competitive devices among a few companies for individual advantage, only to be transformed later into lodestones when they became generally known and followed by imitators. Still other practices of an uneconomic sort have been foisted upon specific industries by ill-conceived legislation. Many have been the sources of wastes that have grown barnacle-fashion about the distribution of goods and services. Whereas analyses by individual companies may frequently reveal the presence and the nature of these common obstructions, only concerted action may at times be competent to remove them.

APPENDIX A

Monthly Sales of W. T. Grant and Company, 1923–38

(In thousands of dollars)

	Jan.	Feb.	March	Apr.	May	June	July	Aug.	Sept.	Oct.	Nov.	Dec.
1923	$1,054	1,147	1,533	1,478	1,687	1,612	1,229	1,322	1,535	2,014	2,052	3,675
1924	1,342	1,474	1,734	1,910	1,940	1,796	1,496	1,553	1,698	2,561	2,710	4,630
1925	1,816	1,796	2,011	2,330	2,293	2,357	1,806	2,006	2,176	3,317	2,922	5,334
1926	2,065	1,951	2,310	2,562	2,867	2,640	2,417	2,371	2,772	3,799	3,726	6,455
1927	2,205	2,248	2,789	3,364	3,160	3,299	3,018	3,114	3,282	4,275	4,366	8,205
1928	2,624	2,843	3,706	3,656	4,096	4,366	3,731	3,996	4,708	5,418	5,515	10,328
1929	3,329	3,516	5,141	4,421	5,089	5,374	4,524	5,066	4,777	6,164	6,511	11,536
1930	3,784	3,911	4,962	5,730	6,153	5,464	4,816	5,383	5,286	7,083	6,677	11,797
1931	4,110	4,347	5,334	6,402	6,606	6,289	5,227	5,395	5,570	7,423	6,485	12,111
1932	4,495	4,837	5,567	5,997	6,085	5,863	5,089	5,055	5,658	5,962	6,334	11,368
1933	4,273	4,492	5,137	6,267	6,553	6,510	5,771	5,750	6,433	7,113	6,899	12,450
1934	4,833	4,550	6,774	5,952	7,179	7,347	5,736	6,292	6,570	7,822	7,493	14,187
1935	5,166	5,578	6,953	7,663	7,430	7,654	6,277	6,767	6,726	8,365	8,581	14,810
1936	5,176	5,754	6,475	7,649	8,328	8,371	7,075	6,925	7,443	9,333	8,492	16,867
1937	5,626	5,615	7,616	7,176	8,514	8,463	7,706	6,780	7,819	8,957	8,373	16,615
1938	5,325	5,523	6,530	8,061	7,214	7,608	6,971	6,834	7,653	8,970	8,635	17,997

APPENDIX B

Mechanics and Principles Governing the Use of the Mail Questionnaire

PRINCIPLES GOVERNING THE FRAMING OF QUESTIONS

1. Ask only what you need to know. After every possible question pertaining to the purpose of the study has been listed, the analyst proceeds to strike out those that are not absolutely essential.

2. Phrase the questions to permit an answer by a check mark or "yes" or "no." In listing a series of possible answers care should be taken to make the list complete, since an omission of any possible answer tends to bias the result in favor of those listed.

3. Avoid questions requiring research or mathematical calculation. Unless the recipient feels legally or morally obligated he is likely to commit such questions to the waste basket.

4. Avoid biased or leading questions. Rephrasing is sometimes all that is needed to correct a leading question. For instance, instead of asking "Do you use Brand X gasoline?" let the informant name the brand by asking "What brand of gasoline do you use?"

5. Avoid ambiguous questions. Since ambiguity is seldom recognized by the person who asks the question, testing of the questionnaire provides the safest means for its detection.

6. Avoid opinion questions, unless by themselves opinions constitute significant information. In a court of law the evidence, not the layman's snap judgment, provides the basis for deciding the guilt or innocence of the accused. Nevertheless the opinions of character witnesses are admitted for the jury's consideration. In many problems of marketing research the opinions of "character witnesses" may represent stubborn facts that have a direct bearing on present and future events. Questionnaires, for instance, asking for opinions on the truth and educational value of advertising or the attitudes of people with regard to the chain stores are significant from this viewpoint. Occasionally the opinion question is justified solely as a means of subtle flattery or as a safety valve to those who enjoy giving their opinions and who feel frustrated if denied the privilege.

7. Avoid personal or embarrassing questions. People answer reluctantly or refuse to commit themselves when questioned about their age, religion, income, habits of personal hygiene, physical defects, and other personal matters.

8. Avoid questions that are likely to elicit exaggerated or biased answers. People frequently resort to a sort of wish-fulfillment in answering questions pertaining to such matters as the newspapers they read, the stores they patronize, the clothes they wear, and the prices they pay for things. The correct information upon these topics must usually be obtained by some indirect method of questioning.

9. Avoid questions involving technical words and those for which there is a dual meaning. The investigator's daily vocabulary may contain words and phrases that are new, misleading, or confusing to those who are asked to answer the questionnaire. A careful testing of the questions provides the only safe means of avoiding this mistake.

10. Avoid questions regarding motives unless you are prepared to study and practice the art of asking why. Reliable information can hardly be expected from people in answering such questions as "Why did you buy Brand X?" or "What influenced you most in the purchase of your automobile?" In discovering motives, the more circuitous method of questioning has often proved successful. The so-called psychological approach involves a series of specific questions in which account is taken of personal tendencies of the buyer, outside influences upon him, and attributes of the product itself.[1]

PRINCIPLES GOVERNING THE ARRANGEMENT OF QUESTIONS

Next in importance to the quality of questions is their arrangement. The effectiveness of a good set of questions can be greatly impaired by an illogical arrangement or poor classification.

1. Arrange the questions in order of interest. The chances of a return are greatly improved by placing the most interesting questions first.

2. Important questions should come first. If this and the first injunction are inconsistent, the sacrifice of importance is not too great a price to pay for interest, since without the latter there is little chance of the questions being answered at all.

3. Arrange the questions in such order that the answer to one question may not bias the respondent's attitude in answering subsequent questions.

4. Group the questions under headings. The more important purposes served by this grouping are: to emphasize the principal topics upon which information is being sought, to give a pleasing appearance to an otherwise monotonous list of questions, to facilitate the respondent's flow of thought in answering and finally, to impress the recipient with the idea that the

[1] Paul Felix Lazarsfeld gives an extensive analysis of the psychological aspects of questionnaire framing in *The Technique of Marketing Research*, chaps. iii and iv.

sender has given the questionnaire thought and by this token has greater moral claim to a thoughtful reply.

5. Sort the questions according to the spheres of interest, knowledge, and experience of those to whom they are to be sent. For example, the market analyst who is seeking the public's opinion on a certain make of automobile might prepare a list of technical questions for engineers, mechanics, and repair men. A second list of questions covering sales policies might be addressed to automobile dealers and salesmen. Finally, questions regarding general performance, appearance, and ease of operation would be reserved for the customers. Sorting and directing brief specific questionnaires to select groups serves both to improve the quality of the information obtained and to increase the percentage of returned schedules.

6. Leave a space for "Don't know" when asking for a reply of "yes" or "no."

7. Provide sufficient space for comments and remarks. Each check list should end with a heading "Others (please specify) . . . ." The side remarks of respondents have sometimes provided research directors with their most helpful information on public attitudes.

8. Number the questions. The numbering will greatly aid the subsequent tabulation.

9. Key the questionnaire. Important differences are frequently revealed when the returns are tabulated by geographical areas, by occupational groups, or by some other basis of division that promises to prove significant.

PHYSICAL DETAILS REGARDING THE FORM OF THE QUESTIONNAIRE

1. Color of paper.—Yellow paper has been found to give the highest percentage of returns, and pink comes second. All dark colors rank low in the scale of effectiveness.[2] The lighter colors used alternately on repeat questionnaires get a greater response than a single color which is repeated.

2. Method of reproduction.—The method that one uses to reproduce a questionnaire is dependent almost entirely upon the number which are to be sent. As one proceeds from a few dozen copies to many thousands of copies, typing, mimeographing, multigraphing, reproprinting, and printing become successively available as economic methods of reproducing the questionnaire.

3. Quality of the paper.—The quality of paper that one uses for the questionnaire is determined very largely by the method of reproduction. For a typed schedule a high quality, perhaps even engraved paper, should be used. The mimeographing and multigraphing processes require a relatively low grade paper with rough finish. Printing is reserved for schedules that are sent out in large numbers, and the grade of paper should vary with the composition of the mailing lists and the amount of money available for the sending.

[2] Reed, *Planned Marketing*.

4. Design of questionnaire.—The postal card often provides a convenient and economical form for a short questionnaire. The double post card arrangement is especially effective for quantity circulation. For longer schedules the booklet form has become very popular. The use of charts, diagrams, and pictures represents a distinctive improvement that has been introduced into questionnaire designing by Henry G. Weaver, Director of the Customer Research Staff of General Motors Corporation. Under his pioneer leadership the pictorial-booklet technique promises to transform the backward methods of asking questions into something of a fine art.

5. Coding of questionnaire.—The coding of a questionnaire relates to the designation of questions by symbols as a means of facilitating the tabulation of replies. Precoding relates to the practice of assigning code marks to questions before the schedules are sent out. The extent to which this is done depends upon the type and quantity of information requested, as well as the number of persons on the mailing list. Questions dealing with motives and attitudes are usually difficult to precode, whereas long questionnaires and long mailing lists make precoding highly desirable as a preliminary step to mechanical tabulation of the returns.

TESTING THE QUESTIONNAIRE

The larger the number of questionnaires to be sent, the greater is the need for making sure that every reasonable provision has been made to insure a successful response. Tests should be made of the questionnaire by submitting it to small groups of persons selected from the mailing list in order to determine what changes are desirable before it is sent out in its final form. In analyzing the preliminary test returns, the following are the principal questions to be considered: (1) Does the questionnaire get the desired information? (2) Does the information come back in a form that is suitable for tabulation? (3) Have the important factors been grasped by those who answer? (4) What additional information, if any, should be obtained?

By the alternate process of testing and revising, the questionnaire is successively improved until the investigator is satisfied that it fulfills the conditions set forth in the plan of the survey. As many as a half dozen drafts and revisions may be necessary before the questionnaire is released for wide distribution.

MECHANICS OF SENDING THE QUESTIONNAIRE

The following are among the more important factors to be considered in the sending of questionnaires:

1. Prepare a selective mailing list. The degree of selectiveness must, of course, be determined by the nature and quality of the information that is being sought.

2. Send to coincide with the convenience of the recipient. Certain types of respondents show a significant difference in the readiness with which

they answer questionnaires received on different days of the week. If there seems to exist any most opportune time at which to make the inquisition, the investigator should strive to find it.

3. Use a dummy company to avoid bias in the results. The tendency of people to say and do the things they think will please others frequently exerts a biasing influence upon the returns secured from questionnaire surveys. Frank and open criticisms of the product and of the policies of a company are possible only if steps are taken to insure that the respondent does not identify the investigator with the company.

4. Enclose a self-addressed envelope and either attach postage or guarantee it. Occasionally a telegram or special delivery letter can be used to bring results. The expense of these exclusive methods of obtaining information precludes their use except with a very small group. Whatever agency of communication the sender of a questionnaire chooses to use, his is the responsibility of paying for the "round trip."

EDITING THE QUESTIONNAIRE

After the return of the questionnaires, the process of editing begins. Each questionnaire is checked on such points as (1) consistency, (2) completeness and (3) truthfulness. Any deficiency that may be found in a personal interview questionnaire is usually referred back to the interviewer, who must either explain the deficiency or correct it. Deficiencies in mail questionnaires are not so easily handled. Usually they result in the questionnaire being discarded unless these deficiencies are of minor importance and limited to some particular section of the schedule.

Various techniques have been employed by questionnaire makers to aid the work of editing. One of these consists in the insertion of questions which approach the same topic from two or more different angles. If the respondent's age, for example, is important, he might be asked to state his age and then to give the date of his birth. Again, if the frequency of purchases as regards a given product is important, the respondent might also be asked the time of his last purchase and when he expected to be in the market again. Examples might be multiplied to show the opportunity which awaits the cross-examiner in marketing research. Questionnaires that are returned with inconsistent answers are, of course, discredited and discarded by the editor.

Another technique for testing the accuracy and truthfulness of a return involves the insertion of one or two quite plausible questions that cannot be answered. An example of this procedure is provided by a brand-familiarity rating scale prepared by Professor H. K. Nixon, of Columbia University. Included in the list of bona fide brands of articles are two fictitious brands that the respondent is expected to rate as "Unknown." Any other answer serves to discredit the truthfulness of his ratings on the bona fide brands.

Corrections and adjustments made by the editors upon a returned questionnaire should appear in colored pencil or ink. Uncoded questions are usually coded as a part of the editing process. The use of a code on which the editor lists and tallies the frequency of each different answer given to each uncoded question on the first few dozen questionnaires serves to reveal the general pattern that the answers on the remaining questionnaires will follow. The editor can then assign a code to each type of response.

Not infrequently the editor of questionnaires encounters trenchant remarks and constructive criticism that either fall outside the code or are too significant to be merged with the general mass of statistical data. These can be marked, in order that verbatim copies can be made of them.

Classified List of References

GENERAL BUDGETARY PLANNING AND CONTROL

American Management Association

Numerous bulletins on the subject of budgeting have been published by the American Management Association and are referred to here only by number.

Annual Convention Series, Nos. 28, 30, 31, 32, 36, 41, 51, 59, 63, 64, 65, 66, 67, 76, 91, 94.

Financial Executive Series, Nos. 2, 4, 6, 7, 17, 24, 30, 31.

General Management Series, Nos. 79, 80.

Industrial Marketing Series, Nos. 5, 21.

Marketing Executive Series, Nos. 40, 52, 56.

Office Executive Series, No. 12.

Office Management Series, No. 52.

Production Executive Series, Nos. 27, 28, 51, 56, 57, 58, 62, 74, 84, 88, 89, 99.

Sales Executive Series, Nos. 9, 21, 22, 31, 36.

Barber, Joseph H., Budgeting to the Business Cycle. New York, Ronald Press, 1925.

Bruère, Henry Jaromir, and Arthur Lazarus, Applied Budgeting. Chicago and New York, Shaw, 1926.

Churchill, William Lucius, Pricing for Profit. New York, Macmillan, 1932.

Controllers Institute of America, Inc., Budget Methods and Procedures of Manufacturing Companies. New York, 1938.

Grisell, Thomas Olen, Budgetary Control of Distribution. New York, Harper, 1929.

Knoeppel, Charles Edward, Profit Engineering. New York, McGraw-Hill, 1933.

Knoeppel, Charles Edward, and Edgar G. Seybold, Managing for Profit. New York, McGraw-Hill, 1937.

McKinsey, James Oscar, Budgetary Control. New York, Ronald Press, 1922.

Metropolitan Life Insurance Company, Policyholders Service Bureau.

The bulletins indexed by the company under the heading "budgets" include many that deal with methods and practices in particular industries and branches of trade. A few deal with specific budget items, such as cash and manufacturing expenses.

National Association of Cost Accountants. Index.

Numerous bulletins on the subject of budgeting are listed in the N. A. C. A. Index.

Rautenstrauch, Walter, The Successful Control of Profits. New York, Forbes, 1930.

Rowland, Floyd Hookway, How to Budget for Profit. New York, Harper, 1933.

Sinclair, Prior, Budgeting. New York, Ronald Press, 1934.

Williams, John H., The Flexible Budget. New York, McGraw-Hill, 1934.

Willsmore, A. W., Business Budgets and Budgetary Control. London, Pitman, 1932.

CLASSIFICATION OF SALES TRANSACTIONS

Altman, George Tilden, Recording Sales Transactions. New York, Ronald Press, 1924.

Childs, A. C., Methods of Analysis of Sales Records. A thesis presented at Massachusetts Institute of Technology, 1931; unpublished.

Dartnell Corporation, Gathering and Arrangement of Sales Data, Dartnell Report No. 138, Dartnell Corporation, Chicago.

Greene, James Henry, Principles and Methods of Retailing. New York, McGraw-Hill, 1924.

McKinsey, James Oscar, Managerial Accounting. Chicago, University of Chicago Press, 1924.

RATIO ANALYSIS

Bliss, James Harris, Financial and Operating Ratios in Management. New York, Ronald Press, 1923.

Foulke, Roy Anderson, Behind the Scenes of Business. Rev. ed. New York, Dun and Bradstreet, 1937.

——— Signs of the Times. New York, Dun and Bradstreet, 1938.

Gilman, Stephen, Analyzing Financial Statements. Rev. ed. New York, Ronald Press, 1934.

Gregory, Homer Ewart, Accounting Reports in Business Management. New York, Ronald Press, 1928.

Guthmann, Harry George, The Analysis of Financial Statements. Rev. ed. New York, Prentice-Hall, 1935.

McNair, Malcolm Perrine, Expenses and Profits of Limited Price Variety Chains in 1936. Boston, 1937. Harvard Business School, Bulletin No. 105.

Metropolitan Life Insurance Company, Policyholders Service Bureau.
A series of bulletins dealing with operating costs and ratios for specific equipment and types of industry.

Myer, John Nicholas, Financial Statement Analysis. New York, The author, 1939.

Schmalz, Carl Nelson, Expenses and Profits of Food Chains in 1934. Boston, 1935. Harvard University, Graduate School of Business Administration, Bulletin No. 99.

——— Operating Results of Department and Specialty Stores in 1936

Boston, 1937. Harvard University, Graduate School of Business Administration, Bulletin No. 104.

Teele, Stanley Ferdinand, Operating Results of Department Store Chains and Department Store Ownership Groups, 1929, 1931–1934. Boston, 1935. Harvard University, Graduate School of Business Administration, Bulletin No. 101.

Wall, Alexander, and Raymond W. Duning, Ratio Analysis of Financial Statements. New York, Harper, 1928.

FUNCTIONAL ANALYSIS

Brown, Lyndon O., "Quantitative Market Analysis," Harvard Business Review, Spring and Autumn Numbers, 1937.

Cowan, Donald Ross Grant, Sales Analysis from the Management Standpoint. Chicago, University of Chicago Press, 1938.

Dean, Joel, Statistical Determination of Costs with Special Reference to Marginal Costs. Chicago, University of Chicago Press, 1936.

Ezekial, Mordecai, Methods of Correlation Analysis. New York, Wiley, 1930.

Hovey, E. F., "Cost Accounting and Budget Making," in Taylor Society Bulletin, XVI (No. 3), 100–103.

Knoeppel, Charles Edward, Profit Engineering. New York, McGraw-Hill, 1933.

Knoeppel, Charles Edward, and Edgar G. Seybold, Managing for Profit. New York, McGraw-Hill, 1937.

Livingston, Robert Teviot, "Control of Operating Expenses—an Application of Statistical Methods," Mechanical Engineering, October, 1932, pp. 711–17.

Rautenstrauch, Walter, The Successful Control of Profits. New York, Forbes, 1930.

DYNAMIC OR TIME SERIES ANALYSIS

Croxton, Frederick Emory, and Dudley Johnstone Cowden, Applied General Statistics. New York, Prentice-Hall, 1939, pp. 363–572.

——— Practical Business Statistics. New York, Prentice-Hall, 1934, pp. 262–361.

Davies, George Reginald, and Walter Frederick Crowder, Methods of Statistical Analysis in the Social Sciences. New York, Wiley, 1933, pp. 132–225.

Kuznets, Simon Smith, Seasonal Variations in Industry and Trade. New York, National Bureau of Economic Research, 1933.

——— Secular Movements in Production and Prices. New York, National Bureau of Economic Research, 1930.

Mills, Frederick Cecil, Statistical Methods Applied to Economics and Business. 2d ed. New York, Holt, 1938, pp. 225–304.

Mitchell, Wesley Clair, Business Cycles—the Problem and Its Setting.

New York, National Bureau of Economic Research, Inc., 1928, chap. iii.

Pearl, Raymond, Studies in Human Biology. Baltimore, Williams and Wilkins, 1924, chaps. xxiv–xxv.

Riggleman, John Randolph, and Ira Nobles Frisbee, Business Statistics. 2d ed. New York, McGraw-Hill, 1938, chap. xvi.

Sasuly, Max, Trend Analysis of Statistics. Washington, D. C., Brookings Institution, 1934.

Snyder, Carl, Business Cycles and Business Measurements. New York, Macmillan, 1927.

Stockton, John R., An Introduction to Business Statistics. Boston, New York, Heath, 1938, pp. 136–249.

FORECASTING

Blake, Edmund G., and Ralph H. Davis, Methods of Forecasting Sales Used in New England Industries. A thesis presented at Massachusetts Institute of Technology, 1931; unpublished.

Bratt, Elmer Clark, Business Cycles and Forecasting. Chicago, Business Publications, Inc., 1937.

Hall, Lincoln Withington, An Approach to Definite Forecasting. Philadelphia, University of Pennsylvania Press, 1929.

Haney, Lewis Henry, Business Forecasting. Boston, New York, Ginn, 1931.

Hardy, Charles Oscar, and Garfield Vestal Cox, Forecasting Business Conditions. New York, Macmillan, 1927.

Hickernell, Warren Fayette, Financial and Business Forecasting. New York, Alexander Hamilton Institute, 1928.

International Labour Office, Economic Barometers; a report submitted to Economic Committee of the League of Nations. Geneva, 1924.

Jordan, David Francis, Business Forecasting. New York, Pitman, 1935.

Karsten, Karl G., Scientific Forecasting. New York, Greenberg, 1931.

Partington, John E., Railroad Purchasing and the Business Cycle. Washington, D. C., Brookings Institution, 1929.

Persons, Warren Milton, Forecasting Business Cycles. New York, Wiley, 1931.

Persons, Warren Milton, and others. The Problem of Business Forecasting. Boston and New York, Houghton Mifflin, 1924.

Richardson, J. H., Business Forecasting. London, Pittman, 1931.

Vance, Ray, Business and Investment Forecasting. 2d ed. New York, Harper, 1925.

Wallace, William, Business Forecasting and Its Practical Application. 3d ed. London, Pitman, 1932.

THEORY OF SAMPLING AND TESTS OF SIGNIFICANCE

Bowley, Arthur Lyon, Elements of Statistics. 6th ed. London, King, 1937.

Conference on Statistical Methods of Sampling Agricultural Data, Ames,

Ia., 1936, Proceedings . . . The Bureau of Agricultural Economics, United States Department of Agriculture, and the Department of Agricultural Economics, the Department of Mathematics, and Statistical Laboratory of Iowa State College Cooperating. Washington, D. C., 1936.

Brown, Theodore H., The Use of Statistical Technique in Certain Problems of Market Research. Boston, 1935. Harvard University Business Research Studies No. 12.

Croxton, Frederick Emory, and Dudley Johnstone Cowden, Applied General Statistics. New York, Prentice-Hall, 1939, pp. 305–62.

——— Practical Business Statistics. New York, Prentice-Hall, 1934, pp. 222–61.

Davies, George Reginald, and Dale Yoder, Business Statistics. New York, Wiley, 1937, pp. 390–436.

Fisher, Ronald Alymer, Statistical Methods for Research Workers. 7th ed. Edinburgh, Oliver and Boyd, 1938, pp. 81–177 and 256–306.

Mills, Frederick Cecil, Statistical Methods Applied to Economics and Business. Rev. ed. New York, Holt, 1938, pp. 452–530 and 618–36.

Pearson, Egon Sharke, "Sampling Problems in Industry," Journal of the Royal Society, Supplement, Vol. I (No. 2, 1934).

Rietz, Henry Lavis, ed., Handbook of Mathematical Statistics. Boston and New York, Houghton Mifflin, 1924, pp. 71–91.

Sarle, C. F., "Statistical Problems of an Annual Census of American Agriculture," in Conference on Statistical Methods of Sampling Agricultural Data, 1936, Proceedings, Washington, D. C.

Smith, John H., Tests of Significance and How to Use Them. Chicago, University of Chicago Press, 1939.

Snedecor, George Waddel, Statistical Methods Applied to Experiments in Agriculture and Biology. Ames, Ia., Collegiate Press, 1937, pp. 134–241.

Tippett, Leonard Henry Caleb, The Methods of Statistics. 2d ed. London, Williams and Norgate, 1937, pp. 41–109.

U. S., Department of Agriculture, Bureau of Agriculture Economics, Proceedings of Conference on Statistical Methods of Sampling Agricultural Data, *see* Conference on Statistical Methods of Sampling Agricultural Data.

Waugh, A. E., Elements of Statistical Method. New York, McGraw-Hill, 1938, pp. 131–159.

Yule, G. Udny, and M. G. Kendall, An Introduction to the Theory of Statistics. 11th ed. London, Griffin, Ltd., 1937, pp. 332–433.

MARKETING RESEARCH

American Marketing Society, Committee on Marketing Research Technique, The Technique of Marketing Research. New York, McGraw-

Bingham, Walter Van Dyke, and Bruce Victor Moore, How to Interview. 4th ed. New York, Harper, 1934.

Borden, Neil Hopper, and Osgood Stevens Lovekin, A Test of the Consumer Jury Method of Ranking Advertisements. Boston, Harvard University, Graduate School of Business Administration, 1935.

Brown, Lyndon O., Market Research and Analysis. New York, Ronald Press, 1937.

Brown, Theodore Henry, The Use of Statistical Techniques in Certain Problems of Market Research. Boston, Harvard University, Graduate School of Business Administration, 1935.

Carroll, Jean F., Standards of Research. Des Moines, Meredith, 1929.

Coutant, Frank Raymond, and John Russell Doubman, Simplified Market Research. Philadelphia, Walther Printing House, 1935.

Dartnell Corporation, Measuring and Forecasting Future Demand. Report No. 162, Dartnell Corporation, Chicago.

Firth, Leo E., Testing Advertisements. New York, McGraw-Hill, 1934.

Fry, Charles Luther, The Technique of Social Investigation. New York, Harper, 1934.

Giles, Ray, The Sales Expansion Question Book. New York, Harper, 1930.

Hensley, Harry Carlyle, and Neil Hopper Borden, Marketing Policies of the California Walnut Growers Association. Washington, D. C., U. S. Govt. Print. Off., 1937. Farm Credit Administration, Coöperative Division, Bulletin No. 10.

Larrabee, Carroll Burton, and Henry William Marks, Check Lists of Advertising, Selling, and Merchandising Essentials. New York, McGraw-Hill, 1937.

Link, Henry Charles, The New Psychology of Selling and Advertising. New York, Macmillan, 1934.

National Management Council, Seventh International Management Congress Distribution Papers. Boston, Waverly Press, 1938.

Phelps, Dudley Maynard, Marketing Research, Its Function, Scope and Method. Ann Arbor, University of Michigan, 1937. University of Michigan Business Studies, Vol. III (No. 2).

Poffenberger, Albert Theodor, Psychology in Advertising. 2d ed. New York, McGraw-Hill, 1932.

Redmayne, Paul, and Hugh Weeks, Market Research. London, Butterworth, 1931.

Reed, Vergil Daniel, Planned Marketing. New York, Ronald Press, 1929.

Reilly, William J., Marketing Investigations. New York, Ronald Press, 1929.

R. O. Eastman, Incorporated, Report of the Eastman Marketing Seminar, held in New York, November, 1927. Cleveland, Eastman, 1928.

Saunders, Mrs. Alta Gwinn, and Chester Reed Anderson, Business Reports, Investigation and Presentation. New York, McGraw-Hill, 1929.

Schluter, William Charles, How to Do Research Work. New York, Prentice-Hall, 1926.

Smith, George C., An Outline for Market Surveys. [St. Louis, Industrial Club of St. Louis, 1930.]

U. S., Bureau of Foreign and Domestic Commerce, Check Sheet—Introduction of New Consumer Products. 1935.

——— Check Sheet—Introduction of New Industrial Products. 1935.

——— Consumer Use of Selected Goods and Services by Income Classes, Austin, Texas, 1935. First of a series of similar reports on cities in several sections of the United States.

——— Consumer Market Data Handbook. [Washington, 1936.]

——— Market Research Sources. Washington, D. C., U. S. Govt. Print. Off., 1938.

White, Percival, Market Analysis, Its Principles and Methods. McGraw-Hill, New York, 1921.

——— Marketing Research Technique. New York, Harper, 1931.

DISTRIBUTION COSTS AND SALES QUOTAS

Blocker, John G., Budgeting in Relation to Distribution Cost Accounting. 1937. University of Kansas Studies in Business, No. 18.

Canfield, Bertrand R., Sales Administration; Principles and Problems. New York, Prentice-Hall, 1938, pp. 430–91.

Castenholz, William Burtis, The Control of Distribution Costs and Sales. New York, Harper, 1930.

Dean, Joel, Statistical Determination of Costs, with Special Reference to Marginal Costs. Chicago, The University of Chicago Press, 1936.

Doubman, John Russell, Fundamentals of Sales Management. New York, Crofts, 1937, pp. 246–73, 284–309.

Griffin, Clare Elmer, Sales Quota Systems. Ann Arbor, University of Michigan, School of Business Administration, 1928. Michigan Business Studies, Vol. I, No. 5.

Hilgert, Joseph Robert, Cost Accounting for Sales. New York, Ronald Press, 1926.

Metropolitan Life Insurance Company, Policyholders Service Bureau, Methods of Determining Distribution Costs. 2d ed. New York, 1933.

Reitell, Charles Ervin, Cost Accounting; Principles and Methods. 2d ed. Scranton, Pa., International Textbook Co., 1937, pp. 326–77.

White, Percival, Sales Quotas; a Manual for Sales Managers. New York, Harper, 1929.

Willcox, Russell Stuart, Cost Accounting. Chicago, Business Publications Company, 1934, pp. 227–60.

Index

Bei Fragen zur Produktsicherheit wenden Sie sich bitte an:
If you have any questions regarding product safety,
please contact:

Walter de Gruyter GmbH
Genthiner Straße 13
10785 Berlin
productsafety@degruyterbrill.com